WORKING

Copyright 2000 by
University of Notre Dame Press
Notre Dame, IN 46556
All Rights Reserved
Manufactured in the United States of America

A record of the Library of Congress Cataloging-in-Publication Data is available
upon request from the Library of Congress.

ISBN 0-268-01961-4 (cloth)
ISBN 0-268-01962-2 (paper)

The paper used in this publication meets the minimum
requirements of the American National Standard for Information
Sciences—Permanence of Paper for Printed Library Materials,
ANSI Z39.48-1984.

# WORKIN

## *Its Meaning and Its Limits*

*Edited by*

## GILBERT C. MEILAENDER

UNIVERSITY OF NOTRE DAME

Notre Dame, Indiana

# THE ETHICS OF EVERYDAY LIFE
## Preface to the Series

This book is one of a series of volumes devoted to the ethics of everyday life. The series has been produced by a group of friends, united by a concern for the basic moral aspects of our common life and by a desire to revive public interest in and attention to these matters, now sadly neglected. We have met together over the past five years, under the auspices of the Institute of Religion and Public Life and supported by a generous grant from the Lilly Endowment. We have been reading and writing, conversing and arguing, always looking for ways to deepen our own understanding of the meaning of human life as ordinarily lived, looking also for ways to enable others to join in the search. These anthologies of selected readings on various aspects of everyday life—courting and marrying, teaching and learning, working, leading, and dying—seem to us very well suited to the task. This preface explains why we think so.

We begin by remembering that every aspect of everyday life is ethically charged. Nearly everything that we do, both as individuals and in relations with others, is colored by sentiments, attitudes, customs, and beliefs concerning "how to live." At work or at play, in word or in deed, with kin or with strangers, we enact, often unthinkingly and albeit imperfectly, our ideas of what it means to live a decent and worthy life. Notions and feelings regarding better and worse, good and bad, right and wrong, noble and base, just and unjust, decent and indecent, honorable and dishonorable, or human and inhuman always influence the way we speak to one another, the way we do our work, the way we control our passions, rear our children, manage our organizations, respond to injustice, treat our neighbors, teach the young, care for the old, court our beloved, and face our deaths.

For many centuries and up through the early part of the twentieth century, there was in the West (as in the East) a large and diverse literature on "living the good life," involving manners, patterns of civility, and the meaning of decency, honor, and virtue as these are manifested in daily life. Moralists, both philosophical and religious, wrote voluminously on the moral dimensions of the life cycle (e.g., growing up and coming of age, courting and marrying, rearing the young, aging and dying); on the virtues of everyday life (e.g., courage, endurance, self-command, generosity, loyalty, forbearance, modesty, industry, neighborliness, patience, hope, forgiveness, repentance); on the moral passions or sentiments (e.g., shame, guilt, sympathy, joy, envy, anger, awe) and their proper expression; on the activities of everyday life (e.g., loving, working, caring, giving, teaching, talking, eating); and on basic moral phenomena (e.g., responsibility, obligation, vocation, conscience, praise and blame). These topics, which once held the attention of great thinkers like Aristotle, Erasmus, and Adam Smith, are now sorely neglected, with sorry social consequences.

The ethics of everyday life have been left behind despite—or perhaps because of—the burgeoning attention given these past few decades to professional ethics and public ethics. Mention ethics today, and the discussion generally turns to medical ethics, legal ethics, journalistic ethics, or some other code of behavior that is supposed to guide the activities of professionals. Or it turns to the need to establish codes of conduct to address and curtail the mischief and malfeasance of members of Congress, generals, bureaucrats, or other public officials. In both cases, the concern for ethics is largely instrumental and protective. The codes are intended to tell people how to stay out of trouble with their professional colleagues and with the law. The latter is especially important in a world in which it is increasingly likely that a challenge or disagreement will be engaged not by civil conversation but by an uncivil lawsuit.

Today's proliferation of codes of ethics, while an expression of moral concern, is at the same time an expression of moral poverty. We write new rules and regulations because we lack shared customs and understandings. Yet the more we resort to such external and contrived codes, the less we can in fact take for granted. "Ethics" and "morality" have their source in "ethos" and "mores," words that refer to the ways and attitudes, manners and habits, sensibilities and customs that shape and define a community. Communities are built on shared understandings, usually tacitly conveyed, not only of what is right and wrong or good and bad, but also of who we are, how we stand, what things mean. These matters are not well taught by ethics codes.

Neither are they communicated, or even much noticed, by the current fashions in the academic study and teaching of ethics or by the proliferating band of professional ethicists. The dominant modes of contemporary ethical discourse and writing, whether conducted in universities or in independent ethics centers, are, by and large, highly abstract, analytically philosophic, interested only in principles or arguments, often remote from life as lived, divorced from the way most people face and make moral decisions, largely deaf to questions of character and moral feeling or how they are acquired, unduly influenced by the sensational or extreme case, hostile to insights from the religious traditions, friendly to fashionable opinion but deaf to deeper sources of wisdom, heavily tilted toward questions of law and public policy, and all too frequently marked by an unwillingness to take a moral stand. Largely absent is the older—and we think richer—practice of moral reflection, which is concrete, rooted in ordinary experience, engaged yet thoughtful, attuned to human needs and sentiments as well as to "rational principles of justification," and concerned for institutions that cultivate and promote moral understanding and moral education. Absent especially is the devoted search for moral wisdom regarding the conduct of life—philosophy's original meaning and goal, and a central focus of all religious thought and practice—a search that takes help from wherever it may be found and that gives direction to a life seriously lived.

Many academic teachers of ethics, formerly professors of moral wisdom, are today purveyors of moral relativism. In the colleges and universities ethics is often taught cafeteria style, with multiple theories and viewpoints, seemingly equal, offered up for the picking. But this apparently neutral approach often coexists with ideologically intolerant teaching. Students are taught that traditional views must give way to the "enlightened" view that all views— except, of course, the "enlightened" one—are culture-bound, parochial, and absolutely dependent on your *point*-of-viewing. The morally charged "givens" of human life—e.g., that we have bodies or parents and neighbors—tend to be regarded not as gifts but as impositions, obstacles to the one true good, unconstrained personal choice. Moral wisdom cannot be taught or even sought, because we already know that we must not constrain freedom, must not "impose" morality. Thus, we insist that our "values" are good because we value them, not that they are valued because they are good. Abstract theories of individual autonomy and self-creation abound, while insights into real life as lived fall into obscurity or disappear altogether. To be sure, not all academic teachers of ethics share these opinions and approaches. But experience and study of the literature convinces us that these generalizations are all too accurate.

The current fashions of ethical discourse are of more than merely academic interest. When teachings of "autonomy" or "self-creation" are disconnected from attention to mores and the cultural ethos and from the search for moral wisdom, we come to know less and less what we are supposed to do and how we are supposed to be. Neither can we take for granted that others know what they are supposed to do and be. Being morally unfettered and unformed may make us feel liberated albeit insecure or lost; but seeing that others are morally unfettered and unformed is downright threatening. Thus, despite our moral codes of ethics with penalties attached, despite the boom in the demand for ethicists and in ethics courses in our colleges, our everyday life declines into relationships of narrow-eyed suspicion. No one can argue that we are as a nation morally better off than we were before professional and academic ethics made such a big splash. Americans of widely differing views recognize the growing incivility and coarseness of public discourse and behavior, the sorry state of sexual mores, the erosion of family life, the disappearance of neighborliness, and the growing friction among, and lack of respect for, peoples of differing ages, races, religions, and social classes. To be sure, contemporary ethicists are not responsible for our cultural and moral difficulties. But they have failed to provide us proper guidance or understanding, largely because they neglect the ethics of everyday life and because they have given up on the pursuit of wisdom.

How to provide a remedy? How to offer assistance to the great majority of decent people who still care about living the good life? How to answer the ardent desires of parents for a better life for their children or the deep longings of undergraduates for a more meaningful life for themselves? How to supply an intellectual defense for the now beleaguered and emaciated teachings of decency and virtue? Any answer to these questions depends on acquiring—or at least seeking—a richer and more profound understanding of the structure of human life and the prospects for its flourishing and enhancement. This series of readings on the ethics of everyday life offers help to anyone seeking such understanding.

The topics considered in the several volumes are central to everyday life. Most of us marry, nearly all of us work (and play and rest), all of us lose both loved ones and our own lives to death. In daily life, many of us teach and all of us learn. In civic life, some of us lead, many of us follow, and, in democratic societies, all of us are called upon to evaluate those who would lead us. Yet rarely do we reflect on the nature and meaning of these activities. The anthologized readings—collected from poets and prophets, philosophers and preachers, novelists and anthropologists, scholars and statesmen; from authors ancient, modern, and contemporary—provide rich materials for such reflection. They are moral, not moralistic; they can yield insights, not maxims. The reader will find here no rules for catching a husband, but rather explorations of the purposes of courting and marrying; no prescriptions for organizing the workplace, but competing accounts of the meaning of work; no discussions of "when to pull the plug," but examinations of living in the face of death; no formulae for "effective leadership," but critical assessments of governance in democratic times; no advice on how to teach, but various meditations on purposes and forms of instruction. The different volumes reflect the differences in their subject matter, as well as the different tastes and outlooks of their editors. But they share a common moral seriousness and a common belief that proper ethical reflection requires a "thick description" of the phenomena of everyday life, with their inherent anthropological, moral, and religious colorations.

The readings in this series impose no morality. Indeed, they impose nothing; they only propose. They propose different ways of thinking about our common lives, sometimes in the form of stories, sometimes in the form of meditations, sometimes in the form of arguments. Some of these proposals will almost certainly "impose" themselves upon the reader's mind and heart as being more worthy than others. But they will do so not because they offer simple abstractable ethical principles or suggest procedures for solving this or that problem of living. They will do so because they will strike the thoughtful reader as wiser, deeper, and more true. We ourselves have had this experience with our readings, and we hope you will also. For the life you examine in these pages is—or could become—your own.

Timothy Fuller
Amy A. Kass
Leon R. Kass
Gilbert C. Meilaender
Richard John Neuhaus
Mark Schwehn

# CONTENTS

## III. Rest

# ACKNOWLEDGMENTS

It would be very hard to describe the process by which one accumulates, sorts through, and organizes a set of readings such as those in this volume, and I do not think I can reconstruct even for myself the gradual way in which these readings came together. Nor can I possibly recall many people who must have made helpful suggestions at various moments along the way.

There are, however, a few people whose help was essential, and I wish to acknowledge that help and thank them. They are: Jody Bottum, Joanne Ciulla, Timothy Fuller, Lee Hardy, Amy Kass, Leon Kass, William F. May, Richard John Neuhaus, Mark Schwehn, and Jane Strohl.

I also owe a debt of thanks to Lori Underhill, whose secretarial assistance was well beyond the call of duty.

# INTRODUCTION

In 1943 some two thousand Westerners were placed by the Japanese in Shantung Compound, an internment camp in northern China. The intent was to control these Westerners, who had been caught in China when the Japanese invaded. In the compound the refugees found themselves within something approaching a state of nature, needing to organize their common life. One important aspect of any community's life is work, and in *Shantung Compound,* a memoir of his time in the compound, Langdon Gilkey notes how central work was to their life, yet how problematic it had become: "Work and life have a strange reciprocal relationship: only if man works can he live, but only if the work he does seems productive and meaningful can he bear the life that his work makes possible."[1]

That strange reciprocity gives rise to some of the most puzzling questions about the place of work in human life. On the one hand, work is necessary to sustain life. An air of obligation surrounds it. On the other hand, we are often dissatisfied to think of work simply as useful and necessary. When we experience our work in that way, we may describe ourselves as alienated rather than engaged. Still more, we may be moved to ask a fundamental question: If I did not need to work in order to live, is there any reason why I nevertheless should work?

We cannot answer such a question without deciding what we mean by work, and in the history of the West work has had no single meaning or significance. St. Augustine once said that he knew what we mean by time until asked to explain it; then he found that he did not really know what it is. Something similar is likely to be true of work. It has been understood in countless different ways, as in the story of the three workers breaking rock into pieces. Asked what they were doing, the first answered, "Making little rocks out of big ones." The second replied, "Making a living." And the third said, "Building a cathedral."[2] The readings gathered together in Part I of this volume represent four somewhat different understandings of human work. Touching each other at points, they are nonetheless different and distinct. One way to explore them would be to attempt to write a history of work.[3] For our purposes, however, as we probe the moral significance of work in everyday life, a typology of approaches may be more helpful.

## I. The Meanings of Work

Work may be understood as "co-creation." The God revealed and depicted in the first chapter of Genesis is at work from the outset. (It is important to note, of course, that this God also rests from work on the seventh day, a fact that will call for further exploration later.) When on the sixth day "man" is created in the image of God, he is made priest of the creation, given "dominion" over it by God. To be in God's image is to work with and under God to care for the creation. That is precisely what the man does in the second chapter of Genesis, when he is placed in the Garden to till the ground. And indeed, if God is, in Kipling's phrase, "the Master of All Good Workmen," it might be hard to imagine a paradise in which each did not work simply "for the joy of the working."

This way of reading Genesis has had a powerful appeal in the modern period, and the readings in this volume should indicate that appeal by drawing on thinkers as otherwise diverse as Dorothy Sayers and Karl Marx. We could, moreover, have expanded our selection of readings more widely still. For example, in his 1981 encyclical letter *Laborem Exercens* (*On Human Work*), Pope John Paul II appeals to "image of God" language to describe the meaning and dignity of work.

> The church finds in the very first pages of the Book of Genesis the source of her conviction that work is a fundamental dimension of human existence on earth.... These truths are decisive for man from the very beginning, and at the same time they trace out the main lines of his earthly existence, both in the state of original justice and also after the breaking, caused by sin, of the creator's original covenant with creation in man.... Man is the image of God partly through the mandate received from his creator to subdue, to dominate, the earth. In carrying out this mandate, man, every human being, reflects the very action of the creator of the universe.[4]

It is quite striking that John Paul should emphasize that work retains its character as co-creation even in a world marred and broken by sin.

Not all readers of the opening chapters of Genesis are likely to agree. For example, Stanley Hauerwas wonders why John Paul did not emphasize other biblical themes in developing a theological perspective on work, such as the Pauline claim that the world is in the grip of principalities and powers, or the Johannine contrast between church and world.[5] And even if we grant the importance of Genesis 1 as a starting point for our reflection, Hauerwas suggests that it should be read in quite a different way. "The good news of the creation account is that God completed his creation and that mankind needs do nothing more to see to its perfection. That is exactly why God could call it good and rest—and, more importantly, invite us to rest within his completed good creation."[6] Beginning in this way, Hauerwas is led to suggest that "we do not need to attribute or find in our work any great significance or salvation," certainly not self-fulfillment, and he claims that we might simply define work as "'that from which the rich are exempt'"—implying that there is no reason to work unless we must work to live.[7] Interestingly, on this question a Catholic thinker as traditional as Josef Pieper is closer to Hauerwas's view than to that of John Paul. For Pieper, noted for his attempt to recapture and articulate the classical concept of leisure, "no one who is without need to support himself is obligated to work."[8] Sherlock Holmes, however, sides with John Paul II. The sheer boredom of life without engaging and challenging work invariably drove Holmes to cocaine—from which habit he could be rescued only by a challenging case.

Hauerwas's challenge to the idea of work as co-creation, if taken seriously, will probably incline us toward a different view of work among those represented in our typology—work as irksome, even if dignified and necessary. For the moment, however, we can permit his challenge to incline us to caution. It might be better—not just theologically better, but more suited to the actual limits of human existence—if we were to speak not of co-creation but of sub-creation. That is, while acknowledging that in our work we may reflect something of the God who is active and creative, fashioning and shaping a world, we may also want to recognize that we participate in this divine creative activity only at a distance.

This slightly chastened view of work might appeal to Dorothy Sayers; nevertheless, there is no doubt that her language is the strong language of co-creation. The worker "must be able to serve God *in* his work, and the work itself must be accepted and respected as the medium of divine creation." Or again, she asserts that in working we fulfill our nature and that the worker's "satisfaction comes, in the god-like manner, from looking upon what he has made and finding it very good." Certainly there is something powerful and appealing in this vision. It is hard to deny that most people, at least, want something meaningful and worthwhile to do with their time—a longing that, if this reading of Genesis 1 is correct, is an understandable expression of a fundamental truth of human nature.

Sayers' picture carries us along in its enthusiasm. If we really understood work as co-creation, as the expression and fulfillment of our person, it would be hard to tear us away from our work. We would struggle to find more time for it, not plot ways to get away from it. As John Julian Ryan puts it, every worker's "joy in his work as an art should be such that there hardly could be a greater punishment for him than being forbidden from his workshop, his laboratory, his desk, his hospital, or his altar."[9] And right about there we should pause. Can this really be true? Is the human being so fundamentally a worker—and is human fulfillment so closely tied to work—that leisure should exist solely to make work possible? That is a question we will have to consider later. But we should be clear from the outset: If this conception of leisure is unsatisfactory, then so must the depiction of work as co-creation be unsatisfactory. There is something tyrannical about this first type, as if we must find fulfillment in work or suffer a meaningless existence. Tyrannical also—and too narrow—is a view that seems to leave little place for those too young, too old, or too disabled to work, not to mention those unable to find employment. (We must grant, though, that those who cannot work are often deeply troubled by this, a fact that may itself suggest the importance of work for human beings.) Those who are not and cannot be workers are not, I think, shut off from human fulfillment. Perhaps Sayers would grant all this. Her vision of the meaning of work is not so much intended to question the dignity of those who cannot work as it is intended to offer a stinging critique of a world in which so many must work in ways that cannot be understood as co-creation.

The same, of course, is true of Marx's famous description in *The German Ideology* of "unalienated," engaged, labor. It is similar to Sayers' enthusiastic celebration of workers who can hardly be torn away from their work, so fulfilling is it. One hunts in the morning and fishes in the afternoon, but what really counts is that one does it not for some extrinsic purpose—not in order to live by selling one's labor—but simply because one wants to, because it gives meaning and satisfaction to life. The idea seems to be that, at least under certain social circumstances, work will lose its necessary character and will no longer be experienced as burdensome or irksome. The more appealing we make this depiction, however, the harder it becomes to distinguish work from play. In the minds of some that may be good. One of the ways in which visions of work differ is the degree to which they seek to unify the whole of life in service of one guiding idea. Certainly work as co-creation moves powerfully in the direction of a unified vision of life in which work at its best can scarcely be distinguished from play. Indeed, the harder we push in this direction the more we may even be led to wonder why Sayers supposes that some leisure should be necessary to refresh us for more work. Why should we need anything other than such fulfilling and invigorating work? Langdon Gilkey noted that the internees in Shantung Compound were free to work for themselves and to organize the work of their community as they saw fit; yet, they did not by any means throw themselves into their work as engaged rather than alienated workers. He found, in fact, "precious little evidence of this sheer love of work." [10] Perhaps they agreed with Dr. Johnson that "No man but a blockhead ever wrote, except for money." [11]

The image of work as co-creation is compelling because it responds to a desire many people have for work that is meaningful and productive—as if, in fact, we ourselves did in some way need to imitate God's own creative work. But the image is also not without its problems. It either downplays the destructive effects of sin on human life or supposes that within human history—after the revolution!—these effects can be overcome. It depicts the worker as the truly fulfilled human being, thereby making more of work than we perhaps ought and making it hard to think of those who cannot work as fully human. It can only with difficulty distinguish work from play.

Nevertheless, let us not forget the degree to which Sayers and Marx offer a critique and an indictment of what work has become in our world. They condemn a world in which work cannot be fulfilling or satisfying, and in doing so they do take their stand beside many who desire meaningful work. When Levin works with the mowers in *Anna Karenina,* the reader is hard-pressed to say whether he is working or playing and relaxing. (Or perhaps, even, a possibility that nudges us in yet another direction, worshipping.) In any case, he is almost freed from time, achieving a kind of self-transcendence. And, of course, he is not engaged in what looks at first to be "creative" work; his is sheer manual labor. Yet, because he is fully "engaged" in his labor, his life seems unified. His work, play, and worship cannot easily be distinguished.

Beyond any doubt, the example of Levin here is a powerful one for testing our own views of work. To the degree that he is truly one with his activity, fulfilled and enriched by it, to the degree that he gladly does this though he has no need at all to do so, I myself am disinclined to describe him as working. Whatever exactly he is doing, it is not work. Others, of course, more drawn to the image or the ideal of work as co-creation, will disagree. Perhaps ultimately the disagreement turns on our sense of what is possible in history. Is a truly unified life, in which work fulfills and enlarges one's self, in which work and play can scarcely be distinguished, genuinely possible for those who, at best, are sinful *sub*creators? That, we may suspect, is a question that must be answered if we are to make up our minds about the vision of work as co-creation.

For a second and quite different view of work, we may turn from biblical to classical roots. For the ancient Greeks—or, at least, for many of the great Greek thinkers—work is important chiefly because it makes possible leisure. Because, however, they may not mean by leisure what we are likely to suppose, we must unpack this view a little more. In doing so we should remember that the view of a thinker such as Aristotle may not, in fact, fully reflect Greek society of his time. The majority of Athenians at Aristotle's time were small farmers or traders who lacked the kind of leisure so central to Aristotle's understanding of human fulfillment. Moreover, the scorn for manual labor and toil that we find in Aristotle cannot be entirely separated from the fact that Athenian society was built upon the institution of slavery.

The classical attitude is captured nicely by Plutarch at the beginning of his life of Pericles. Contrasting attention to work with attention to virtue (which he thinks much more significant), Plutarch notes that we may be pleased with a piece of work but still think little of the workman. "[F]or instance, in perfumes and purple dyes, we are taken with the things themselves well enough, but do not think dyers and perfumers otherwise than low and sordid people." And similarly, he suggests, no virtuous young man, seeing and admiring the statue of Jupiter at Pisa, would ever desire to be Phidias, its sculptor. The work is good, but to be a workman toiling away with hammer and chisel is not. "For it does not necessarily follow, that, if a piece of work please for its gracefulness, therefore he that wrought it deserves our admiration."[12] Similarly, in Plato's *Gorgias* (512c), Socrates expresses disdain for the work of engineering, asking Callicles whether he would permit his daughter to marry the son of an engineer. On this view, work—even creative work—is not the purpose of life, although, of course, it is necessary for life. In Hesiod's description of the Golden Age, men lived like gods, and the gods did not work. That is quite unlike the story in Genesis, in which God is at work from the outset and human beings are placed in the Garden to till it and keep it.[13]

Plutarch's is a succinct expression of the view represented in our readings by selections from Aristotle and Xenophon. Aristotle understands well that a community requires various kinds of work for its sustenance and survival. It will need agricultural workers and craftsmen, but such work is not to be done by citizens. A well-structured community must have slaves or serfs to serve as farmers, craftsmen, and traders. At different stages of life citizens see to public tasks such as defense of the city, deliberation about their shared public life, and what Arisotle terms "public worship." The ancient Greek thinkers used the term *banausos* (usually translated 'mechanic') to describe those who toiled with their hands to make a living, toil generally regarded as inimical to the life of a free citizen.[14]

Thus, one way to characterize Aristotle's view is to think of him as distinguishing between several different kinds of occupation—some suited for free citizens who can flourish as human beings, and others needing to be done by those who will necessarily fall short of full humanity. This is probably what we, influenced by more modern notions of work as co-creation, tend to emphasize in his thought. But for Aristotle himself the important distinction is not between kinds of work. It is a distinction between occupation and leisure. The reason some kinds of work are regarded as servile or menial is that they do not fit one for the enjoyment of leisure. It is common to note that the Greek term for 'leisure' is *scholē,* and to be occupied with work is *ascholia* ("unleisurely"). Conceptually, leisure is the primary notion. Occupation is simply lack of leisure.[15] Hence, leisure is not time away from work or relaxation that refreshes us to return to work. As Ernest Barker puts it, commenting on Aristotle, "Amusement and recreation mean rest after occupation, and preparation for new occupation: they are thus both essentially connected with the idea of occupation. Leisure stands by itself, in its own independent right."[16] Hence, for Aristotle, forms of "play" are simply necessary moments of rest that are part of the cycle of work, whereas leisure has its own value entirely apart from the world of work. This is not precisely a contrast between the active and the contemplative life, although, obviously, it is closely related to that contrast. Aristotle clearly regards the contemplative life as superior, but just as clearly he emphasizes that it is itself a form of activity, indeed the highest form. Leisure is not rest; it is activity, though not the activity of menial toil. It is cultivation of the mind through activities that are intrinisically worthwhile—theoretical reflection, listening to good music and poetry, conversation with friends.

Although we today probably tend to think of leisure simply as freedom from work or as amusement that refreshes us to return to work, Witold Rybczynski's history of the idea of the weekend suggests that a faint hint of the classical view may still be alive among us. As he notes, the weekend has become a time of "strenuous activity," which may even be on the verge of enslaving us. The work week becomes merely an "irritating interference" with the "real" life of the weekend, and that real life is taken up with more passion, with less carelessness, and sometimes with a greater sense of obligation than is our work. But, of course, this is not really the classical meaning of leisure, and we might well attend to Josef Pieper's attempt to recapture that classical understanding of leisure as "a form of silence" and an "attitude of total receptivity toward, and willing immersion in, reality."

A third view of work within Western thought is very different from either of the first two. P. D. Anthony recounts the "apocryphal tale of the chronic absentee colliery-worker who was asked by his exasperated manager why he worked only four shifts every week. 'Because,' replied the man, 'I can't live on three.'"[17] On this view, work need not lack dignity, but it is certainly irksome and toilsome. Indeed, in many European languages the word for "labor" is closely associated with pain—as in the Greek *ponos*, the French *travail*, and the German *Arbeit*. Echoing the associations found in Genesis 3, the pain of work is closely associated with the labor pangs of birth.[18] From a perspective not unlike this, Anthony Trollope "deconstructs" an exalted notion of work as creative—as, for example, in the famous comparison he makes between his labor of writing and the work of a shoemaker.

If the idea of work as co-creation is sometimes derived from the teaching in Genesis 1 of the creation of humankind in God's image, this third view can be grounded in Genesis 3. The man who has fallen into sin is now condemned to toil for the bread he eats—and, indeed, his toil is made more difficult by a recalcitrant earth that brings forth thorns and thistles. The brief selection in our reading from George Foot Moore aptly summarizes the rabbinic view of work that grows out of these opening chapters of Genesis. Work is dignified and necessary. Even the scholar is to support himself by manual labor and not to suppose that the toilsome aspects of work are beneath him or can be avoided in sinful human history. The rabbi known to Christians as St. Paul seems to have felt this way. "If any will not work, let him not eat," Paul writes, urging those who are living in idleness to earn their own living.[19] Commenting on 1 Thessalonians 2:9, in which Paul writes that he had labored day and night in order not to burden the Thessalonians with his support, Wayne Meeks writes: "For Paul's pride in his self-support by handwork (according to Acts, tent-making) cf. 1 Cor. 9 and 2 Cor. 11:7–11. Propagandists for religious or philosophical cults [in the Hellenistic world] were normally expected to live from the contributions of their audiences or converts. These passages show that this was the norm also in Christianity. Paul's contrasting practice agrees with that of Pharisaic teachers of Torah."[20] That even irksome toil is not without dignity is clearly indicated when the prophet Isaiah describes the new creation Israel's God will bring about as one in which such work still has a place: "They shall build houses and inhabit them; they shall plant vineyards and eat their fruit."[21]

One does not, however, need anything other than ordinary human experience to learn that work is often burdensome. Certainly any who doubt this might profit from reading George Orwell's description of the work of coal miners. In his characteristically sparse and direct prose, Orwell takes us unforgettably into the life of a laborer—and reminds us how much we owe to those who daily take up such tasks. "You can never forget that spectacle once you have seen it—the line of bowed, kneeling figures, sooty black all over, driving their huge shovels under the coal with stupendous force and speed." No one, I think, having read Orwell would say of ditch-digging, as John Julian Ryan does, that for it as "for most other jobs, much of the boredom apparent in the job results from a failure on the part of the worker to approach it with the right attitude and expectancy—namely, that of artistic achievement and *all* its attendant joys."[22] It is difficult—perhaps impossible—to think of such work as co-creation, and it is hard to imagine that those who engaged in it could have thought of leisure as anything other than sheer rest from labor. Yet, this work is not without its dignity. "It is impossible to watch the 'fillers' at work without feeling a pang of envy for their toughness," Orwell writes. And again, "it is even humiliating to watch coal-miners working. It raises in you a momentary doubt about your own status as an 'intellectual' and a superior person generally." In short, it raises a doubt about wherein true human dignity lies.

Why would anyone do such work? Would we do it if we had no need to? One might argue that we have a social obligation to work. Lawrence Becker puts such a claim directly: "People who are able to work, and do not work, are parasites, however unattractive and emotionally loaded that label is."[23] Perhaps some work simply because, as Orwell notes, the worker has a kind of dignity in his work. More likely, though, such work is done because it must be. One works to live. There may be camaraderie to be found with one's fellow workers, but probably not fulfillment in the work itself. Perhaps, too, much of the satisfaction of such work comes from providing for one's family and loved ones. If true, of course, this would mean that the significance of work comes in considerable measure from something extrinsic to the activity itself. Advocates of work as co-creation, who seek the worth in the work itself, would not be likely to agree. They might argue, as Sayers seems to, that no one should have to do work that cannot be done as humanly fulfilling activity. But, then, Genesis 3 may be read to suggest that we do not—and will not—live in a world where that is possible. In the world we inhabit, a certain nobility may come from hard work, even drudgery and toil, by which one provides for one's family and others. Advocates of the classical view, who thought of work as necessary for leisure, did see something of the truth of this third view; for they did not suppose that work was intrinsically satisfying. It existed to make possible what was worthwhile for its own sake—namely, leisure. But in adopting this view they necessarily deprived those who had to carry out such toil—Orwell's miners—of a dignity they seem, in fact, to possess. Sobering as this third view is, there is much to be said for it. The worker may achieve considerable dignity in work that, although necessary, cannot be fulfilling or satisfying.

Over against Tolstoy's depiction of Levin "working" in the field with the mowers, we may therefore want to set a different novelist's view in which there is no spiritualization of labor. Nathaniel Hawthorne's description of the life of the Blithedale community forces us to ask with Coverdale whether it is true that "the yeoman and the scholar . . . are two distinct individuals, and can never be melted or welded into one substance." That more sober view is argued by the late lay theologian Jacques Ellul. He contends that it is impossible in the modern world to see work as meaningful or fulfilling. In a capitalistic economy of wage earners, the person's work becomes a commodity to be bought and sold. Hence, his work "cannot be an expression of his personality." Furthermore, mechanization means that no worker sees the task or the product whole. Each does his specialized part, and any larger reflection on the meaning or purposes of this work becomes nearly impossible. And finally, technological advance means that the only thing that counts in work is competence. A desire to serve others, a call from God, a search for purpose and meaning in life—none of these counts for much when a technically skilled worker is what is needed. Perhaps Ellul presses this third understanding of work too far. In his

eagerness to depict its irksomeness we may miss an affirmation of its dignity.
But we need not deny the power of his critique. It raises for us once more the
difficult question whether work, in order to have the character of work, must
be irksome—or whether it is simply the case that much work is, in fact, irksome.
Would the best workers feel themselves at one with their work and find it plea-
surable, as Levin does? Clearly, the advocates of work as co-creation think so,
but this third view invites us to qualify their optimistic picture. Perhaps at least
we should say, as Yves Simon does, that even if we do not include irksomeness
in the definition of work, the very fact that work is connected with the world
of necessity means that "there exists in work a permanent foundation for irksomeness."[24] It will always be something that *has* to be done, even though this
necessary work can be done in joy rather than in sorrow.[25]

Our fourth and last image of work came to powerful articulation in the
Protestant Reformation. As men and women fled in droves from monasteries
and nunneries—where, it was thought, only the "religious" had a "calling" from
God—they came to think of their everyday life in the world as God's call that
sanctified their work and gave significance to it. Thus Luther loved to say that
the maid sweeping the steps does a work as pleasing to God as the monk at
his prayers. Just as combatively, Robert Louis Stevenson, reflecting (as W. R.
Forrester puts it) the "activism" of the very Calvinist background he also rejected, wrote in his poem *Our Lady of Snows:*

> And ye, O brethren, what if God,
> When from Heav'n's top He spies abroad,
> And sees on this tormented stage
> The noble war of mankind rage:
> What if His vivifying eye,
> O monks, should pass your corner by?
> For still the Lord is Lord of might;
> In deeds, in deeds, He takes delight;
> The plough, the spear, the laden barks,
> The field, the founded city, marks;
> He marks the smiler of the streets,
> The singer upon garden seats;
> He sees the climber in the rocks;
> To him, the shepherd folds his flocks.
> For those He loves that underprop
> With daily virtues Heaven's top,
> And bear the falling sky with ease,
> Unfrowning caryatides.
> Those he approves that ply the trade,

That rock the child, that wed the maid,
That with weak virtues, weaker hands,
Sow gladness on the peopled lands,
And still with laughter, song and shout,
Spin the great wheel of earth about.

But ye?—O ye who linger still
Here in your fortress on the hill,
With placid face, with tranquil breath,
The unsought volunteers of death,
Our cheerful General on high
With careless looks may pass you by.[26]

A less combative mood, and a more helpful one, is captured in what is also a better poem: George Herbert's "The Elixir," included in the collection of readings. In a few short stanzas of great beauty, Herbert captures the power of the idea of vocation. The elixir that turns the base metal of drudgery into the gold of something divine is the sense that one is called to the work by God. When God reaches down to touch both work and worker, the work can no longer be described simply as "mean." For then the drudgery is "divine."

This understanding of work proved powerful indeed. "God loveth adverbs," said the Puritan thinker quoted by Charles Taylor, and those shaped by the Reformation worked dutifully and diligently because they believed that to do so was God-pleasing. Hence, Taylor writes, a "full human life is now defined in terms of labour and production, on one hand, and marriage and family life, on the other." The "good life" is now available to everyone, for each person has a calling from God. Taylor's discussion traces this revolutionary affirmation of ordinary life to the thought of the Reformers, and, like all who do this, he ultimately draws from the well of Max Weber. Whatever the defects of Weber's thesis in *The Protestant Ethic and the Spirit of Capitalism*, he sensed the powerful impact of the Reformation's affirmation of everyday life. Our readings include just a short selection in which Weber contrasts the quite different conclusions of Dante's *Divine Comedy* and Milton's *Paradise Lost* and, having contrasted them, notes of Milton: "One feels at once that this powerful expression of the Puritan's serious attention to the world, his acceptance of life in the world as a task, could not possibly have come from the pen of a mediaeval writer."

Perhaps the archetype of diligent, methodical labor in one's calling was John Wesley, the great eighteenth-century preacher and founder of Methodism, described as "the Lord's horseman" by one of his biographers because he logged thousands of miles on horseback bringing the gospel to the laboring class. The energizing source of his activity is captured succinctly in the well-known hymn by his brother Charles, "Forth in thy name, O Lord, I go."

> Forth in thy name, O Lord, I go,
> My daily labor to pursue.
> Thee, only thee resolved to know.
> In all I think, or speak, or do.

For those moved by such beliefs, daily work became a vocation, a calling from God. The task of the believer was not simply worship, but preeminently work. One sought not the vision of God but the transformation of the world in accordance with God's will. Or, to put it in the Protestant jargon nicely captured by C. S. Lewis, the Christian was to focus not on doing good works, but on doing good work—on faithfulness and diligence in the calling.[27]

One of the classic discussions of work as vocation can be found in a treatise by William Perkins, a great sixteenth-century Puritan theologian in England. Portions of Perkins' treatise are included in our collection of readings, and even in this relatively short selection one can see many of the implications that were drawn from the concept of vocation: the need for diligence in the calling and the repudiation of sloth and idleness; the sense that one's work, however seemingly humble, makes a difference because one is called to it by God; the strong emphasis that the point of vocation is neither self-advancement nor self-fulfillment, but service of God and the neighbor; the sense that every person must have a calling within society in order to be what God asks a person to be; an emphasis upon joy and contentment in the calling, because one knows that it is in service of God's will. Perkins distinguishes the general calling to be a Christian (which requires one to offer prayer and thanksgiving to God, to further the cause of the church, to show love to all, and to live a righteous life) from the particular callings that we identify with our work in the world. Each person's calling is, in fact, personal—it is his or her calling from God, and no one else's. It is God who fits together and orders these several callings in order that the larger, common good may be served. Hence, thinking of work as a vocation within a whole system of vocations emphasizes that work is a social activity contributing in some way to the common good of all. Thus, Yves Simon notes wittily that "the activity of a burglar digging a hole is not work."[28] We might, he notes, describe the burglar as "at work" digging the hole, but we would still not be likely to describe him as engaged in what we are prepared to call "work."

This vision of work as a calling from God is clearly a powerful one whose impact on our culture has been profound. It is not without its dangers, however. Indeed, in some respects it floats rather uncertainly between the emphases of the first and third members of our typology (work as co-creation, and work as irksome but dignified). Undergirding the idea that work is co-creation, the concept of vocation gives an enhanced religious aura to the world of work—reinforcing and perhaps in part giving rise to the modern idea that work is integral to human identity and fulfillment. Indeed, even among religious thinkers, the idea of vocation has often lost much of its original accent and has been transmuted into an emphasis upon work as the sphere in which one fulfills oneself. Perkins would have been astonished. In this way, the concept of vocation may reinforce the dubious idea that the human being is essentially and primarily a worker. But an emphasis upon the calling may also be allied with the sense that work, however hard and irksome, retains dignity. Surely this was part of the original vision of the Reformers when they called people into the tasks of ordinary life and asserted that "God loveth adverbs." Here again, however, by undergirding the dignity of irksome work in powerful religious language, we may too easily be invited to overlook just how hard and unsatisfying much toil is. We may recommend such work as service to the neighbor or, even, as spiritual discipline, but we should be careful lest this religious language lead us to ignore the empirical realities of the work many people must do.

## II. The Limits of Work

Precisely because several of the meanings we give to work—in particular, under the rubrics of co-creation and vocation—exalt its place in life, we may easily forget some of the ways in which work has and ought to have only limited significance. Without denying its enormous importance for human survival and flourishing, we need to remind ourselves that the human being is not merely a worker. The readings gathered in Part II of this volume direct our attention to some of these limits. They encourage us to remember reasons why work should not occupy the whole of life.

"For everything there is a season," the well-known passage from Ecclesiastes says, and that is true also of work. In a thoughtful selection from her classic *Gift from the Sea,* Anne Morrow Lindbergh demonstrates how just one day of a life may incorporate many different kinds of work—some of them of great significance, others seemingly humdrum and trivial. Moreover, the rhythm of life, its movement through a defined series of stages in some of which work is more central than in others, sets a clear limit to the place of work. The young child is not a worker in any ordinary sense, nor is the person who in old age has again become dependent. Moreover, the character of our attention to work shifts at different moments in life.

Not everyone will agree with this claim, of course. Thus, for example, the rather poignant selection from an address given by Oliver Wendell Holmes on

the occasion of his ninetieth birthday asserts forcefully that "to live is to function." Perhaps it is not entirely surprising that this should be said by one who
himself functioned vigorously into a very old age, but other selections in our
reading lead in different directions. Mickey Kaus reflects upon the attitude
toward work which he finds among his middle-age compatriots. They are "getting sleepy." This tendency to lose some of the energy needed to work at one's
previous pace Kaus describes as "part of the natural human life cycle." Insight-
fully, he explores the problem this life cycle creates for an economy such as
ours. To recognize that work is not the whole of life is only the beginning; for,
having seen this, we must then consider how to give meaning and purpose to
life in a world where work alone has tended to supply such meaning.

One of the problems, however, with Kaus's witty and insightful commentary on our times is that it so readily buys into the current rather narcissistic
idea that work primarily serves the worker. St. Augustine, who after his con-
version to the Christian faith longed for a quiet life of philosophical conversation among friends, found himself drawn instead into the priesthood and,
eventually, into a busy and demanding life as a bishop of the church. In a famous passage from Book XIX of his *City of God*, Augustine takes up the classical contrast between the active and contemplative lives and shows us how one
may deal with the relation of work to life's rhythms. Longing for "sanctified
leisure," one might hope to be freed from the "burden" of "righteous engagement in affairs," and Augustine finds nothing wrong in seizing such freedom
should it be given us. But if that is not our fate, if this burden is laid upon
us, "it is to be undertaken because of the compulsion of love." Even so, however, Augustine will not allow that work alone should occupy our life. The
whole of life must display a kind of rhythm in which leisure and action each
has its place; it should not be a life of work alone, "lest compulsion should
overwhelm us." Karl Barth, himself as great a theologian in the twentieth century as Augustine had been in the fourth and fifth centuries, reminds us in his
characteristically assertive prose that the meaning of work must change with
different stages of life. The necessary rhythm is not simply one between action
and leisure but between different moments of life. At each age we are related
in distinctive ways to the world of work and invited to grasp the opportunity
of that age.

Work is also limited in other ways. When discussing above the scene from
*Anna Karenina* in which Levin joins his workers in mowing the field, I noted
that it may be hard to say whether he is working or playing. And, in fact, work
must in some way be contrasted with play if we are to understand its meaning
and limits. The contrast is, however, a puzzling one and not easy to make
clearly, as Mark Twain demonstrates unforgettably in the famous fence whitewashing scene in chapter 2 of *Tom Sawyer*. As Tom carries out the task Aunt

Polly has set him, applying whitewash to a fence thirty yards long and nine feet high, Ben Rogers passes by on his way to go swimming. Ben taunts Tom because he has to stay and work, and Tom poses our problem.

> "What do you call work?"
> "Why ain't *that* work?"
> Tom resumed his whitewashing, and answered carelessly:
> "Well, maybe it is, and maybe it ain't. All I know, is, it suits Tom Sawyer."

And the chapter concludes with Twain's observation that had Tom been "a great and wise philosopher . . . he would now have comprehended that Work consists of whatever a body is *obliged* to do, and that Play consists of whatever a body is not obliged to do. And this would help him to understand why constructing artificial flowers or performing on a treadmill is work, while rolling tenpins or climbing Mont Blanc is only amusement."

Engaging as Twain's chapter is, the distinction between work and play is more complicated than this summary sentence suggests. Not that Twain's summary lacks insight. I noted above that work seems to have about it a necessary and obligatory quality. One may perhaps take pleasure in that necessity, even when it is irksome, but it does have the element of necessity to which Twain calls attention. Adequately to characterize work in distinction from play, however, probably requires us to note several other features of work. It is, for example, what Yves Simon has called a "transitive activity"—that is, even if it has an effect on the worker himself, it also produces an external effect on something else. If its sole point becomes the effect it has on the worker, we are likely to call the activity something else—play, sport, or even "make-work." "Movements which might be the acts of workers often are repeated by people at play, or by people who want to lose weight, or by people who want to discipline their passions."[29] Moreover, work has not only an element of necessity in it but also an element of usefulness. We do it not for its own sake—in which case it is more like a hobby—but for the sake of the useful good in which it terminates.[30] In these ways work must be distinguished from play. There are, to be sure, instances in which the distinction is hard to make, as in intellectual work done by the scientific researcher or the philosopher. Even in such cases, however, the worker's attention is focused not on the sheer pleasure of the activity but on the work itself.

In our readings a view somewhat different from Simon's is represented in the selection from Adriano Tilgher. Focusing in particular on the cases of intellectual and artistic work, he declines to distinguish work from play on the basis of a supposed distinction between an effect external to the worker (in work) and the sheer joy of the activity itself (in play). For him the distinction focuses on the "seriousness" of the activity. "Play—if it is real play—always has something of triviality in it." Thus, for example, the story of the young Babe Ruth who, having signed his first contract, said, "You mean they *pay* you to play baseball?"[31] Likewise, Tilgher is reluctant to connect work too closely with the realm of necessity and obligation. "No play, no sport, can bring such joy as loving labor." Some of the questions we have been pondering come into focus here. Could playing baseball—for a living—really be work? If not, why not? Because it lacks the element of necessity? Because it is not, in Simon's phrase, a transitive activity? Because it lacks seriousness? These are different attempts to characterize work in terms of the kind of activity it is. Or, perhaps, is the crucial factor not the kind of activity but the attitude we bring to it? George Will almost suggests as much when he titles his book about professional baseball players: *Men at Work*. The men who play this game, Will says, achieve "at least intermittently, the happy condition of the fusion of work and play." We might want to ponder this a bit more, however. True as it obviously is that these men earn their living by playing baseball, and true as it is that their craft is (as both Will and Roger Angell emphasize) a demanding one which fully engages their energy and imagination, these truths alone may not qualify their activity as work. I, at least, admit to doubting that it does.

However precisely we contrast work with play, and however careful we are to distinguish play from leisure (in the classical sense), most thinkers who make the distinction will eventually argue that the good life must contain elements of both work and play. Thus, granting that no life can be occupied solely with the seriousness and passion of work as he understands it, Tilgher argues for a balance between work and play in one's life. That balance was notably expressed by Shakespeare's Prince Hal:

> If all the year were playing holidays,
> To sport would be as tedious as to work;
> But when they seldom come, they wished-for come,
> And nothing pleaseth but rare accidents.

At various periods in our history many people have carried out their daily work from their home. Indeed, before the rise of industry and technology, probably the largest amount of work was done within the sphere of the family. Our term 'economy' comes from the Greek *oikos*, which means household. Nevertheless, the demands of work and the demands of domestic life are different, they may sometimes conflict, and, hence, domestic life constitutes a third kind of limit to the supremacy of work.

I noted above that one of the reasons we might undertake hard and burdensome work is the desire to provide for the needs of our family. The irony is, however, that, either because these needs are great or because the work turns out to have its own attractions, it may come to occupy the bulk of our life. Indeed, Arlie Hochschild's essay strikingly questions our notion of home as a place to retreat from work. In late-twentieth-century America, going to work feels for some people more like being at "home," and, by contrast, home becomes a place from which one seeks to escape by ever greater devotion to work. Perhaps, however, this has always been true.

Tolstoy's depiction of Ivan Ilyich is a biting—and in some respects, perhaps, unkind and uncharitable—depiction of a man for whom work has become everything. Ilyich separates his official duties from his private life and "fence[s] off a world for himself outside the family," using it almost as a retreat from the demands and vexations of private life. Although Ilyich does this more and more as the years pass, the tendency had been there from the start. Even when he married he did so with the hope that marriage would not disrupt the life he had fashioned for himself with work at its center. Readers of the novella almost inevitably feel that Ilyich's life is a shallow and truncated one, and he himself comes to believe that before his death. At least part of his life's inadequacy seems to lie in the fact that he has permitted himself to be entirely absorbed in his official duties, in his work, and has left no time or energy for personal, private bonds.

The simple fact that work is often undertaken to support one's family reminds us that there is more to life than work—that the sphere of the private and personal constitutes one of the limits to work's domain. Just as we may recommend some sort of balance between work and play, so also people often seek such balance between work and the private realms of family and friendships. Judith Martin, known to most readers as "Miss Manners," wittily dissects our society's attitude toward the public world of work. She is at her best in demonstrating how we blur the distinction between the private realm of personal ties and the public world of work. Thus, we treat personal matters as if they were best handled with business practices, and we inappropriately use private social forms in business situations. It may surprise us, however, to note that she is recommending what Ivan Ilyich did: he made a firm and distinct separation between the domestic sphere and the world of work. Martin differs from Ilyich, of course, in recommending balance between these spheres of life. Earlier generations had different ways of achieving a certain balance—a "diachronic" balance in which one generation worked hard so that the next generation could in more leisurely fashion enjoy inherited wealth, and a "synchronic" balance in which men saw to the public world of work and women attended to the domestic sphere.

Neither of these kinds of balance satisfies Miss Manners. The former is, she thinks, inappropriate for a society in which equality is highly prized. The latter "leaves a lot of dissatisfied people—overburdened men and bored women." Why? Evidently because their lives lack balance between work and family. Such balance is Martin's ideal: "[E]veryone needs a reasonable amount of challenging work in his or her life, and also a personal life, complete with noncompetitive leisure." The ideal of balance is hard to argue with, so appealing is it to our natural tendency to favor well-roundedness. Nevertheless, we should question it. At least some of the meanings work has in life—as co-creative activity in which we step forth as those made in God's image, as vocation in which we respond to a summons to devote ourselves to work that is uniquely ours, and even as irksome labor undertaken in service of those who depend upon us— may challenge us to devote the whole of our powers to work that lies before us. And such devotion may seem to leave little time or place for other aspects of life. In the face of a seeming need to place the whole of one's powers in service of one's work, the call to a "balanced" life seems rather pale and anemic. No doubt most of us, most of the time, will still seek lives in which such balance exists, but we should not imagine that the balanced life is a satisfactory life for everyone. What every thoughtful person must do, however, is contemplate whether and how our work should be limited by bonds that are personal and private.

The ever-present tension between these spheres of life is succinctly and, even, poignantly captured in the brief selection from William F. May. He is not writing about the tension between work and the family, but simply about the broader tension between work and private ties of various sorts. And although this selection discusses in particular the way in which such a tension affects the lives of physicians, it has a wider range and broader applicability. May insists that we give the world of work its due. It is an important world, for through work the needs of many are served. Because that is true, the relative impersonality required in the world of work is a price worth paying. We cannot be friends with everyone if we want to do our work well, and if we attempt the impossible we are likely to succeed only in failing those who depend upon our work.

Like Tolstoy and Martin, May sees the need for a certain separation between the worlds of work and personal ties. He notes how awkward and painful are our attempts to import a style appropriate to one realm into a different realm where life must be structured in different ways. But May also probes deeply enough to get beyond the ideal of balance. We cannot, on his view, give the whole of our attention to our work. That would be self-destructive. Nor can we devote all our energies to private bonds, such as the family. That too would be self-destructive, for neither of these spheres can bear that much weight. Neither can become "the sole arena of self-realization." Shall we then balance them? Not exactly. A person's life can be fulfilled in neither sphere, nor in both of them taken together and balanced. Even in tandem they cannot bear the whole weight of a life's meaning and significance. What we need, rather, is a way of living with the permanent tension between the worlds of work and private bonds. We need, May writes, a sense of "the final extraterritoriality of the person"—the sense that, because we live in relation to God, neither our work nor our personal ties can divulge the ultimate significance of a human life. Understanding this, we will be free to live with the tension between several spheres of life, free "to function in a 'hardship post,' as it were, without being annihilated thereby."

For the first time since the rise of large-scale industry, work may be returning to the home. Recent technological advances now often make it possible to work from one's home, which is, in some respects, a return to an earlier pattern. Whether this will be good for either work or family remains to be seen, but it illustrates nicely the fact that the form work takes is subject to continual transformation within history. The place of work in our life and its significance for us are limited by the fact that the shape of work never stands still. It is constantly being transformed and restructured. And although it is always a dangerous enterprise to predict what the future will bring, there can be little doubt that the structure of much work is being radically altered at the present time.

Such transformations occur, paradoxically enough, because the human being is more than a worker. "The heart of capitalism is *caput* [head]," Michael Novak has written.[32] Few authors have written more compellingly about or celebrated more highly the role played by creative human intelligence in the world of work. He echoes in certain respects the words and vision of Dorothy Sayers when he suggests that founding a business "rivals, in its way, artistic creativity" and "participates from afar in the source of all knowledge, the Creator."

Being almost godlike in our creative powers is not an unmixed blessing, however. For we are not godlike in our ability to foresee the full range of consequences that flow from the transformations creative minds bring to the world of work. Peter Drucker charts some of these transformations—from a world in which most workers were farmers or domestic servants, through an industrialized world populated largely by blue-collar workers, to a presently emerging society dominated by "knowledge workers." In this world *caput* will count for a great deal indeed, and it may not always be a kinder, gentler world. "The knowledge society," Drucker writes, "will inevitably become far more competitive than any society we have yet known—for the simple reason that with knowledge being universally accessible, there will be no excuses for nonperformance." As organizations become of necessity "leaner and meaner," as the workplace and the workforce are constantly restructured, we will continually be reminded how important work is in people's lives and how much they suffer without it. In such circumstances we will probably be tempted to turn away from the dynamism of a world in which work is continually transformed—tempted, that is, to trade in creativity for security. If we think that a bad exchange, we will have to ponder, as Michael Novak does, what can be done to mitigate the undesirable consequences that inevitably accompany some of the contemporary transformations of work.

In celebrating the creativity of work, we should not fail to think critically about the forms work takes in our world. Drucker writes that "the central and distinctive organ" of work in the emerging knowledge society is "management." Whereas both he and Novak seem quite optimistic about the possibilities for managerial expertise within the world of work, Alasdair MacIntyre unleashes a powerful philosophical critique of the very possibility of such managerial expertise. Interestingly, a part of his argument depends precisely on the very human capacity for innovation and new creation that Novak celebrates. MacIntyre does not see our capacity for unpredictable innovation as godlike. On the contrary, he finds in the radical unpredictability of human life the sign that we are not gods. The very concept of managerial expertise, as it has been developed in our time, is for him a "fiction" that disguises manipulation under the cloak of expertise. MacIntyre's critique has about it a prophetic quality, and it challenges us to be clear—clearer than we often are—about the transformations of work in our time.

### III. Rest

Anyone who works must eventually rest as well. That much is sheer physiological fact. The rhythms of life discussed above also require rest, and play is often seen as a form of rest from work. But in our history there is a deeper meaning to the idea of "rest," and that deeper meaning is grounded in the creation story in Genesis where God is said to have "rested on the seventh day from all his work which he had done" and to have "blessed the seventh day and hallowed it." As God is not simply a "worker," neither are his creatures, and it may be that to rest is, in the deepest sense, to rest in God. That, at any rate, is the suggestion of George Herbert's poem, "The Pulley."

> When God at first made man,
> Having a glass of blessings standing by;
> Let us (said he) pour on him all we can:
> Let the world's riches, which dispersed lie,
>     Contract into a span.

So strength first made a way;
Then beauty flow'd, then wisdom, honor, pleasure:
When almost all was out, God made a stay,
Perceiving that alone of all his treasure
Rest in the bottom lay.

For if I should (said he)
Bestow this jewel also on my creature,
He would adore my gifts instead of me,
And rest in Nature, not the God of Nature:
So both should losers be.

Yet let him keep the rest,
But keep them with repining restlessness:
Let him be rich and weary, that at least,
If goodness lead him not, yet weariness
May toss him to my breast.[33]

The need for rest that characterizes human beings is not just physiological fact; it is, the poem suggests, a divine gift. It reminds us that, however significant or useful our work may be, it is not the chief purpose or the final goal of human life. Restlessness, the need to rest not just from labor but from longing and anxiety, is the pulley that draws us toward God.

We, of course, do not always recognize this; hence, the Bible records that God had to command a sabbath, a prescribed day of rest in the weekly cycle reminding workers that they do not sustain their existence. As the Israelites marching through the desert could rest on the sabbath from gathering manna, confident that this one day of the week it would keep without spoiling, so we all are commanded to anticipate the goal of human life by learning even now to rest, trusting in God to care for us.

In the history of Judaism, in particular, this insight has been most fully developed in practices that shape a way of life. And then, in turn, the practices themselves unfold an ever deeper understanding of the meaning of rest. For example, Abraham Joshua Heschel, in one of our selections, develops (in the most poetic of prose) an understanding of the sabbath as a temple in time rather than space, a temple in which "the goal is not to have but to be." The sabbath is, therefore, intimately connected with that long, gradual process by which ancient Israel emancipated itself (or was emancipated) from the natural cycles of death and rebirth in nature and from the gods and goddesses all around it who were thought to reside in space—the process, that is, by which Israel came to understand her God as transcendent. If Heschel perhaps overstates his case on occasion—Israel, after all, also came to know of Zion, the holy hill of her Lord—he is nevertheless profound in drawing out the significance of a cathedral built in time rather than space. What it means, he suggests, is freedom to trust God, freedom from enslavement to the world of things upon which we depend for so much of life. (That an insight at least akin to this has not, however, been hidden from thinkers in that other great—Greek and Roman—strand of Western tradition is made clear in the brief selection from Josef Pieper included in our readings.)

Almost inevitably, of course, such an understanding gives rise to a complicated casuistry. One must know when and how to rest, what exceptions the commandment to rest permits—in general, how rigorously the commandment is to be observed. Christians, believing that observance of God's law could never become the means of salvation and concerned also to draw Gentiles into the community of believers, gradually lost this elaborate casuistry and, in recent times, even lost a sense that the sabbath was a day for rest from work. (And, of course, they shifted their sabbath from the seventh day to the first day of the week, the day on which Jesus had risen.) George Herbert's description (this time in prose) of "The Parson in Circuit" captures an earlier period in which Christians too paid attention to such sabbath observance. Although commending his parishioners to their respective callings, the parson admonishes them not so to give themselves to their labor that they become anxious or distrustful, "as if it were in their own hands to thrive, or not to thrive." The parson recognizes some exceptions to the command to rest from work on the sabbath—for example, when the seed must be sown or the crop harvested in an agricultural society. But he still advises that no "unnecessary" work be done on the sabbath.

So insistent has Christian culture been on the importance of work, however, and so eager have we moderns been to think of human beings as essentially "workers," that it may sometimes seem hard to justify resting from work. The Good Samaritan in Jesus' story, who devoted himself without reserve to the needs of the man who had been beaten by thieves, may easily come to represent the whole of life—as if the service our work renders to others could not itself be idolized, and as if rest could be justified only as a means to further service. One may easily forget that the Gospel of Luke seems deliberately to pair that Good Samaritan story with another in which Jesus commends Mary for sitting and listening to his teaching while her sister Martha, seeing to the needs of her guest, is "distracted with much serving." The tension between work or service and worship is a perennial one. The selection from Pieper notes succinctly how it was recognized in Greek philosophy, and the excerpt from Kenneth Kirk's classic work, *The Vision of God*, argues that worship—

understood as an end in itself and not simply as a means to further work—is essential to true service.

Whatever the roots of our day of rest from work, it has, of course, taken on its own shape over the centuries. It has also acquired competitors, alternative forms of rest. Michael Walzer contrasts the idea of the sabbath (or, more generally, the public holiday) with the more recent idea of the vacation. He finds in the sabbath a more egalitarian distribution of free time than in the vacation—an observation which might encourage us to think critically about the manner in which our society now regularly attaches its holidays to weekends so that they may become part of longer vacations. That, in turn, might, as Walzer notes, make us see some point in "blue laws," since it is "difficult to guarantee rest to everyone without imposing it on everyone." If I rest from the labors of meal preparation on Sunday by eating dinner at a restaurant, others, of course, must labor. They cannot experience the "pulley" that draws the heart to rest in God. And even at its best and most enticing—as Joseph Epstein depicts it in his remembrances of childhood Sundays and description of his adult Sundays—the sabbath becomes simply a day on which, as Epstein puts it, the pace slackens. If that slackened pace may sometimes draw us into pleasures that become Herbert's "pulley," it may also serve as nothing more than the relaxation that is needed in order to work more efficiently. That, surely, would be to lose the human wisdom of Genesis, a wisdom which suggests that the goal of life is, finally, to rest from one's labors as God did.

## Notes

1. Langdon Gilkey, *Shantung Compound* (San Francisco: Harper & Row, 1966), p. 52.

2. Readers may have encountered this story, or one like it, in different places. I have taken it from John Julian Ryan, "Humanistic Work: Its Philosophical and Cultural Implications," in W. J. Heisler and John W. Houck, eds., *A Matter of Dignity: Inquiries into the Humanization of Work* (Notre Dame and London: University of Notre Dame Press, 1977), p. 11.

3. See especially Sebastian de Grazia, *Of Time, Work, and Leisure* (New York: Twentieth Century Fund, 1962). Also helpful are Adriano Tilgher, *Homo Faber* (Chicago: Henry Regnery Co., 1958) and Yves R. Simon, *Work, Society, and Culture* (New York: Fordham University Press, 1971).

4. John Paul II, *On Human Work* (Washington, D.C.: United States Catholic Conference, 1981), pp. 9–10.

5. Stanley Hauerwas, *In Good Company* (Notre Dame and London: University of Notre Dame Press, 1995), p. 110.

6. Ibid., p. 112.

7. Ibid., pp. 115, 117.

8. Keith A. Breclaw, "*Homo Faber* Reconsidered: Two Thomistic Reflections on Work," *The Thomist* 57 (October 1993): 579–607.

9. Ryan, p. 18.

10. Gilkey, p. 132.

11. *Boswell's Life of Johnson,* ed. George Birkbeck Hill (New York: Bigelow, Brown & Co., n.d.), vol. 3, p. 22.

12. Plutarch, *The Lives of the Noble Grecians and Romans,* translated by John Dryden and revised by Arthur Hugh Clough (New York: Modern Library, n.d.), pp. 182–83.

13. W. R. Forrester, *Christian Vocation* (London: Lutterworth Press, 1951), pp. 121–22.

14. The term is derived from words for "furnace" and for "lighting a fire." Hence, it must first have designated those who carried out their work with fire, but it is also used of artisans more generally. See the notes of Sarah Pomeroy in her translation of Xenophon's *Oeconomicus* (Oxford: Clarendon Press, 1994), pp. 235–6.

15. The same is true in Latin, where *negotium* (work) is the lack of *otium* (leisure). Cf. Vukan Kuic, "Work, Leisure and Culture," *Review of Politics* 43 (1981): 446.

16. Aristotle, *The Politics,* translated with an introduction by Ernest Barker (London: Oxford University Press, 1958), pp. 323–24.

17. P. D. Anthony, *The Ideology of Work* (London: Tavistock Publications, 1977), p. 6.

18. Simon, p. 18.

19. The little red hen seems to agree!

20. Wayne A. Meeks, *The Writings of St. Paul* (New York and London: W. W. Norton, 1972), p. 5.

21. Isaiah 65:21.

22. Ryan, p. 17.

23. Lawrence C. Becker, "The Obligation to Work," *Ethics* 91 (October 1980): 43. For example, the 1936 constitution of the Soviet Union (cited by Becker, p. 36) stated: "Work in the U.S.S.R. is a duty and a matter of honour for every able-bodied citizen, in accordance with the principle: 'He who does not work, neither shall he eat.'" The 1977 constitution made the same point a little more gently: "Conscientious labor in one's chosen field of socially useful activity and observance of labor discipline is the duty and a matter of honor for every Soviet citizen who is able to work. Avoiding socially useful work is incompatible with the principles of a socialist society" (ibid.). I should note that, although Becker defends the notion of an obligation to work, he is seeking to provide a much more nuanced account of that notion.

24. Simon, p. 32.

25. Ibid., p. 31.

26. Cited in Forrester, pp. 141–42.

27. Cf. C. S. Lewis, *The World's Last Night and Other Essays* (New York: Harcourt Brace Jovanovich, 1960), pp. 71–81.

28. Simon, p. 33.

29. Simon, p. 6.

30. Ibid., p. 8.

31. Ryan, pp. 16–17.

32. Michael Novak, *Business as a Calling: Work and the Examined Life* (New York: Free Press, 1996), p. 144.

33. George Herbert, "The Pulley," in *The Country Parson, The Temple,* ed. John N. Wall, Jr. (New York: Paulist Press, 1981), pp. 384f.

# I. THE MEANINGS OF WORK

## IA. Work as Co-Creation

1. Genesis 1:26–31. Translation is the Revised Standard Version.

2. Alice Cary, "Work," pp. 72–73 in *The Poetical Works of Alice and Phoebe Cary* (Boston and New York: Houghton, Mifflin & Co., 1882). Alice Cary (1829–1871) lived in Cincinnati and later New York. She published prose sketches of country life and several volumes of poetry, almost always working together with her sister Phoebe, who also published two volumes of poetry.

3. Karl Marx, pp. 123–24 in *The Grundrisse,* edited and translated by David McLellan (New York: Harper Torchbooks, 1971). Marx (1818–1883) worked off and on for many years on the *Grundrisse der Kritik der politischen Ökonomie* ("Outline of the Critique of Political Economy"). Parts of it were incorporated into his famous *Capital,* the first volume of which was published in 1867, but the *Grundrisse,* which included material of far wider scope—more truly philosophical and less purely economic in character—was never completed. David McLellan's was the first translation into English of parts of the *Grundrisse.*

4. Karl Marx, p. 124 in "The German Ideology: Part I," in Robert C. Tucker, ed., *The Marx-Engels Reader* (New York: W. W. Norton & Co., 1972). Marx, together with Engels, wrote *The German Ideology* in 1845–1846. The two short selections from Marx exemplify his vision of human beings as workers, whose greatest fulfillment is to be found in work that involves them fully.

5. Leo Tolstoy, *Anna Karenina,* the Maude Translation, backgrounds and sources, essays in criticism, edited by George Gibian (Oxford: Oxford University Press, 1918, revised 1939), Part III, chapters 4–6. Tolstoy (1828–1910) is, of course, one of the greatest novelists, and Anna Karenina (published 1875–1877) is one of

his two greatest novels. The selection reprinted here involves Constantine Levin, an anguished character tormented by questions about the point of life. He finds some measure of peace through devotion to his family and to his work.

6. Rudyard Kipling, "When Earth's Last Picture Is Painted," pp. 131–32 in *Collected Verse* (Garden City, N.Y.: Doubleday & Co., 1907). The reputation of Kipling (1865–1936) has been somewhat eclipsed because he has been perceived as a supporter of British imperialism. Nevertheless, Kipling's stories and poems were once very widely read.

7. Dorothy L. Sayers, selections from "Why Work?", pp. 47–64 in *Creed or Chaos?* (London: Methuen & Co., 1947). Dorothy Sayers (1893–1957) is known as a writer of detective stories, religious drama, and theological essays, and as a translator of Dante.

8. Sir Arthur Conan Doyle, selection from "The Sign of Four," pp. 89–90 in *The Complete Sherlock Holmes,* vol. 1 (Garden City, N.Y.: Doubleday & Co., 1930). Although his interests and writings were wide-ranging, Sir Arthur Conan Doyle (1859–1930) is known today as the creator of Sherlock Holmes. In the opening lines from "The Sign of Four," reprinted here, Holmes, in conversation with Dr. Watson, explains how work alone can offer him relief from boredom.

# Genesis 1:26–31

Then God said, "Let us make man in our image, after our likeness; and let them have dominion over the fish of the sea, and over the birds of the air, and over the cattle, and over all the earth, and over every creeping thing that creeps upon the earth." So God created man in his own image, in the image of God he created him; male and female he created them. And God blessed them and God said to them, "Be fruitful and multiply, and fill the earth and subdue it; and have dominion over the fish of the sea and over the birds of the air and over every living thing that moves upon the earth." And God said, "Behold, I have given you every plant yielding seed which is upon the face of all the earth, and every tree with seed in its fruit; you shall have them for food. And to every beast of the earth, and to every bird of the air, and to everything that creeps on the earth, everything that has the breath of life, I have given every green plant for food." And it was so. And God saw everything that he had made, and behold, it was very good. And there was evening and there was morning, a sixth day.

# Alice Cary, "Work"

Down and up, and up and down,
  Over and over and over;
Turn in the little seed, dry and brown,
  Turn out the bright red clover.
Work, and the sun your work will share,
  And the rain in its time will fall;
For Nature, she worketh everywhere,
  And the grace of God through all.

With hand on the spade and heart in the sky,
  Dress the ground, and till it;
Turn in the little seed, brown and dry,
  Turn out the golden millet.
Work, and your house shall be duly fed;
  Work, and rest shall be won;
I hold that a man had better be dead
  Than alive, when his work is done!

Down and up, and up and down,
  On the hill-top, low in the valley;
Turn in the little seed, dry and brown,
  Turn out the rose and lily.
Work with a plan, or without a plan,
  And your ends they shall be shaped true;
Work, and learn at first hand like a man,—
  The best way to *know* is to *do!*

Down and up till life shall close,
  Ceasing not your praises;
Turn in the wild white winter snows,
  Turn out the sweet spring daisies.
Work, and the sun your work will share,
  And the rain in its time will fall;
For Nature, she worketh everywhere,
  And the grace of God through all.

# Karl Marx, *The Grundrisse*

'Thou shalt labour by the sweat of thy brow!' was Jehovah's curse that he bestowed upon Adam. A. Smith conceives of labour as such a curse. 'Rest' appears
to him to be the fitting state of things, and identical with 'liberty' and 'happiness'. It seems to be far from A. Smith's thoughts that the individual, 'in his
normal state of health, strength, activity, skill and efficiency', might also require a normal portion of work, and of cessation from rest. It is true that the
quantity of labour to be provided seems to be conditioned by external circumstances, by the purpose to be achieved, and the obstacles to its achievement
that have to be overcome by labour. But neither does it occur to A. Smith that
the overcoming of such obstacles may itself constitute an exercise in liberty,
and that these external purposes lose their character of mere natural necessities
and are established as purposes which the individual himself fixes. The result
is the self-realisation and objectification of the subject, therefore real freedom,
whose activity is precisely labour. Of course he is correct in saying that labour
has always seemed to be repulsive, and forced upon the worker from outside,
in its historical forms of slave-labour, bond-labour and wage-labour, and that
in this sense non-labour could be opposed to it as 'liberty and happiness'. This
is doubly true of this contradictory labour which has not yet created the sub-
jective and objective conditions (which it lost when it abandoned pastoral conditions) which make it into attractive labour and individual self-realisation.
This does not mean that labour can be made merely a joke, or amusement, as
Fourier naively expressed it in shop-girl terms. Really free labour, the compos-
ing of music for example, is at the same time damned serious and demands
the greatest effort. The labour concerned with material production can only
have this character if (1) it is of a social nature, (2) it has a scientific character
and at the same time is general work, i.e. if it ceases to be human effort as a
definite, trained natural force, gives up its purely natural, primitive aspects and
becomes the activity of a subject controlling all the forces of nature in the production process.

# Karl Marx, *The German Ideology*

[T]he division of labour offers us the first example of how, as long as man remains in natural society, that is, as long as a cleavage exists between the particular and the common interest, as long, therefore, as activity is not voluntarily, but naturally, divided, man's own deed becomes an alien power opposed to him, which enslaves him instead of being controlled by him. For as soon as the distribution of labour comes into being, each man has a particular, exclusive sphere of activity, which is forced upon him and from which he cannot escape. He is a hunter, a fisherman, a shepherd, or a critical critic, and must remain so if he does not want to lose his means of livelihood; while in communist society, where nobody has one exclusive sphere of activity, but each can become accomplished in any branch he wishes, society regulates the general production and thus makes it possible for me to do one thing today and another tomorrow, to hunt in the morning, fish in the afternoon, rear cattle in the evening, criticise after dinner, just as I have a mind, without ever becoming hunter, fisherman, shepherd or critic. This fixation of social activity, this consolidation of what we ourselves produce into an objective power above us, growing out of our control, thwarting our expectations, bringing to naught our calculations, is one of the chief factors in historical development up till now.

* Karl Marx is the father of communism. This is basically stating that in a communist state you can do or be whatever you would like, or choose. (career oriented)

# Leo Tolstoy, *Anna Karenina*

## Chapter IV

The personal matter that occupied Levin while he was talking with his brother was this. The year before, when visiting a field that was being mown, he had lost his temper with his steward, and to calm himself had used a remedy of his own—he took a scythe from one of the peasants and himself began mowing.

He liked this work so much that he went mowing several times: he mowed all the meadow in front of his house, and when spring came he planned to devote several whole days to mowing with the peasants. Since his brother's arrival, however, he was in doubt whether to go mowing or not. He did not feel comfortable at the thought of leaving his brother alone all day long, and he also feared that Koznyshev might laugh at him. But while walking over the meadow he recalled the impression mowing had made on him and almost made up his mind to do it. After his irritating conversation with his brother he again remembered his intention.

'I need physical exercise; without it my character gets quite spoilt,' thought he, and determined to go and mow, however uncomfortable his brother and the peasants might make him feel.

In the evening Constantine went to the office and gave orders about the work, sending round to the villages to tell the mowers to come next day to the Kalina meadow, the largest and finest he had.

'And please send my scythe to Titus to be sharpened, and have it taken to the meadow to-morrow: I may go mowing myself,' he said, trying to overcome his confusion.

The steward smiled and said, 'All right, sir.'

That evening, at tea, Levin said to his brother:

'The weather looks settled; to-morrow we begin mowing.'

'I like that work very much,' said Koznyshev.

'I like it awfully too. I have mown with the peasants now and then, and to-morrow I want to mow all day.'

Koznyshev looked up at his brother in surprise.

'How do you mean? All day, just like the peasants?'

'Yes, it is very pleasant,' replied Levin.

'It is splendid physical exercise, but you will hardly be able to hold out,' remarked Koznyshev, without the least sarcasm.

'I have tried it. At first it seems hard, but one gets drawn into it. I don't think I shall lag behind . . . '

'Dear me! But tell me, how do the peasants take it? I expect they laugh at their crank of a master?'

'No, I don't think so; but it is such pleasant work, and at the same time so hard, that one has no time for thinking.'

But how can you dine with them? It would not be quite the thing to send you claret and roast turkey out there?'

'No; I will just come home at their dinner-time.'

Next morning Constantine got up earlier than usual, but giving instructions about the farming delayed him, and when he came to the meadow each man was already mowing his second swath.

From the hill, as he came to his first swath, he could see, in the shade at his feet, a part of the meadow that was already mown, with the green heaps of grass and dark piles of coats thrown down by the mowers.

As he drew nearer, the peasants—following each other in a long straggling line, some with coats on, some in their shirts, each swinging his scythe in his own manner—gradually came into sight. He counted forty-two of them.

They moved slowly along the uneven bottom of the meadow, where a weir had once been. Levin recognized some of his own men. Old Ermil, wearing a very long white shirt, was swinging his scythe, with his back bent; young Vaska, who had been in Levin's service as coachman, and who at each swing of his scythe cut the grass the whole width of his swath and Titus, Levin's mowing master, a thin little peasant, who went along without stopping, mowing his wide swath as if in play.

Levin dismounted and, tethering his horse by the roadside, went up to Titus, who fetched another scythe from behind a bush and gave it to Levin.

'It's ready, master! Like a razor, it will mow of itself,' said Titus, taking off his cap and smiling as he handed the scythe.

Levin took it and began to put himself in position. The peasants, perspiring and merry, who had finished their swaths came out onto the road one after another and laughingly exchanged greetings with the master. They all looked at him, but no one made any remark until a tall, shrivelled, beardless old man, wearing a sheepskin jacket, stepped out on to the road and addressed him:

'Mind, master! Having put your hand to the plough, don't look back!'

And Levin heard the sound of repressed laughter among the mowers.

'I will try not to lag behind,' he said, taking his place behind Titus and waiting his turn to fall in.

'Mind!' repeated the old man.

Titus made room for Levin, and Levin followed him. By the roadside the grass was short and tough, and Levin, who had not done any mowing for a long time and was confused by so many eyes upon him, mowed badly for the first ten minutes, though he swung his scythe with much vigour. He heard voices behind him:

'It's not properly adjusted, the grip is not right. See how he has to stoop!' said one.

'Hold the heel lower,' said another.

'Never mind! It's all right: he'll get into it,' said the old man. 'There he goes . . . '

'You are taking too wide a swath, you'll get knocked up.' . . . 'He's the master, he must work; he's working for himself!' . . . 'But look how uneven!' . . . 'That's what the likes of us used to get a thump on the back for.'

They came to softer grass, and Levin, who was listening without replying, followed Titus and tried to mow as well as possible. When they had gone some hundred steps Titus was still going on without pausing, showing no signs of fatigue, while Levin was already beginning to fear he would not be able to keep up, he felt so tired.

He swung his scythe, feeling almost at the last gasp, and made up his mind to ask Titus to stop. But just at that moment Titus stopped of his own accord, stooped, took up some grass and wiped his scythe with it. Levin straightened himself, sighed, and looked back. The peasant behind him was still mowing but was obviously tired too, for he stopped without coming even with Levin and began whetting his scythe. Titus whetted his own and Levin's, and they began mowing again.

The same thing happened at Levin's second attempt. Titus swung his scythe, swing after swing, without stopping and without getting tired. Levin followed, trying not to lag behind, but it became harder and harder until at last the moment came when he felt he had no strength left, and then Titus again stopped and began whetting his scythe. So they finished the first row. And this long row seemed to Levin particularly difficult; but when it was done and Titus with his scythe over his shoulder turned about and slowly retraced his steps, placing his feet on the marks left on the mown surface by the heels of his boots, and Levin went down his own swath in the same way, then—in spite of the perspiration that ran down his face in streams and dripped from his nose, and though his back was as wet as if the shirt had been soaked in water—he felt very light-hearted. What gave him most pleasure was the knowledge that he would be able to keep up with the peasants.

The only thing marring his joy was the fact that his swath was not well mown. 'I must swing the scythe less with my arms and more with the whole of my body,' he thought, comparing Titus's swath, cut straight, as if by measure, with his own, on which the grass lay scattered and uneven.

As Levin was aware, Titus had been mowing his swath with special rapidity, probably to put his master to the test, and it chanced to be a very long one. The next swaths were easier, but still Levin had to work with all his might to keep even with the peasants. He thought of nothing and desired nothing, except not to lag behind and to do his work as well as possible. He heard only the swishing of the scythes and saw only the receding figure of Titus, the convex half-circle of the mown piece before him, and the grasses and heads of flowers falling in waves about the blade of his scythe, and ahead of him the end of the swath where he would rest.

Suddenly he was conscious of a pleasant coolness on his hot perspiring shoulders, without knowing what it was or whence it came. He glanced up at the sky whilst whetting his scythe. A dark cloud was hanging low overhead, and large drops of rain were falling. Some of the peasants went to put on their coats; others as well as Levin felt pleasure in the refreshing rain and merely moved their shoulders up and down.

They came to the end of another swath. They went on mowing long and short rows, good and poor grass. Levin had lost all count of time and had really no idea whether it was late or early. His work was undergoing a change which gave him intense pleasure. While working he sometimes forgot for some minutes what he was about, and felt quite at ease; then his mowing was nearly as even as that of Titus. But as soon as he began thinking about it and trying to work better, he at once felt how hard the task was and mowed badly.

He finished a swath and was about to start another when Titus paused and went up to the old man, and both looked at the sun.

'What are they talking about, and why don't they start another swath?' thought Levin. It did not occur to him that the peasants who had been mowing unceasingly for four hours, wanted their breakfast.

'Breakfast-time, master,' said the old man.

'Is it time? Well, then, breakfast!'

Levin handed his scythe to Titus, and with the peasants, who were going to fetch the bread that lay with their coats, went across the swaths of the long mown portion of the meadow, slightly sprinkled with rain. Only then he remembered that he had not been right about the weather and that the rain was wetting the hay.

'The hay will be spoilt,' said he.

'It won't hurt, master. "Mow in the rain, rake when it's fine!"'

Levin untied his horse and rode home to his coffee.

By the time Levin had finished breakfast Koznyshev had only just got up, and Levin went back to the meadow before Koznyshev had come to table.

## Chapter V

After breakfast Levin got placed between a humorous old man who invited him to be his neighbour and a young peasant who had only got married last autumn and was now out for his first summer's mowing.

The old man went along holding himself erect, moving with regular, long steps, turning out his toes, and with a precise and even motion that seemed to cost him no more effort than swinging his arms when walking, he laid the grass in a level high ridge, as if in play or as if the sharp scythe of its own accord whizzed through the juicy grass.

Young Mishka went behind Levin. His pleasant young face, with a wisp of grass tied round the forehead over his hair, worked all over with the effort; but whenever anyone glanced at him he smiled. Evidently he would have died rather than confess that the work was trying.

Between these two went Levin. Now, in the hottest part of the day, the work did not seem so hard to him. The perspiration in which he was bathed was cooling, and the sun which burnt his back, his head and his arm—bare to the elbow—added to his strength and perseverance in his task, and those unconscious intervals when it became possible not to think of what he was doing recurred more and more often. The scythe seemed to mow of itself. Those were happy moments. Yet more joyous were the moments when, reaching the river at the lower end of the swaths, the old man would wipe his scythe with the wet grass, rinse its blade in the clear water, and dipping his whetstone-box in the stream, would offer it to Levin.

'A little of my kvas? It's good!' said he, with a wink.

And really Levin thought he had never tasted any nicer drink than this lukewarm water with green stuff floating in it and a flavour of the rusty tin box. And then came the ecstasy of a slow walk, one hand resting on the scythe, when there was leisure to wipe away the streams of perspiration, to breathe deep, to watch the line of mowers, and to see what was going on around in forest and field.

The longer Levin went on mowing, the oftener he experienced those moments of oblivion when his arms no longer seemed to swing the scythe, but the scythe itself his whole body, so conscious and full of life; and as if by magic, regularly and definitely without a thought being given to it, the work accomplished itself of its own accord. These were blessed moments.

It was difficult only at those times when it was necessary to interrupt the movement which had become unconscious, and to think in order to mow around a molehill or a space where the hard sorrel stalks had not been weeded out. The old man accomplished this with ease. When he came to a molehill he would change his action, and with a short jerk of the point and then of the heel of his scythe he would mow all around the molehill. And while doing this he noted everything he came to: now he plucked a sorrel stalk and ate it, or offered it to Levin; now he threw aside a branch with the point of his scythe, or examined a quail's nest from which the hen bird had flown up, almost under the scythe; or he caught a snake, lifting it with the scythe-point as with a fork, and after showing it to Levin, threw it away.

Levin and the young fellow on the other side of him found such changes of action difficult. Both of them, having got into one strained kind of movement, were in the grip of feverish labour and had not the power to change the motion of their bodies and at the same time to observe what lay before them.

Levin did not notice how time passed. Had he been asked how long he had been mowing, he would have answered 'half an hour,' although it was nearly noon. As they were about to begin another swath the old man drew Levin's attention to the little boys and girls approaching from all sides along the road and through the long grass, hardly visible above it, carrying jugs of kvas stoppered with rags, and bundles of bread which strained their little arms.

'Look at the midges crawling along!' he said, pointing to the children and glancing at the sun from under his lifted hand. They completed two more swaths and then the old man stopped.

'Come, master! It's dinner-time,' said he with decision. All the mowers on reaching the river went across the swaths to where their coats lay, and where the children who had brought their dinners sat waiting for them. The men who had driven from a distance gathered in the shadow of their carts; those who lived nearer sheltered under the willow growth, on which they hung grass.

Levin sat down beside them; he did not want to go away.

All the peasants' restraint in the presence of the master had vanished. The men began preparing for dinner. Some had a wash. The young lads bathed in the river; others arranged places for their after-dinner rest, unfastened their bags of bread and unstoppered their jugs of kvas. The old man broke some rye bread into a bowl, mashed it with a spoon handle, poured over it some water from his tin, broke more bread into it and salted it, and then, turning to the East, said grace.

'Come, master, have some of my dinner,' said he, kneeling in front of his bowl.

The bread and water was so nice that Levin gave up all intention of going home to lunch. He shared the old man's meal and got into conversation with him about his domestic affairs, taking a lively interest in them and telling him about his own, giving him all the particulars which would interest the old peasant. When the old man got up and, having said grace, lay down beneath the willows with an armful of grass under his head, Levin did the same, regardless of the flies, importunate and persistent in the sunshine, and of the crawling insects that tickled his perspiring face and body. He at once fell asleep, waking only when the sun touched the opposite side of the willows and reached him. The old man had already been long awake and sat setting the scythes for the young men.

Levin looked round and hardly recognized the place, everything was so altered. A wide expanse of the meadow was already mown, and with its swaths of grass already giving off perfume, shone with a peculiar fresh brilliance in the oblique rays of the descending sun. The bushes by the river where the grass had been cut and the river itself with its curves, previously invisible, were now glittering like steel; and the people getting up and moving about, the steep wall of yet uncut grass, and the hawks soaring over the bare meadow, struck him as something quite new. When he was fully awake Levin began to calculate how much had been done and how much could still be done that day.

An extraordinary amount had been done by the forty-two men. The larger meadow, which in the days of serfdom had taken thirty men two days to mow, was all finished except some short patches at the corners. But Levin wanted to get as much as possible done that day, and it was vexatious to see the sun already declining. He was not feeling at all tired and was only longing to work again and to accomplish as much as he could.

'What do you think—could we manage to get Mashkin Heights mown today?' he asked the old man.

'Well, God willing, we might! The sun is not very high though. Perhaps—if the lads could have a little vodka!'

At half-time, when they sat down again and those who smoked were lighting their pipes, the old man informed the young fellows that if they mowed the Mashkin Heights there would be vodka.

'What? Not mow that? Come along, Titus; we'll get it clear in no time!'

'You can eat your fill at night. Let's begin!' shouted different voices, and the mowers took their places, finishing their bread as they went.

'Now then, lads! Keep going!' said Titus, starting off ahead almost at a trot.

'Go on, go on!' said the old man, hurrying after him and easily catching him up. 'Take care, I'll mow you down!'

And young and old vied with each other at mowing. But in spite of their haste they did not spoil the grass, and the swaths fell just as evenly and exactly as before. The small patch that was left in the last corner was mown in five minutes; and whilst the last mowers were finishing their swaths, those in front, carrying their coats over their shoulders, were already crossing the road toward Mashkin Heights.

The sun was already setting toward the trees when, with their tin boxes rattling, they entered the wooded ravine of the Heights.

The grass that in the middle of the ravine reached to their waists was delicate, soft, and broad-bladed, speckled here and there with cow-grass.

After a short consultation as to whether they should mow the ravine across or lengthwise, Prokhor—a gigantic dark man and a famous mower—took the lead. He went in front, mowed a swath, turned around and restarted; following him all the others took their places, going downhill along the creek and back up to the very skirts of the wood. The sun had set behind the wood and now shone only on the mowers at the top of the hill, while in the valley, where the mists were rising, they were in cool, dewy shade. The work proceeded briskly.

The scented grass, cut down with a sound that showed how juicy it was, fell in high ridges. On the short swaths the mowers crowded together, their tin boxes clattering, their scythes ringing whenever they touched, the whetstones whistling upon the blades, and their merry voices resounding as they urged each other on.

Levin was again mowing between the old man and the lad. The old man, who had put on his sheepskin jacket, was still as jolly, witty, and easy in his movements as before. In the wood their scythes continually cut down wood mushrooms, grown plump amid the juicy grass. The old man stooped each time he came upon one, picked it up, and put it inside his jacket, saying, 'Another treat for my old woman.'

It was easy to cut the wet soft grass, but on the other hand it was very difficult to go up and down the steep slopes of the ravine. This, however, did not trouble the old man. Swinging his scythe just as usual, taking short steps with feet shod in large bast-plaited shoes, he slowly climbed the slopes; and though his whole body and his loosely-hanging trousers shook, he did not miss a single mushroom or a curious grass, and continued joking with the other peasants and with Levin. Levin followed, and often thought he would certainly fall when climbing a mound with his scythe in his hand—a mound so steep that it would have been hard to climb even unencumbered. Still, he managed to climb it and to do all that had to be done; and he felt as if some external force were urging him on.

## Chapter VI

Mashkin Heights were mown, and the peasants, having completed their last swaths, put on their coats and went home in high spirits. Levin, having regretfully taken leave of them, mounted and rode home. He looked back from the top of the hill. He could not see the men, for the mist rising from the hollow hid them; but he heard their merry rough voices, laughter, and the clanking of the scythes.

Koznyshev had long had his dinner, and was in his room drinking iced water with lemon, while looking over the papers and magazines just arrived by post, when Levin rushed in, his tangled hair clinging to his moist brow, his shirt saturated back and front and dark with perspiration, and cried out joyfully:

'We have finished the whole of the meadow! How delightful it is! wonderful! And how have you got on?' Levin had quite forgotten the unpleasant conversation of the previous day.

'Dear me, what a sight you are!' said Koznyshev, turning to his brother with a momentary look of vexation. 'The door—the door! Shut it!' he exclaimed. 'You've certainly let in a whole dozen!' Koznyshev could not bear flies, and opened the windows in his room only at night, keeping the door carefully closed.

'No, not one, I swear. And if I have, I'll catch it! . . . You would not believe what enjoyment it was! And how have you spent the day?'

'Quite well. But have you really been mowing all day? You must be as hungry as a wolf. Kuzma has everything ready for you.'

'No, I don't want to eat; I have had something there. But I'll go and wash.'

'Yes, yes, go; and I will come presently.' Koznyshev shook his head as he looked at his brother. 'Go, go, and be quick!' he added with a smile, as, gathering together his books, he prepared to go too. He also felt suddenly quite cheerful and did not wish to part from his brother. 'And where were you when it rained?'

'What rain was that? Only a few drops. . . . Well, then, I'll come back directly. So you have spent the day all right? That's good.' And Levin went off to dress.

Five minutes later the brothers met again in the dining-room. Though Levin had imagined that he was not hungry, and sat down to table only not to offend Kuzma, yet when he began eating he thought everything delicious. Koznyshev smiled as he looked at him.

'Oh, yes, there's a letter for you,' said he. 'Kuzma, please bring it. It's downstairs. And mind you shut the door.'

The letter was from Oblonsky. Levin read it aloud. Oblonsky wrote from Petersburg: 'I have had a letter from Dolly. She is in Ergushevo, and everything is out of gear there. Please go and see her and help her with your advice—you know all about everything. She will be so glad to see you. She is quite alone, poor thing; my mother-in-law is still abroad.'

'That's splendid! I will certainly go and see her,' said Levin. 'Or shall we both go? She is such a good woman; don't you think so?'

'Is it far from here?'

'A little over twenty-five miles or maybe even thirty, but the road is excellent. We'll have a fine drive.'

'I shall be very glad,' replied Koznyshev, still smiling. The sight of his younger brother had a distinctly cheering influence on him.

'I must say you have an appetite!' he said, glancing at the sunburnt ruddy face bent over the plate.

'Fine! You would hardly believe what a remedy it is for every kind of folly. I am thinking of enriching Medicine with a new word: *Arbeitskur!*

'You would hardly require it, I should say.'

'No, but those who suffer from their nerves do.'

'Yes, it ought to be tested. You know, I thought of coming to the meadow to have a look at you, but it was so unbearably hot that I got only as far as the forest! I sat there a little, and then went through the forest to the village, where I met your old wet-nurse and sounded her as to what the peasants think of you. From her I understood that they do not approve of your doing it. She said: "It's not gentlefolk's work." It seems to me that on the whole, in the people's opinion, a very decided demand for what they call "gentlefolk's work" exists, and they don't approve of the gentry going outside the bounds they set for them.'

'Possibly; but it is a pleasure such as I have never in my life experienced before, and there is nothing wrong in it. Don't you think so too?' replied Levin. 'If they don't like it, it can't be helped. Besides, I think it's all right. Eh?'

'I see that on the whole you are well satisfied with your day.'

'Very well indeed! We finished the meadow. And I chummed up with a fine old man! You can't imagine what a charming fellow he is.'

'Well, then, you are satisfied with your day, and so am I. First of all I solved two chess problems—one a very good one, beginning with a pawn move. I'll show it you. And afterwards I thought over our yesterday's conversation.'

'What about yesterday's conversation?' asked Levin, who had finished dinner and sat blissfully blinking and puffing, quite unable to remember what yesterday's conversation had been about.

'I think you are partly right. Our disagreement lies in the fact that you consider personal interests the motive power, while I think every man with a certain degree of education ought to be interested in the general welfare. You may be right in thinking that activity backed by material interest is best; but your nature is altogether *primesautiere* as the French say: you want passionate, energetic activity, or nothing at all.'

Levin listened to his brother but understood absolutely nothing and did not wish to understand. He was only afraid his brother might put some question which would elicit the fact that he was not paying attention.

"That's what it is, old chap,' said Koznyshev, patting Constantine's shoulder.

'Yes, of course! But what matter? I don't insist on my view,' replied Levin, with a guilty, childlike smile. 'What can I have been disputing about?' he thought. 'Of course I was right, and he was right too, so it's all right! . . . But I must go round to the office.' He rose, stretching himself and smiling. Koznyshev smiled too.

'Shall we go for a stroll together?' he said, not wishing to part from his brother, who seemed to be exhaling freshness and vigour; 'Come along! We could call in at the office if you want to.'

'Oh, dear me!' exclaimed Levin, so loudly that he scared Koznyshev.

'What's the matter?'

'How's Agatha Mikhaylovna's arm?' asked Levin, slapping his head. 'I had forgotten all about it.'

'Much better.'

'Well, I'll run and see her, all the same. You won't have got your hat before I am back.'

And his heels clattered swiftly down the stairs, making a noise like a rattle.

# Rudyard Kipling,
## "When Earth's Last Picture Is Painted"

When Earth's last picture is painted and the tubes are
    twisted and dried,
When the oldest colours have faded, and the youngest critic
    has died,
We shall rest, and, faith, we shall need it—lie down for an
    aeon or two,
Till the Master of All Good Workmen shall put us to work
    anew.

And those that were good shall be happy: they shall sit in a
    golden chair;
They shall splash at a ten-league canvas with brushes of
    comets' hair;
They shall find real saints to draw from—Magdalene, Peter,
    and Paul;
They shall work for an age at a sitting and never be tired at
    all!

And only the Master shall praise us, and only the Master
    shall blame;
And no one shall work for money, and no one shall work for
    fame,
But each for the joy of the working, and each, in his separate
    star,
Shall draw the Thing as he sees It for the God of Things as
    They are!

# Dorothy Sayers, "Why Work?"

I have already, on a previous occasion, spoken at some length on the subject of Work and Vocation. What I urged then was a thorough-going revolution in our whole attitude to work. I asked that it should be looked upon—not as a necessary drudgery to be undergone for the purpose of making money, but as a way of life in which the nature of man should find its proper exercise and delight and so fulfil itself to the glory of God. That it should, in fact, be thought of as a creative activity undertaken for the love of the work itself; and that man, made in God's image, should make things, as God makes them, for the sake of doing well a thing that is well worth doing. . . .

What is the Christian understanding of work? . . . I should like to put before you two or three propositions arising out of the doctrinal position which I stated at the beginning: namely, that work is the natural exercise and function of man—the creature who is made in the image of his Creator. You will find that any one of them, if given in effect everyday practice, is so revolutionary (as compared with the habits of thinking into which we have fallen), as to make all political revolutions look like conformity.

The first, stated quite briefly, is that work is not, primarily, a thing one does to live, but the thing one lives to do. It is, or it should be, the full expression of the worker's faculties, the thing in which he finds spiritual, mental, and bodily satisfaction, and the medium in which he offers himself to God.

Now the consequences of this are not merely that the work should be performed under decent living and working conditions. That is a point we have begun to grasp, and it is a perfectly sound point. But we have tended to concentrate on it to the exclusion of other considerations far more revolutionary.

(a) There is, for instance, the question of profits and remuneration. We have all got it fixed in our heads that the proper end of work is to be paid for—to produce a return in profits or payment to the worker which fully or more than compensates the effort he puts into it. But if our proposition is true, this does not follow at all. So long as Society provides the worker with a sufficient return in real wealth to enable him to carry on the work properly, then he has his reward. For his work is the measure of his life, and his satisfaction is found in the fulfilment of his own nature, and in contemplation of the perfection of his work. That, in practice, there is this satisfaction, is shown by the mere fact that a man will put loving labour into some hobby which can never bring him in any economically adequate return. His satisfaction comes, in the god-like manner, from looking upon what he has made and finding it very

43

good. He is no longer bargaining with his work, but serving it. It is only when work has to be looked on as a means to gain that it becomes hateful; for then, instead of a friend, it becomes an enemy from whom tolls and contributions have to be extracted. What most of us demand from society is that we should always get out of it a little more than the value of the labour we give to it. By this process, we persuade ourselves that society is always in our debt—a conviction that not only piles up actual financial burdens, but leaves us with a grudge against society.

(b) Here is the second consequence. At present we have no clear grasp of the principle that every man should do the work for which he is fitted by nature! The employer is obsessed by the notion that he must find cheap labour, and the worker by the notion that the best-paid job is the job for him. Only feebly, inadequately, and spasmodically do we ever attempt to tackle the problem from the other end, and inquire: What type of worker is suited to this type of work? People engaged in education see clearly that this is the right end to start from; but they are frustrated by economic pressure, and by the failure of parents on the one hand and employers on the other to grasp the fundamental importance of this approach. And that the trouble results far more from a failure of intelligence than from economic necessity is seen clearly under war conditions, when, though competitive economics are no longer a governing factor, the right men and women are still persistently thrust into the wrong jobs, through sheer inability on everybody's part to imagine a purely vocational approach to the business of fitting together the worker and his work.

(c) A third consequence is that, if we really believed this proposition and arranged our work and our standard of values accordingly, we should no longer think of work as something that we hastened to get through in order to enjoy our leisure; we should look on our leisure as the period of changed rhythm that refreshed us for the delightful purpose of getting on with our work. And, this being so, we should tolerate no regulations of any sort that prevented us from working as long and as well as our enjoyment of work demanded. We should resent any such restrictions as a monstrous interference with the liberty of the subject. How great an upheaval of our ideas that would mean I leave you to imagine. It would turn topsy-turvy all our notions about hours of work, rates of work, unfair competition, and all the rest of it. We should all find ourselves fighting, as now only artists and the members of certain professions fight, for precious time in which to get on with the job—instead of fighting for precious hours saved from the job.

(d) A fourth consequence is that we should fight tooth and nail, not for mere employment, but for the quality of the work that we had to do. We should clamour to be engaged on work that was worth doing, and in which we could take a pride. The worker would demand that the stuff he helped to turn out

*[Handwritten marginal notes in left margin:]*

*Not what he/she is fitted by nature to do. Not what society dictates through the economy what most of us do.*

*b. The worker should do what he/she is fitted by nature to do. Not what pays the most. Sayer is frustrated that society dictates through the economy what most of us do.*

*c. We should think of work as a vocation not a vacation.*

d. Take pride in what you do and with the product you produced. Also don't relinquish the product after you produce it, see it through to the end.

Dorothy Sayers, "Why Work?"                                    45

should be good stuff—he would no longer be content to take the cash and let the credit go. Like the shareholders in the brewery, he would feel a sense of personal responsibility, and clamour to know, and to control, what went into the beer he brewed. There would be protests and strikes—not only about pay and conditions, but about the quality of the work demanded and the honesty, beauty, and usefulness of the goods produced. The greatest insult which a commercial age has offered to the worker has been to rob him of all interest in the end-product of the work and to force him to dedicate his life to making badly things which were not worth making.

This first proposition chiefly concerns the worker as such. My second *2nd prop.* proposition directly concerns Christians as such, and it is this: It is the business of the Church to recognize that the secular vocation, as such, is sacred. Christian people, and particularly perhaps the Christian clergy, must get it firmly into their heads that when a man or woman is called to a particular job of secular work, that is as true a vocation as though he or she were called to specifically religious work. The Church must concern herself not only with such questions as the just price and proper working conditions: she must concern herself with seeing that the work itself is such as a human being can perform without degradation—that no one is required by economic or any other considerations to devote himself to work that is contemptible, soul-destroying, or harmful. It is not right for her to acquiesce in the notion that a man's life is divided into the time he spends on his work and the time he spends in serving God. He must be able to serve God in his work, and the work itself must be accepted and respected as the medium of divine creation. . . .

The Church's approach to an intelligent carpenter is usually confined to exhorting him not to be drunk and disorderly in his leisure hours, and to come to church on Sundays. What the Church should be telling him is this: that the very first demand that his religion makes upon him is that he should make good tables. . . .

Let the Church remember this: that every maker and worker is called to serve God in his profession or trade—not outside it. The Apostles complained rightly when they said it was not meet they should leave the word of God and serve tables; their vocation was to preach the word. But the person whose vocation it is to prepare the meals beautifully might with equal justice protest: It is not meet for us to leave the service of our tables to preach the word. The official Church wastes time and energy, and, moreover, commits sacrilege, in demanding that secular workers should neglect their proper vocation in order to do Christian work—by which she means ecclesiastical work. The only Christian work is good work well done. Let the Church see to it that the workers are Christian people and do their work well, as to God: then all the work will be Christian work, whether it is Church embroidery, or sewage-farming. . . .

This brings me to my third proposition; and this may sound to you the most revolutionary of all. It is this: the worker's first duty is to *serve the work*. The popular 'catch' phrase of to-day is that it is everybody's duty to serve the community. It is a well-sounding phrase, but there is a catch in it: It is the old catch about the two great commandments. 'Love God—and your neighbour; on those two commandments hang all the Law and the Prophets.' The catch in it, which nowadays the world has largely forgotten, is that the second commandment depends upon the first, and that without the first, it is a delusion and a snare. Much of our present trouble and disillusionment have come from putting the second commandment before the first. If we put our neighbour first, we are putting man above God, and that is what we have been doing ever since we began to worship humanity and make man the measure of all things. Whenever man is made the centre of things, he becomes the storm-centre of trouble—and that is precisely the catch about serving the community. It ought perhaps to make us suspicious of that phrase when we consider that it is the slogan of every commercial scoundrel and swindler who wants to make sharp business practice pass muster as social improvement. 'Service' is the motto of the advertiser, of big business, and of fraudulent finance. . . .

There is, in fact, a paradox about working to serve the community, and it is this: that to aim directly at serving the community is to falsify the work; the only way to serve the community is to forget the community and serve the work.

# Sir Arthur Conan Doyle, "The Sign of Four"

Sherlock Holmes took his bottle from the corner of the mantelpiece, and his hypodermic syringe from its neat morocco case. With his long, white, nervous fingers he adjusted the delicate needle and rolled back his left shirtcuff. For some little time his eyes rested thoughtfully upon the sinewy forearm and wrist, all dotted and scarred with innumberable puncture-marks. Finally, he thrust the sharp point home, pressed down the tiny piston, and sank back into the velvet-lined armchair with a long sigh of satisfaction.

Three times a day for many months I had witnessed this performance, but custom had not reconciled my mind to it. . . . Again and again I had registered a vow that I should deliver my soul upon the subject; but there was that in the cool, nonchalant air of my companion which made him the last man with whom one would care to take anything approaching to a liberty. . . .

Yet upon that afternoon, whether it was the Beaune which I had taken with my lunch or the additional exasperation produced by the extreme deliberation of his manner, I suddenly felt that I could hold out no longer.

"Which is it to-day?" I asked, "morphine or cocaine?"

He raised his eyes languidly from the old black-letter volume which he had opened.

"It is cocaine," he said, "a seven-per-cent solution. Would you care to try it?"

"No indeed," I answered brusquely, "My constitution has not got over the Afghan campaign yet. I cannot afford to throw any extra strain upon it."

He smiled at my vehemence. "Perhaps you are right, Watson," he said. "I suppose that its influence is physically a bad one. I find it, however, so transcendently stimulating and clarifying to the mind that its secondary action is a matter of small moment."

"But consider!" I said earnestly. "Count the cost! Your brain may, as you say, be roused and excited, but it is a pathological and morbid process which involves increased tissue-change and may at last leave a permanent weakness. You know, too, what a black reaction comes upon you. Surely the game is hardly worth the candle. Why should you, for a mere passing pleasure, risk the loss of those great powers with which you have been endowed? Remember that I speak not only as one comrade to another but as a medical man to one for whose constitution he is to some extent answerable."

He did not seem offended. On the contrary, he put his finger-tips together, and leaned his elbows on the arms of his chair, like one who has a relish for conversation.

"My mind," he said, "rebels at stagnation. Give me problems, give me work, give me the most abstruse cryptogram, or the most intricate analysis, and I am in my own proper atmosphere. I can dispense then with artificial stimulants."

# IB. Work as Necessary for Leisure

1. Hesiod, "Works and Days," pp. 5, 7, 9, 11, 13 in *The Homeric Hymns and Homerica,* rev. ed., translated by Hugh G. Evelyn-White, Loeb Classical Library (London: William Heinemann, 1982). Hesiod, who is one of the earliest Greek poets known to us, lived around 700 B.C. His epic poem, *Works and Days*—addressed to his brother Perses, who had gotten an unfair share of their inheritance—recounts several myths that teach the importance of hard and honest work.

2. Aristotle, selections from Book X, chapters 6-8 (pp. 286-94) in *Nicomachean Ethics,* translated by Martin Ostwald (Indianapolis: Bobbs-Merrill, 1962). Aristotle (384-322 B.C.) was certainly one of the most influential philosophers in Western history, and the *Nicomachean Ethics* is his most important ethical writing. The selections here discuss the place of contemplation in "happiness," that is, in a flourishing human life.

3. Aristotle, selections from Books VII and VIII (pp. 289, 301, 335-36) in *The Politics,* translated by Ernest Barker (London and New York: Oxford University Press, 1958). The *Politics* is less a single treatise than a collection of essays on political themes. It is worth noting that Aristotle was himself a tutor for six years to the young (age 13-19) Alexander the Great. The brief selections included here develop Aristotle's concept of leisure as distinct from both occupation and recreation.

4. Xenophon, selection from Book IV (pp. 121, 123) in *Xenophon Oeconomicus: A Social and Historical Commentary,* with English translation by Sarah B. Pomeroy (Oxford: Clarendon Press, 1994). Xenophon (431-350 B.C.) is generally described as a Greek historian, was a contemporary of Socrates, and served as a mercenary under the Persian king Cyrus. His *Oeconomicus* is a discussion of how best to manage one's estate.

5. Josef Pieper, selection from pp. 137-40 of "Leisure and Its Threefold Opposition," in Josef Pieper, *An Anthology* (San Francisco: Ignatius Press, 1989). Pieper (1904-1997) was a German philosopher and a Roman Catholic, whose book *Leisure: The Basis of Culture* is a classic discussion of its subject.

6. Angela Morgan, "Buttons and Trash," pp. 168–69 in *Creator Man* (New York: Dodd, Mead & Co., 1929). Angela Morgan (1874–1957) was an American poet, widely read in the early twentieth century, who wrote a number of poems dealing with the place of work in life.

7. Witold Rybczynski, "Waiting for the Weekend," pp. 35–37 in *The Atlantic Monthly* (August 1991). Rybczynski (1943–) is a professor of architecture who, as is clear from this selection, writes on a wide range of topics.

# Hesiod, *Works and Days*

For the gods keep hidden from men the means of life. Else you would easily do work enough in a day to supply you for a full year even without working; soon would you put away your rudder over the smoke, and the fields worked by ox and sturdy mule would run to waste. But Zeus in the anger of his heart hid it [fire], because Prometheus the crafty deceived him; therefore he planned sorrow and mischief against men. He hid fire; but that the noble son of Iapetus stole again for men from Zeus the counsellor in a hollow fennel-stalk, so that Zeus who delights in thunder did not see it. But afterwards Zeus who gathers the clouds said to him in anger:

"Son of Iapetus, surpassing all in cunning, you are glad that you have out-witted me and stolen fire—a great plague to you yourself and to men that shall be. But I will give men as the price for fire an evil thing in which they may all be glad of heart while they embrace their own destruction."

So said the father of men and gods, and laughed aloud. And he bade famous Hephaestus make haste and mix earth with water and to put in it the voice and strength of human kind, and fashion a sweet, lovely maiden-shape, like to the immortal goddesses in face; and Athene to teach her needlework and the weaving of the varied web; and golden Aphrodite to shed grace upon her head and cruel longing and cares that weary the limbs. And he charged Hermes the guide, the Slayer of Argus, to put in her a shameless mind and a deceitful nature.

So he ordered. And they obeyed the lord Zeus the son of Cronos. Forthwith the famous Lame God moulded clay in the likeness of a modest maid, as the son of Cronos purposed. And the goddess bright eyed Athene girded and clothed her, and the divine Graces and queenly Persuasion put necklaces of gold upon her, and the rich-haired Hours crowned her head with spring flowers. And Pallas Athene bedecked her form with all manner of finery. Also the Guide, the Slayer of Argus, contrived within her lies and crafty words and a deceitful nature at the will of loud thundering Zeus, and the Herald of the gods put speech in her. And he called this woman Pandora, because all they who dwelt on Olympus gave each a gift, a plague to men who eat bread.

But when he had finished the sheer, hopeless snare, the Father sent glorious Argus-Slayer, the swift messenger of the gods, to take it to Epimetheus as a gift. And Epimetheus did not think on what Prometheus had said to him, bidding him never take a gift of Olympian Zeus, but to send it back for fear it might prove to be something harmful to men. But he took the gift, and afterwards, when the evil thing was already his, he understood.

For ere this the tribes of men lived on earth remote and free from ills and hard toil and heavy sicknesses which bring the Fates upon men; for in misery men grow old quickly. But the woman took off the great lid of the jar with her hands and scattered all these and her thought caused sorrow and mischief to men. Only Hope remained there in an unbreakable home within under the rim of the great jar, and did not fly out at the door; for ere that, the lid of the jar stopped her, by the will of Aegis-holding Zeus who gathers the clouds. But the rest, countless plagues, wander amongst men; for earth is full of evils and the sea is full. Of themselves diseases come upon men continually by day and by night, bringing mischief to mortals silently; for wise Zeus took away speech from them. So is there no way to escape the will of Zeus.

Or if you will, I will sum you up another tale well and skilfully—and do you lay it up in your heart,—how the gods and mortal men sprang from one source.

First of all the deathless gods who dwell on Olympus made a golden race of mortal men who lived in the time of Cronos when he was reigning in heaven. And they lived like gods without sorrow of heart, remote and free from toil and grief: miserable age rested not on them; but with legs and arms never failing they made merry with feasting beyond the reach of all evils. When they died, it was as though they were overcome with sleep, and they had all good things; for the fruitful earth unforced bare them fruit abundantly and without stint. They dwelt in ease and peace upon their lands with many good things, rich in flocks and loved by the blessed gods.

But after the earth had covered this generation—they are called pure spirits dwelling on the earth, and are kindly, delivering from harm, and guardians of mortal men; for they roam everywhere over the earth, clothed in mist and keep watch on judgements and cruel deeds, givers of wealth; for this royal right also they received;—then they who dwell on Olympus made a second generation which was of silver and less noble by far. It was like the golden race neither in body nor in spirit. A child was brought up at his good mother's side an hundred years, an utter simpleton, playing childishly in his own home. But when they were full grown and were come to the full measure of their prime, they lived only a little time and that in sorrow because of their foolishness, for they could not keep from sinning and from wronging one another, nor would they serve the immortals, nor sacrifice on the holy altars of the blessed ones as it is right for men to do wherever they dwell. Then Zeus the son of Cronos was angry and put them away, because they would not give honour to the blessed gods who live on Olympus.

But when earth had covered this generation also—they are called blessed spirits of the underworld by men, and, though they are of second order, yet honour attends them also—Zeus the Father made a third generation of mortal men, a brazen race, sprung from ash-trees; and it was in no way equal to the silver age, but was terrible and strong. They loved the lamentable works of Ares and deeds of violence; they ate no bread, but were hard of heart like adamant fearful men. Great was their strength and unconquerable the arms which grew from their shoulders on their strong limbs. Their armour was of bronze, and their houses of bronze, and of bronze were their implements: there was no black iron. These were destroyed by their own hands and passed to the dank house of chill Hades, and left no name: terrible though they were, black Death seized them, and they left the bright light of the sun.

But when earth had covered this generation also, Zeus the son of Cronos made yet another, the fourth, upon the fruitful earth, which was nobler and more righteous, a god-like race of hero-men who are called demi-gods, the race before our own, throughout the boundless earth. Grim war and dread battle destroyed a part of them, some in the land of Cadmus at seven-gated Thebe when they fought for the flocks of Oedipus, and some, when it had brought them in ships over the great sea gulf to Troy for rich-haired Helen's sake: there death's end enshrouded a part of them. But to the others father Zeus the son of Cronos gave a living and an abode apart from men, and made them dwell at the ends of earth. And they live untouched by sorrow in the islands of the blessed along the shore of deep swirling Ocean, happy heroes for whom the grain-giving earth bears honey-sweet fruit flourishing thrice a year, far from the deathless gods, and Cronos rules over them; for the father of men and gods released him from his bonds. And these last equally have honour and glory.

And again far-seeing Zeus made yet another generation, the fifth, of men who are upon the bounteous earth.

Thereafter, would that I were not among the men of the fifth generation, but either had died before or been born afterwards. For now truly is a race of iron, and men never rest from labour and sorrow by day, and from perishing by night; and the gods shall lay sore trouble upon them. But, notwithstanding, even these shall have some good mingled with their evils. And Zeus will destroy this race of mortal men also when they come to have grey hair on the temples at their birth. The father will not agree with his children, nor the children with their father, nor guest with his host, nor comrade with comrade; nor will brother be dear to brother as aforetime. Men will dishonour their parents as they grow quickly old, and will carp at them, chiding them with bitter words, hard-hearted they, not knowing the fear of the gods. They will not repay their aged parents the cost of their nurture, for might shall be their right: and one man will sack another's city. There will be no favour for the man who keeps his oath or for the just or for the good; but rather men will praise the evil-doer and his violent dealing. Strength will be right and reverence will cease to be; and the wicked will hurt the worthy man, speaking false words against him, and will swear an oath upon them. Envy, foul-mouthed, delighting in evil, with scowling face, will go along with wretched men one and all. And then Aidos and Nemesis, with their sweet forms wrapped in white robes, will go from the wide-pathed earth and forsake mankind to join the company of the deathless gods: and bitter sorrows will be left for mortal men, and there will be no help against evil.

# Aristotle, *Nicomachean Ethics*

### 6. Happiness and activity

Now that we have completed our discussion of the virtues, and of the different kinds of friendship and pleasure, it remains to sketch an outline of happiness, since, as we assert, it is the end or goal of human (aspirations). Our account will be more concise if we recapitulate what we have said so far.

We stated, then, that happiness is not a characteristic; (if it were,) a person who passes his whole life in sleep, vegetating like a plant, or someone who experiences the greatest misfortunes could possess it. If, then, such a conclusion is unacceptable, we must, in accordance with our earlier discussion, classify happiness as some sort of activity. Now, some activities are necessary and desirable only for the sake of something else, while others are desirable in themselves. Obviously, happiness must be classed as an activity desirable in itself and not for the sake of something else. For happiness lacks nothing and is self-sufficient. Activities desirable in themselves are those from which we seek to derive nothing beyond the actual exercise of the activity. Actions in conformity with virtue evidently constitute such activities; for to perform noble and good deeds is something desirable for its own sake. Pleasant amusements, too, (are desirable for their own sake). We do not choose them for the sake of something else, since they lead to harm rather than good when we become neglectful of our bodies and our property. But most of those who are considered happy find an escape in pastimes of this sort, and this is why people who are well versed in such pastimes find favor at the courts of tyrants; they make themselves pleasant by providing what the tyrants are after, and what they want is amusement. Accordingly, such amusements are regarded as being conducive to happiness, because men who are in positions of power devote their leisure to them. But perhaps such persons cannot be (regarded as) evidence. For virtue and intelligence, which are the sources of morally good activities, do not consist in wielding power. Also, if these men, who have never tasted pure and generous pleasure, find an escape in the pleasures of the body, this is no sufficient reason for thinking that such pleasures are in fact more desirable. For children, too, think that what they value is actually the best. It is, therefore, not surprising that as children apparently do not attach value to the same things as do adults, so bad men do not attach value to the same things as do good men. Accordingly, as we have stated repeatedly, what is valuable and pleasant to a morally good man actually is valuable and pleasant. Each individual considers that activity most desirable which corresponds to his own proper characteristic condition, and a morally good man, of course, so considers activity in conformity with virtue.

Consequently, happiness does not consist in amusement. In fact, it would be strange if our end were amusement, and if we were to labor and suffer hardships all our life long merely to amuse ourselves. For, one might say, we choose everything for the sake of something else—except happiness; for happiness is an end. Obviously, it is foolish and all too childish to exert serious efforts and toil for purposes of amusement. Anacharsis seems to be right when he advises to play in order to be serious; for amusement is a form of rest, and since we cannot work continuously we need rest. Thus rest is not an end, for we take it for the sake of (further) activity. The happy life is regarded as a life in conformity with virtue. It is a life which involves effort and is not spent in amusement. . . .

### 7. Happiness, intelligence, and the contemplative life

Now, if happiness is activity in conformity with virtue, it is to be expected that it should conform with the highest virtue, and that is the virtue of the best part of us. Whether this is intelligence or something else which, it is thought, by its very nature rules and guides us and which gives us our notions of what is noble and divine; whether it is itself divine or the most divine thing in us; it is the activity of this part (when operating) in conformity with the excellence or virtue proper to it that will be complete happiness. That it is an activity concerned with theoretical knowledge or contemplation has already been stated.

This would seem to be consistent with our earlier statements as well as the truth. For this activity is not only the highest—for intelligence is the highest possession we have in us, and the objects which are the concern of intelligence are the highest objects of knowledge—but also the most continuous: we are able to study continuously more easily than to perform any kind of action. Furthermore, we think of pleasure as a necessary ingredient in happiness. Now everyone agrees that of all the activities that conform with virtue activity in conformity with theoretical wisdom is the most pleasant. At any rate, it seems that (the pursuit of wisdom or) philosophy holds pleasures marvellous in purity and certainty, and it is not surprising that time spent in knowledge is more pleasant than time spent in research. Moreover, what is usually called "self-sufficiency" will be found in the highest degree in the activity which is concerned with theoretical knowledge. Like a just man and any other virtuous man, a wise man requires the necessities of life; once these have been adequately provided, a just man still needs people toward whom and in company with whom to act justly, and the same is true of a self-controlled man, a courageous man, and all the rest. But a wise man is able to study even by himself, and the wiser he is the more is he able to do it. Perhaps he could do it better if he had colleagues to work with him, but he still is the most self-sufficient of all. Again, study seems to be the only activity which is loved for its own sake. For while we derive a greater or a smaller advantage from practical pursuits beyond the action itself, from study we derive nothing beyond the activity of studying. Also, we regard happiness as depending on leisure; for our purpose in being busy is to have leisure, and we wage war in order to have peace. Now, the practical virtues are activated in political and military pursuits, but the actions involved in these pursuits seem to be unleisurely. This is completely true of military pursuits, since no one chooses to wage war or foments war for the sake of war; he would have to be utterly bloodthirsty if he were to make enemies of his friends simply in order to have battle and slaughter. But the activity of the statesman, too, has no leisure. It attempts to gain advantages beyond political action, advantages such as political power, prestige, or at least happiness for the statesman himself and his fellow citizens, and that is something other than political activity: after all, the very fact that we investigate politics shows that it is not the same (as happiness). Therefore, if we take as established (1) that political and military actions surpass all other actions that conform with virtue in nobility and grandeur; (2) that they are unleisurely, aim at an end, and are not chosen for their own sake; (3) that the activity of our intelligence, inasmuch as it is an activity concerned with theoretical knowledge, is thought to be of greater value than the others, aims at no end beyond itself, and has a pleasure proper to itself—and pleasure increases activity; and (4) that the qualities of this activity evidently are self-sufficiency, leisure, as much freedom from fatigue as a human being can have, and whatever else falls to the lot of a supremely happy man; it follows that the activity of our intelligence constitutes the complete happiness of man, provided that it encompasses a complete span of life; for nothing connected with happiness must be incomplete. . . .

## 8. The advantages of the contemplative life

A further indication that complete happiness consists in some kind of contemplative activity is this. We assume that the gods are in the highest degree blessed and happy. But what kind of actions are we to attribute to them? Acts of justice? Will they not look ridiculous making contracts with one another, returning deposits, and so forth? Perhaps acts of courage—withstanding terror and taking risks, because it is noble to do so? Or generous actions? But to whom will they give? It would be strange to think that they actually have currency or something of the sort. Acts of self-control? What would they be?

Surely, it would be in poor taste to praise them for not having bad appetites. If we went through the whole list we would see that a concern with actions is petty and unworthy of the gods. Nevertheless, we all assume that the gods exist and, consequently, that they are active; for surely we do not assume them to be always asleep like Endymion. Now, if we take away action from a living being, to say nothing of production, what is left except contemplation? Therefore, the activity of the divinity which surpasses all others in bliss must be a contemplative activity, and the human activity which is most closely akin to it is, therefore, most conducive to happiness. . . .

But we shall also need external well-being, since we are only human. Our nature is not self-sufficient for engaging in study: our body must be healthy and we must have food and generally be cared for. Nevertheless, if it is not possible for a man to be supremely happy without external goods, we must not think that his needs will be great and many in order to be happy; for self-sufficiency and moral action do not consist in an excess (of possessions). It is possible to perform noble actions even without being ruler of land and sea; a man's actions can be guided by virtue also if his means are moderate. That this is so can be clearly seen in the fact that private individuals evidently do not act less honorably but even more honorably than powerful rulers. It is enough to have moderate means at one's disposal, for the life of a man whose activity is guided by virtue will be happy.

# Aristotle, *The Politics*

*~ state of being happy*

"If we are right in our view, and felicity should be held to consist in 'well-*doing*', it follows that the life of action is best, alike for every state as a whole and for each individual in his own conduct. But the life of action need not be, as is sometimes thought, a life which involves relations to others. Nor should our thoughts be held to be active only when they are directed to objects which have to be achieved by action. Thoughts with no object beyond themselves, and speculations and trains of reflection followed purely for their own sake, are far more deserving of the name of active." (VII, iii)

---

"[A] state with an ideal constitution . . . cannot have its citizens living the life of mechanics or shopkeepers, which is ignoble and inimical to goodness. Nor can it have them engaged in farming: leisure is a necessity, both for growth in goodness and for the pursuit of political activities." (VII, ix)

*of low aims    . unfriendly*

---

"[I]t is the power to use leisure rightly, as we would once more repeat, which is the basis of all our life. It is true that both occupation and leisure are necessary; but it is also true that leisure is higher than occupation, and is the end to which occupation is directed. Our problem, therefore, is to find modes of activity which fill our leisure. We can hardly fill our leisure with play. To do so would be to make play the be-all and end-all of life. That is an impossibility. Play is a thing to be chiefly used in connexion with one side of life—the side of occupation. (A simple argument shows that this is the case. Occupation is the companion of work and exertion: the worker needs relaxation: play is intended to provide relaxation.) We may therefore conclude that play and games should only be admitted into our state at the proper times and seasons, and should be applied as restoratives. The feelings which play produces in the mind are feelings of relief from exertion; and the pleasure it gives provides relaxation. Leisure is a different matter: we think of it as having in itself intrinsic pleasure, intrinsic happiness, intrinsic felicity. Happiness of that order does not belong to those who are engaged in occupation: it belongs to those who have leisure. Those who are engaged in occupation are so engaged with a view to some end which they regard as still unattained. But felicity is a present end. . . . " (VIII, iii)

*Play is intended to provide relaxation .... leisure is used to recharge the inner self.*

# Xenophon, *Oeconomicus*

CRITOBULUS. But show me the branches of knowledge which are considered to be most honourable and which I might most suitably concern myself with. Show me these and those who practise them, and you yourself, too—to the best of your ability—instruct me and help me to learn them.

SOCRATES. Very well said, Critobulus. In fact, the so-called 'banausic' occupations are both denounced and, quite rightly, held in very low esteem by states. For they utterly ruin the bodies of those who work at them and those of their supervisors, by forcing them to lead a sedentary life and to stay indoors, and some of them even to spend the whole day by the fire. When their bodies become effeminate, their souls too become much weaker. Furthermore, the so-called 'banausic' occupations leave a man no spare time to be concerned about his friends and city. Consequently such men seem to treat their friends badly and to defend their countries badly too. In fact, in some cities, especially in those reputed to excel in war, none of the citizens is permitted to work at banausic occupations.

CRITOBULUS. Then, Socrates, which occupations do you advise us to practise?

SOCRATES. Surely we ought not to be ashamed to imitate the king of the Persians? For they say that he classifies farming and the art of war among the noblest and most essential concerns, and he is seriously concerned about both of them.

# Josef Pieper, "Leisure and Its Threefold Opposition"

Whoever advocates leisure nowadays may already be on the defensive. We have to face an opposition that at first seems to prevail. Things are not made easier by the fact that this opposition does not come from "someone else" but indeed springs from a conflict within ourselves. Worse yet, when put on the spot, we are not even able to define exactly what we are trying to defend. For example, when Aristotle says, "We work so we can have leisure", we must admit in all honesty that we do not know what this offensive statement means.

This, I think, is our situation.

The first question, therefore, is: What is leisure? How is this concept defined in our great philosophical tradition?

I deem it advisable to attempt an answer in such a way as to deal first with those opposing forces that could be labeled "overvaluation of work". This is admittedly a tentative expression. For "work" can mean several things, at least three. "Work" can mean "activity as such". Second, "work" can mean "exertion, effort, drudgery". And third is the usage of "work" for all "useful activity", especially in the sense "useful for society". Which of the three concepts do I have in mind when I speak of the "overvaluation of work"? I would say: all three! We encounter overvaluation of activity for its own sake, as well as overvaluation of exertion and drudgery, and—last but not least—overvaluation of the social function of work. This specifically is the three-faced demon everyone has to deal with when setting out to defend leisure.

*Overvaluation of activity for its own sake.* By this I mean the inability to let something simply happen; the inability to accept a kindness graciously, to be on the receiving end in general. This is the attitude of "absolute activity" that, according to Goethe, always ends bankrupt. The most extreme expression so far of this heresy can be found in a statement by Adolf Hitler: "Any activity is meaningful, even a criminal activity; all passivity, in contrast, is meaningless." This, of course, is an insane formulation, simply absurd. But "milder" forms of such insanity, I surmise, are typical of our contemporary world.

*Overvaluation of exertion and drudgery.* Strangely enough, this too can be found. Yes, we may even assert that the average ethical understanding of "decent" modern people is to a large extent colored by such an overvaluation of drudgery: goodness is by nature difficult, and whatever is gained without effort cannot have moral value. [The German poet] Friedrich Schiller has ridiculed this attitude in a ditty aimed at Kant:

*Handwritten margin note: Don't overanalyze everything or try to control every situation, try to let things happen and enjoy them*

Readily do I help all my friends—
Too bad, I do so with pleasure;
Much am I grieved that I, with this,
Can gain no virtuous treasure.

*He helps all his friends with ease, but he says his friends don't appreciate it because no work or drudgery went into it.*

The ancients—who are for me the great Greeks Plato and Aristotle but also the famous teachers of Western Christianity—did not hold that goodness is difficult by nature and therefore will always and necessarily be so. They were well aware of the fact that the highest forms of applied goodness are indeed always effortless because they essentially flow from love. In this same way the highest forms of perception—the sudden flash of ingenious insight or true contemplation—do not really require mental labor but come without effort because they are by nature gifts. "Gifts"—this may well be the key concept. If we consider the strange propensity toward hardship that is engraved into the face of our contemporaries as a distinct expectation of suffering (a more typical trait, I believe, than the oft deplored craving for pleasure)—if we consider this, then to our surprise we may face the question: Could perhaps the deepest reason be the people's refusal to accept a gift, no matter where it comes from? *is what?*

*Overvaluation of the social function of work.* Not much has to be said to show how this trait dominates contemporary societies. We should, however, think not just of those totalitarian "five-year plans" whose infamy lies not so much in their attempt to order everything as rather in their claim to provide the exclusive value standards for all aspects of life, not only industrial production but the personal life of individuals as well. Oh yes, the nontotalitarian world, too, can effectively be dominated by the dictatorship of "social usefulness".

At this point we should recall the ancient distinction between *artes liberales* and *artes serviles,* between "free" and "servile" activities. This distinction states that some human activities contain their purpose in themselves and other activities are ordered toward a purpose outside themselves and thus are merely "useful". This idea may at first appear rather *out of style* outmoded and *makes a show* pedantic. And yet it deals with something of contemporary political relevance. The question, "Are there 'free' activities?", translated into the jargon of totalitarian societies would ask: "Are there human activities that in themselves neither require nor accept any justification based on the provisions of a five-year plan?" The ancients have answered this question with a decisive "yes". The answer in a totalitarian environment would be an equally decisive: "No! Humans are defined by their function. Any 'free' activity that does not serve a socially useful purpose is undesirable and should therefore be liquidated."

If we now direct our attention from the threefold overvaluation of work toward the concept of "leisure", then one thing becomes immediately clear: there is no room for it in such a world. The idea of leisure here is not only preposterous but morally suspect. As a matter of fact, it is absolutely incompatible with the prevailing attitude. The idea of leisure is diametrically opposed to the totalitarian concept of the "worker", and this under each of the three aspects of work we have considered.

[1] *Against the idolizing of "activity".* Leisure is essentially "nonactivity"; it is a form of silence. Leisure amounts to that precise way of being silent which is a prerequisite for listening in order to hear; for only the listener is able to hear. Leisure implies an attitude of total receptivity toward, and willing immersion in, reality; an openness of the soul, through which alone may come about those great and blessed insights that no amount of "mental labor" can ever achieve.

*Against the overvaluation of drudgery.* Leisure means an attitude of celebration. And celebration is the opposite of exertion. Those who are basically suspicious of achievement without effort are by the same token as unable to enjoy leisure as they are usable to celebrate a feast. To truly celebrate, however, something else is required; more on this shortly.

*Against the overvaluation of social usefulness.* Leisure implies that a person is freed for this period of time from any social function. Yet leisure does not mean the same as a "break". A break, whether for an hour or three weeks, is designed to provide a respite from work in anticipation of more work; it finds its justification in relation to work. Leisure is something entirely different. The essence of leisure is not to assure that we may function smoothly but rather to assure that we, embedded in our social function, are enabled to remain fully human. That we may not lose the ability to look beyond the limits of our social and functional station, to contemplate and celebrate the world as such, to become and be that person who is essentially oriented toward the whole of reality. And that all this be achieved through our own free disposition, which contains its own significance and is not "geared toward" anything.

1. Leisure allows one to listen and truly hear. Being able to hear opens ones mind to reality.

# Angela Morgan, "Buttons and Trash"

I lost my soul to-day
For the sake of scrubbing and buttons and trash.
It was a wonder-day of beauty.
Rapturous leaves afire in the sun besought me;
Butterflies beckoned, birds entreated with song;
The great mother sky, wide and blue as the ocean,
Implored me to drift on the miracle tide
Of gladness and renewing.

But I turned away.
There were chairs to be dusted, floors to be
       swept. . . .
Floors, mind you! Common boards, dirt-covered,
That must absorb my being.
And the ecstatic world without
Pleaded with me in vain.
A book lay open on the table.
In it were hidden jewel-truths
More wonderful than gems in the depths of the
      earth.
"Gather us! Take us! Be comforted and
      inspired!"
But there were buttons to be sewn upon garments,
Buttons to be sorted and stowed in boxes;
Buttons, mind you, that must absorb my soul!

A master musician there was—
I might have heard him had I paused to think it.
This golden afternoon, the music of angels. . . .
But there was trash in the cellar that must be
      cleared away—
Trash, mind you! Papers and dust and rags
That must smother my soul.
And the great musician played, unheeded.
Had I gone a few rods, I might have listened;
Had I gone a few paces from the fettered
      path. . . .

But I lost my soul to-day,
For scrubbing and buttons and trash.
There will be many, many days when I may scrub
    and sew and clean.
I traded Beauty for an hour of rubbish,
I sold my birthright for a drudge's dole.
O Beauty, stand once more upon my threshold!
O Day of Wonder, beckon me again!
That I, the penitent, may open wide my dwelling
And plead with Loveliness as she has plead with
    me.

# Witold Rybczynski, "Waiting for the Weekend"

The word "weekend" started life as "week-end" but lost its hyphen somewhere along the way, ceasing to be merely the end of the week and acquiring, instead, an autonomous and sovereign existence. "Have a good weekend," we say to one another—never "Have a good week." Where once the week consisted of week-days and Sunday, it now consists of weekdays and weekend. Ask most people to name the first day of the week and they will answer, Monday, of course; fifty years ago the answer would have been Sunday. Wall calendars still show Sunday as the first day of the week, and children are taught the days of the week start-ing with Sunday, but how long will these conventions last? Sunday, once the day of rest, has become merely one of two days of what is often strenuous activity. Although we continue to celebrate the traditional religious and civic holidays—holy days—these now account for only a small portion of our total nonworking days, and are overshadowed by the 104 days of secular weekends.

For most of us life assumes a different rhythm on the weekend; we sleep in, cut the grass, wash the car. We also go to the movies, especially during hot weather. We travel. And of course we exercise and play games. Some of these pastimes, like tennis, have an old history and a newfound popularity; oth-ers, like whitewater canoeing, windsurfing, and hang-gliding, are more recent. Most are distinguished from nineteenth-century recreations such as croquet and golf by their relative arduousness and even riskiness.

Although the weekend is a time for sports, for shopping, and for house-hold chores, it is foremost a manifestation of the structure of our leisure. The chief *Oxford English Dictionary* definition of leisure is "time which one can spend as one pleases." That is, "free" time. But in one of his popular columns in *The Illustrated London News*—a Saturday paper—G. K. Chesterton pointed out that leisure should not be confused with liberty. Contrary to most people's expectations, the presence of the first by no means assures the availability of the second. This confusion arose, according to Chesterton, because the term "leisure" is used to describe three different things: "The first is being allowed to do something. The second is being allowed to do anything. And the third (and perhaps most rare and precious) is being allowed to do nothing." The first, he acknowledged, was the most common form of leisure, and the one that of late—he was writing in the early 1890s—had shown the greatest quantitative increase. The second—the liberty to fashion what one willed out of one's lei-sure time—was more unusual and tended to be the province of artists and other creative individuals. It was the third, however, that was obviously his favorite, because it allowed idleness—in Chesterton's view, the truest form of leisure.

Chesterton argued that a man compelled by lack of choice—or by social pressure—to play golf when he would rather be attending to some solitary hobby was not so different from the slave who might have several hours of leisure while his overseer slept but had to be ready to work at a moment's notice. Neither could be said to be the master of his leisure. Both had free time but not freedom. To press this parallel further, have we become enslaved by the weekend?

At first glance it is an odd question, for surely it is our work that enslaves us, not our free time. We call people who become obsessed by their jobs workaholics, but we don't have a word for someone who is possessed by recreation. Maybe we should. I have many acquaintances for whom weekend activities seem more important than workaday existence, and who behave as if the week were merely an irritating interference in their real, extracurricular lives. I sometimes have the impression that to really know these weekend sailors, mountain climbers, and horsewomen, I would have to accompany them on their outings and excursions—see them in their natural habitat, so to speak. But would I see a different person, or merely the same one governed by different conventions of comportment, behavior, accoutrement, and dress?

I'm always charmed by old photographs of skiers which show groups of people in what appear to be street clothes, with uncomplicated pieces of bent wood strapped to sturdy walking boots. These men and women have a playful and unaffected air. Today every novice is caparisoned in skintight spandex, like an Olympic racer, and even crosscountry skiing, a simple enough pastime, has been infected by a preoccupation with correct dress, authentic terminology, and up-to-date equipment. This reflects an attitude toward play which is different from what it was in the past. Most outdoor sports, once simply muddled through, are now undertaken with a high degree of seriousness. "Professional" used to be a word that distinguished someone who was paid for an activity from the sportsman; today the word has come to denote anyone with a high degree of proficiency; "professional-quality" equipment is available to—and desired by—all. Conversely, "amateur," a wonderful word literally meaning "lover," has been degraded to mean a rank beginner or anyone without a certain level of skill. "Just an amateur," we say; it is not, as it once was, a compliment.

The lack of carelessness in our recreation, the sense of obligation to get things right, and the emphasis on protocol and decorum do represent an enslavement of a kind. People used to "play" tennis; now they "work" on their backhand. It is not hard to imagine what Chesterton would have thought of such dedication; this is just the sort of laborious pursuit of play that he so often derided. "If a thing is worth doing," he once wrote, "it is worth doing badly."

Chesterton held the traditional view that leisure was different from the type of recreation typically afforded by the modern weekend. His own leisure pastimes included an eclectic mix of the unfashionable and the bohemian—sketching, collecting weapons, and playing with the cardboard cutouts of his toy theater. Leisure was the opportunity for personal, even idiosyncratic, pursuits, not for ordered recreation; it was for private reverie rather than for public spectacles. If a sport was undertaken, it was for the love of playing—not of winning, nor even of playing well. Above all, free time was to remain that: free of the encumbrance of convention, free of the need for busyness, free for the "noble habit of doing nothing at all." That hardly describes the modern weekend.

# IC. Work as Dignified but Irksome

1. Genesis 3:8–19. Translation is the Revised Standard Version.

2. 1 Thessalonians 4:10b–12. Translation is the Revised Standard Version.

3. 2 Thessalonians 3:6–12. Translation is the Revised Standard Version.

4. George Foot Moore, p. 177 in *Judaism in the First Centuries of the Christian Era,* vol. 2 (New York: Schocken Books, 1971). This very short selection from Moore (1851–1931) is taken from his classic discussion of the development of rabbinic Judaism.

5. "The Little Red Hen," though scarcely a great work of literature, may be one of the places where many children have first learned the importance of work.

6. Nathaniel Hawthorne, pp. 83–90 of *The Blithedale Romance* (New York: W. W. Norton, 1958). Hawthorne (1804–1864) is surely one of the greatest fiction writers in American history. *The Blithedale Romance,* a novel about an experiment in communal living, is based in part on Hawthorne's own experience living at Brook Farm, a famous commune in nineteenth-century America.

7. Henry Wadsworth Longfellow, "The Village Blacksmith," pp. 14–15 in Horace E. Scudder, ed., *The Complete Poetical Works of Henry Wadsworth Longfellow* (Boston and New York: Houghton Mifflin, 1893). Longfellow's (1807–1882) reputation has been somewhat eclipsed, but he was the most popular nineteenth-century American poet.

8. John Ruskin, pp. 54–56 of *The Crown of Wild Olive* (New York: F. M. Lupton, n.d.). Ruskin (1819–1900) was an influential Victorian thinker who first made his reputation as an art critic. Later in life he turned to topics more political and economic in character.

9. Anthony Trollope, pp. 94–106, 108–110 of *An Autobiography* (New York: Harper & Brothers, 1883). Trollope (1815–1882) is now considered among the great English novelists. He is famous for the "workmanlike" attitude he took to his writing, an attitude displayed in the selections here.

10. George Orwell, chapter 2 of *The Road to Wigan Pier* (New York: Harcourt Brace, 1958). George Orwell was the pseudonym of the Englishman Eric Blair (1903–1950). He is famous especially as an essayist and critic, but Orwell's *Road to Wigan Pier* is typical of much of his writing. Based on his study of the life of miners in northern England, the book argues the case for socialism while simultaneously offering biting criticism of the socialist movement of Orwell's time.

11. Jacques Ellul, selections from pp. 495–506 of *The Ethics of Freedom* (Grand Rapids, Mich.: William B. Eerdmans, 1976). Ellul (1912–1994) was a lay French theologian who is perhaps best known for his writings on the dangers of technology.

# Genesis 3:8–19

And they heard the sound of the LORD God walking in the garden in the cool of the day, and the man and his wife hid themselves from the presence of the LORD God among the trees of the garden. But the LORD God called to the man, and said to him, "Where are you?" And he said, "I heard the sound of thee in the garden, and I was afraid, because I was naked; and I hid myself." He said, "Who told you that you were naked? Have you eaten of the tree of which I commanded you not to eat?" The man said, "The woman whom thou gavest to be with me, she gave me fruit of the tree, and I ate." Then the LORD God said to the woman, "What is this that you have done?" The woman said, "The serpent beguiled me, and I ate." The LORD God said to the serpent,

> "Because you have done this,
>> cursed are you above all cattle,
>> and above all wild animals;
> upon your belly you shall go,
>> and dust you shall eat
>> all the days of your life.
> I will put enmity between you and the woman,
>> and between your seed and her seed;
> he shall bruise your head,
>> and you shall bruise his heel."
> To the woman he said,
> "I will greatly multiply your pain in childbearing;
>> in pain you shall bring forth children,
> yet your desire shall be for your husband,
>> and he shall rule over you."
> And to Adam he said,
> "Because you have listened to the voice of your wife,
>> and have eaten of the tree
> of which I commanded you,
>> 'You shall not eat of it,'
> cursed is the ground because of you;
>> in toil you shall eat of it all the days of your life;
> thorns and thistles it shall bring forth to you;
>> and you shall eat the plants of the field.
> In the sweat of your face
>> you shall eat bread

till you return to the ground,
>    for out of it you were taken;
you are dust,
>    and to dust you shall return."

# 1 Thessalonians 4:10b–12

But we exhort you, brethren, to do so more and more, to aspire to live quietly, to mind your own affairs, and to work with your hands, as we charged you; so that you may command the respect of outsiders, and be dependent on nobody.

# 2 Thessalonians 3:6–12

Now we command you, brethren, in the name of our Lord Jesus Christ, that you keep away from any brother who is living in idleness and not in accord with the tradition that you received from us. For you yourselves know how you ought to imitate us; we were not idle when we were with you, we did not eat any one's bread without paying, but with toil and labor we worked night and day, that we might not burden any of you. It was not because we have not that right, but to give you in our conduct an example to imitate. For even when we were with you, we gave you this command: If any one will not work, let him not eat. For we hear that some of you are living in idleness, mere busybodies, not doing any work. Now such persons we command and exhort in the Lord Jesus Christ to do their work in quietness and to earn their own living.

# G. F. Moore, *Judaism in the First Centuries of the Christian Era*

Men should make every effort not to become a public charge. Rather make your sabbath a week day (by foregoing the sabbatical luxury) than become a burden to your fellow men. A pointed application of this principle is made by Rab: "Skin the carcass of a dead beast in the market place for hire, and do not say, I am a great man, it is beneath my dignity." Earn your own living even by the most repugnant employment.

Many of the most eminent scholars, as is well known, supported themselves and their families by manual labor, some of them by unskilled labor. Every father was enjoined to teach his son a trade, not only because it secured him a livelihood but because of the moral influence of labor. Shemaiah's motto was, "Love labor, shun office, and do not cultivate intimacy with the authorities." The dignity and the blessings of labor are a frequent theme in the literature of all periods.

# The Little Red Hen

One day a little red hen found a grain of wheat. "Who will plant this wheat?" she said.

"I won't," said the dog.

"I won't," said the cat.

"I won't," said the pig.

"I won't," said the turkey.

"Then I will," said the little red hen. "Cluck, cluck." So she planted the grain of wheat.

Very soon the wheat began to grow out of the ground. The sun shone and the rain fell and the wheat kept on growing until it was tall, strong, and ripe. "Who will cut this wheat?" said the little red hen.

"I won't," said the dog.

"I won't," said the cat.

"I won't," said the pig.

"I won't," said the turkey.

"Then I will," said the little red hen. "Cluck, cluck." So she cut the wheat.

"Who will thresh this wheat?" said the little red hen.

"I won't," said the dog.

"I won't," said the cat.

"I won't," said the pig.

"I won't," said the turkey.

"Then I will," said the little red hen. "Cluck, cluck." So she threshed the wheat.

"Who will take this wheat to the mill to have it ground into flour?" said the little red hen.

"I won't," said the dog.

"I won't," said the cat.

"I won't," said the pig.

"I won't," said the turkey.

"Then I will," said the little red hen. "Cluck, cluck." So she took the wheat to the mill, and soon she came back with the flour.

"Who will bake this flour?" said the little red hen.

"I won't," said the dog.

"I won't," said the cat.

"I won't," said the pig.

"I won't," said the turkey.

"Then I will," said the little red hen. "Cluck, cluck." So she baked the flour and made a fine loaf of bread.

"Who will eat this bread?" said the little red hen.

"I will," said the dog.

"I will," said the cat.

"I will," said the pig.

"I will," said the turkey.

"No, I will," said the little red hen. "Cluck, cluck." And she ate up the loaf of bread.

# Nathaniel Hawthorne, *The Blithedale Romance*

I was now on my legs again. My fit of illness had been an avenue between two existences; the low-arched and darksome doorway, through which I crept out of a life of old conventionalisms, on my hands and knees, as it were, and gained admittance into the freer region that lay beyond. In this respect, it was like death. And, as with death, too, it was good to have gone through it. No otherwise could I have rid myself of a thousand follies, fripperies, prejudices, habits, and other such worldly dust as inevitably settles upon the crowd along the broad highway, giving them all one sordid aspect before noontime, however freshly they may have begun their pilgrimage in the dewy morning. The very substance upon my bones had not been fit to live with in any better, truer, or more energetic mode than that to which I was accustomed. So it was taken off me and flung aside, like any other worn-out or unseasonable garment; and, after shivering a little while in my skeleton, I began to be clothed anew, and much more satisfactorily than in my previous suit. In literal and physical truth, I was quite another man. I had a lively sense of the exultation with which the spirit will enter on the next stage of its eternal progress, after leaving the heavy burthen of its mortality in an earthly grave, with as little concern for what may become of it as now affected me for the flesh which I had lost.

Emerging into the genial sunshine, I half fancied that the labors of the brotherhood had already realized some of Fourier's predictions. Their enlightened culture of the soil and the virtues with which they sanctified their life, had begun to produce an effect upon the material world and its climate. In my new enthusiasm, man looked strong and stately,—and woman, O how beautiful!—and the earth a green garden blossoming with many-colored delights. Thus Nature, whose laws I had broken in various artificial ways, comported herself towards me as a strict but loving mother, who uses the rod upon her little boy for his naughtiness, and then gives him a smile, a kiss, and some pretty playthings, to console the urchin for her severity.

In the interval of my seclusion, there had been a number of recruits to our little army of saints and martyrs. They were mostly individuals who had gone through such an experience as to disgust them with ordinary pursuits, but who were not yet so old, nor had suffered so deeply, as to lose their faith in the better time to come. On comparing their minds one with another, they often discovered that this idea of a Community had been growing up, in silent and unknown sympathy, for years. Thoughtful, strongly-lined faces were among them; sombre brows, but eyes that did not require spectacles, unless prematurely dimmed by the student's lamplight, and hair that seldom showed a thread of silver. Age, wedded to the past, incrusted over with a stony layer of habits, and retaining nothing fluid in its possibilities, would have been absurdly out of place in an enterprise like this. Youth, too, in its early dawn, was hardly more adapted to our purpose; for it would behold the morning radiance of its own spirit beaming over the very same spots of withered crass and barren sand whence most of us had seen it vanish. We had very young people with us, it is true—downy lads, rosy girls in their first teens, and children of all heights above one's knee—but these had chiefly been sent hither for education, which it was one of the objects and methods of our institution to supply. Then we had boarders, from town and elsewhere, who lived with us in a familiar way, sympathized more or less in our theories, and sometimes shared in our labors.

On the whole, it was a society such as has seldom met together; nor, perhaps, could it reasonably be expected to hold together long. Persons of marked individuality—crooked sticks, as some of us might be called—are not exactly the easiest to bind up into a fagot. But, so long as our union should subsist, a man of intellect and feeling, with a free nature in him, might have sought far and near without finding so many points of attraction as would allure him hitherward. We were of all creeds and opinions, and generally tolerant of all, on every imaginable subject. Our bond, it seems to me, was not affirmative, but negative. We had individually found one thing or another to quarrel with in our past life, and were pretty well agreed as to the inexpediency of lumbering along with the old system any further. As to what should be substituted, there was much less unanimity. We did not greatly care—at least, I never did— for the written constitution under which our millennium had commenced. My hope was, that, between theory and practice, a true and available mode of life might be struck out; and that, even should we ultimately fail, the months or years spent in the trial would not have been wasted, either as regarded passing enjoyment, or the experience which makes men wise.

Arcadians though we were, our costume bore no resemblance to the be-ribboned doublets, silk breeches and stockings, and slippers fastened with artificial roses, that distinguish the pastoral people of poetry and the stage. In outward show, I humbly conceive, we looked rather like a gang of beggars, or banditti, than either a company of honest laboring men, or a conclave of philosophers. Whatever might be our points of difference, we all of us seemed to have come to Blithedale with the one thrifty and laudable idea of wearing out our old clothes. Such garments as had an airing, whenever we strode a-field! Coats with high collars and with no collars, broad-skirted or swallow-tailed, and with the waist at every point between the hip and armpit; pantaloons of a dozen successive epochs, and greatly defaced at the knees by the humiliations of the wearer before his ladylove;—in short, we were a living epitome of defunct fashions, and the very raggedest presentment of men who had seen better days. It was gentility in tatters. Often retaining a scholarlike or clerical air, you might have taken us for the denizens of Grub-street, intent on getting a comfortable livelihood by agricultural labor; or, Coleridge's projected Pantisocracy in full experiment; or, Candide and his motley associates, at work in their cabbage-garden; or anything else that was miserably out at elbows, and most clumsily patched in the rear. We might have been sworn comrades to Falstaff's ragged regiment. Little skill as we boasted in other points of husbandry, every mother's son of us would have served admirably to stick up for a scarecrow. And the worst of the matter was, that the first energetic movement essential to one downright stroke of real labor was sure to put a finish to these poor habiliments. So we gradually flung them all aside, and took to honest homespun and linsey-woolsey, as preferable, on the whole, to the plan recommended, I think, by Virgil,—"*Ara nudus; sere nudus,*"—which, as Silas Foster remarked, when I translated the maxim, would be apt to astonish the women-folks.

After a reasonable training, the yeoman life throve well with us. Our faces took the sunburn kindly; our chests gained in compass, and our shoulders in breadth and squareness; our great brown fists looked as if they had never been capable of kid gloves. The plough, the hoe, the scythe, and the hay-fork, grew familiar to our grasp. The oxen responded to our voices. We could do almost as fair a day's work as Silas Foster himself, sleep dreamlessly after it, and awake at daybreak with only a little stiffness of the joints, which was usually quite gone by breakfast-time.

To be sure, our next neighbors pretended to be incredulous as to our real proficiency in the business which we had taken in hand. They told slanderous fables about our inability to yoke our own oxen, or to drive them a-field when yoked, or to release the poor brutes from their conjugal bond at night-fall. They had the face to say, too, that the cows laughed at our awkwardness at milking-time, and invariably kicked over the pails; partly in consequence of our putting the stool on the wrong side, and partly because, taking offence at the whisking of their tails, we were in the habit of holding these natural fly-flappers with one hand, and milking with the other. They further averred that we hoed up whole acres of Indian corn and other crops, and drew the earth carefully about the weeds; and that we raised five hundred tufts of burdock, mistaking them for cabbages; and that, by dint of unskilful planting, few of our seeds ever came up at all, or, if they did come up, it was stem-foremost; and that we spent the better part of the month of June in reversing a field of beans, which had thrust themselves out of the ground in this unseemly way. They quoted it as nothing more than an ordinary occurrence for one or other of us to crop off two or three fingers, of a morning, by our clumsy use of the hay-cutter. Finally, and as an ultimate catastrophe, these mendacious rogues circulated a report that we communitarians were exterminated, to the last man, by severing ourselves asunder with the sweep of our own scythes!—and that the world had lost nothing by this little accident.

But this was pure envy and malice on the part of the neighboring farmers. The peril of our new way of life was not lest we should fail in becoming practical agriculturists, but that we should probably cease to be anything else. While our enterprise lay all in theory, we had pleased ourselves with delectable visions of the spiritualization of labor. It was to be our form of prayer and ceremonial of worship. Each stroke of the hoe was to uncover some aromatic root of wisdom, heretofore hidden from the sun. Pausing in the field, to let the wind exhale the moisture from our foreheads, we were to look upward, and catch glimpses into the far-off soul of truth. In this point of view, matters did not turn out quite so well as we anticipated. It is very true that, sometimes, gazing casually around me, out of the midst of my toil, I used to discern a richer picturesqueness in the visible scene of earth and sky. There was, at such moments, a novelty, an unwonted aspect, on the face of Nature, as if she had been taken by surprise and seen at unawares, with no opportunity to put off her real look, and assume the mask with which she mysteriously hides herself from mortals. But this was all. The clods of earth, which we so constantly belabored and turned over and over, were never etherealized into thought. Our thoughts, on the contrary, were fast becoming cloddish. Our labor symbolized nothing, and left us mentally sluggish in the dusk of the evening. Intellectual activity is incompatible with any large amount of bodily exercise. The yeoman and the scholar—the yeoman and the man of finest moral culture, though not the man of sturdiest sense and integrity—are two distinct individuals, and can never be melted or welded into one substance.

Zenobia soon saw this truth, and gibed me about it, one evening, as Hollingsworth and I lay on the grass, after a hard day's work.

"I am afraid you did not make a song, to-day, while loading the hay-cart," said she, "as Burns did, when he was reaping barley."

"Burns never made a song in haying-time," I answered, very positively. "He was no poet while a farmer, and no farmer while a poet."

"And, on the whole, which of the two characters do you like best?" asked Zenobia. "For I have an idea that you cannot combine them any better than Burns did. Ah, I see, in my mind's eye, what sort of an individual you are to be, two or three years hence. Grim Silas Foster is your prototype, with his palm of sole-leather and his joints of rusty iron (which all through summer keep the stiffness of what he calls his winter's rheumatize), and his brain of—I don't know what his brain is made of, unless it be a Savoy cabbage: but yours may be cauliflower, as a rather more delicate variety. Your physical man will be transmuted into salt beef and fried pork, at the rate, I should imagine, of a pound and a half a day; that being about the average which we find necessary in the kitchen. You will make your toilet for the day (still like this delightful Silas Foster) by rinsing your fingers and the front part of your face in a little tin-pan of water at the door-step, and teasing your hair with a wooden pocket-comb before a seven-by-nine-inch looking-glass. Your only pastime will be to smoke some very vile tobacco in the black stump of a pipe."

"Pray, spare me!" cried I. "But the pipe is not Silas's only mode of solacing himself with the weed."

"Your literature," continued Zenobia, apparently delighted with her description, "will be the Farmer's Almanac; for I observe our friend Foster never gets so far as the newspaper. When you happen to sit down, at odd moments, you will fall asleep, and make nasal proclamation of the fact, as he does; and invariably you must be jogged out of a nap, after supper, by the future Mrs. Coverdale, and persuaded to go regularly to bed. And on Sundays, when you put on a blue coat with brass buttons, you will think of nothing else to do, but to go and lounge over the stone walls and rail fences, and stare at the corn growing. And you will look with a knowing eye at oxen, and will have a tendency to clamber over into pig-sties, and feel of the hogs, and give a guess how much they will weigh after you shall have stuck and dressed them. Already I have noticed you begin to speak through your nose, and with a drawl. Pray, if you really did make any poetry to-day, let us hear it in that kind of utterance!"

"Coverdale has given up making verses now," said Hollingsworth, who never had the slightest appreciation of my poetry. "Just think of him penning a sonnet with a fist like that! There is at least this good in a life of toil, that it takes the nonsense and fancy-work out of a man, and leaves nothing but what truly belongs to him. If a farmer can make poetry at the plough-tail, it must be because his nature insists on it; and if that be the case, let him make it, in Heaven's name!"

"And how is it with you?" asked Zenobia, in a different voice; for she never laughed at Hollingsworth, as she often did at me. "You, I think, cannot have ceased to live a life of thought and feeling."

"I have always been in earnest," answered Hollingsworth. "I have hammered thought out of iron, after heating the iron in my heart! It matters little what my outward toil may be. Were I a slave at the bottom of a mine, I should keep the same purpose, the same faith in its ultimate accomplishment, that I do now. Miles Coverdale is not in earnest, either as a poet or a laborer."

"You give me hard measure, Hollingsworth," said I, a little hurt. "I have kept pace with you in the field; and my bones feel as if I had been in earnest, whatever may be the case with my brain!"

"I cannot conceive," observed Zenobia, with great emphasis,—and, no doubt, she spoke fairly the feeling of the moment,—"I cannot conceive of being so continually as Mr. Coverdale is within the sphere of a strong and noble nature, without being strengthened and ennobled by its influence!"

This amiable remark of the fair Zenobia confirmed me in what I had already begun to suspect, that Hollingsworth, like many other illustrious prophets, reformers and philanthropists, was likely to make at least two proselytes among the women to one among the men. Zenobia and Priscilla! These, I believe (unless my unworthy self might be reckoned for a third), were the only disciples of his mission; and I spent a great deal of time, uselessly, in trying to conjecture what Hollingsworth meant to do with them—and they with him!

# Henry Wadsworth Longfellow, "The Village Blacksmith"

Under a spreading chestnut-tree
  The village smithy stands;
The smith, a mighty man is he,
  With large and sinewy hands;
And the muscles of his brawny arms
  Are strong as iron bands.

His hair is crisp, and black, and long,
  His face is like the tan;
His brow is wet with honest sweat,
  He earns whate'er he can,
And looks the whole world in the face,
  For he owes not any man.

Week in, week out, from morn till night,
  You can hear his bellows blow;
 You can hear him swing his heavy sledge,
  With measured beat and slow,
Like a sexton ringing the village bell,
  When the evening sun is low.

And children coming home from school
  Look in at the open door;
They love to see the flaming forge,
  And hear the bellows roar,
And catch the burning sparks that fly
  Like chaff from a threshing-floor.

He goes on Sunday to the church,
  And sits among his boys;
He hears the parson pray and preach,
  he hears his daughter's voice,
Singing in the village choir,
  And it makes his heart rejoice.

It sounds to him like her mother's voice,
  Singing in Paradise!
He needs must think of her once more,
  How in the grave she lies;
And with his hard, rough hand he wipes
  A tear out of his eyes.

Toiling,—rejoicing,—sorrowing,
  Onward through life he goes;
Each morning sees some task begin,
  Each evening sees it close;
Something attempted, something done,
  Has earned a night's repose.

Thanks, thanks to thee, my worthy friend,
  For the lesson thou hast taught!
Thus at the flaming forge of life
  Our fortunes must be wrought;
Thus on its sounding anvil shaped
  Each burning deed and thought.

# John Ruskin, *The Crown of Wild Olive*

I pass now to our third condition of separation, between the men who work with the hand, and those who work with the head.

And here at we have at last an inevitable distinction. There *must* be work done by the arms, or none of us could live. There *must* be work done by the brains, or the life we get would not be worth having. And the same men cannot do both. There is rough work to be done, and rough men must do it; there is gentle work to be done, and gentlemen must do it; and it is physically impossible that one class should do, or divide, the work of the other. And it is of no use to try to conceal this sorrowful fact by fine words, and to talk to the workman about the honorableness of manual labor, and the dignity of humanity. That is a grand old proverb of Sancho Panza's, "Fine words butter no parsnips;" and I can tell you that, all over England just now, you workmen are buying a great deal too much butter at that dairy. Rough work, honorable or not, takes the life out of us; and the man who has been heaving clay out of a ditch all day, or driving an express train against the north wind all night, or holding a collier's helm in a gale on a lee-shore, or whirling white-hot iron at a furnace mouth, that man is not the same at the end of his day, or night, as one who has been sitting in a quiet room, with everything comfortable about him, reading books, or classing butterflies, or painting pictures. If it is any comfort to you to be told that the rough work is the more honorable of the two, I should be sorry to take that much of consolation from you; and in some sense I need not. The rough work is at all events real, honest, and, generally, though not always, useful; while the fine work is, a great deal of it, foolish and false as well as fine, and therefore dishonorable: but when both kinds are equally well and worthily done, the head's is the noble work, and the hand's the ignoble; and of all hand work whatsoever, necessary for the maintenance of life, those old words, "In the sweat of thy face thou shalt eat bread," indicate that the inherent nature of it is one of calamity; and that the ground, cursed for our sake, casts also some shadow of degradation into our contest with its thorn and its thistle; so that all nations have held their days honorable, or "holy," and constituted them "holy-days," or "holidays," by making them days of rest; and the promise, which, among all our distant hopes, seems to cast the chief brightness over death, is that blessing of the dead who die in the Lord, that "they rest from their labors, and their works do follow them."

# Anthony Trollope, *An Autobiography*

I received my £100 [for *Barchester Towers*], in advance, with profound delight. It was a positive and most welcome increase to my income, and might probably be regarded as a first real step on the road to substantial success. I am well aware that there are many who think that an author in his authorship should not regard money,—nor a painter, or sculptor, or composer in his art. I do not know that this unnatural self-sacrifice is supposed to extend itself further. A barrister, a clergyman, a doctor, an engineer, and even actors and architects, may without disgrace follow the bent of human nature, and endeavour to fill their bellies and clothe their backs, and also those of their wives and children, as comfortably as they can by the exercise of their abilities and their crafts. They may be as rationally realistic, as may the butchers and the bakers; but the artist and the author forget the high glories of their calling if they condescend to make a money return a first object. They who preach this doctrine will be much offended by my theory, and by this book of mine, if my theory and my book come beneath their notice. They require the practice of a so-called virtue which is contrary to nature, and which, in my eyes, would be no virtue if it were practised. They are like clergymen who preach sermons against the love of money, but who know that the love of money is so distinctive a characteristic of humanity that such sermons are mere platitudes called for by customary but unintelligent piety. All material progress has come from man's desire to do the best he can for himself and those about him, and civilisation and Christianity itself have been made possible by such progress. Though we do not all of us argue this matter out within our breasts, we do all feel it; and we know that the more a man earns the more useful he is to his fellow-men. The most useful lawyers, as a rule, have been those who have made the greatest incomes,—and it is the same with the doctors. It would be the same in the Church if they who have the choosing of bishops always chose the best man. And it has in truth been so too in art and authorship. Did Titian or Rubens disregard their pecuniary rewards? As far as we know, Shakespeare worked always for money, giving the best of his intellect to support his trade as an actor. In our own century what literary names stand higher than those of Byron, Tennyson, Scott, Dickens, Macaulay, and Carlyle? And I think I may say that none of those great men neglected the pecuniary result of their labours. Now and then a man may arise among us who in any calling, whether it be in law, in physic, in religious teaching, in art, or literature, may in his professional enthusiasm utterly disregard money. All will honour his enthusiasm, and if he be wifeless and childless, his disregard of the great objects of men's work will be blameless. But it is a mistake to suppose that a man is a better man because he despises money. Few do so, and those few in doing so suffer a defect. Who does not desire to be hospitable to his friends, generous to the poor, liberal to all, munificent to his children, and to be himself free from the carking fears which poverty creates? The subject will not stand an argument;—and yet authors are told that they should disregard payment for their work, and be content to devote their unbought brains to the welfare of the public. Brains that are unbought will never serve the public much. Take away from English authors their copyrights, and you would very soon take away also from England her authors.

I say this here, because it is my purpose as I go on to state what to me has been the result of my profession in the ordinary way in which professions are regarded, so that by my example may be seen what prospect there is that a man devoting himself to literature with industry, perseverance, certain necessary aptitudes, and fair average talents, may succeed in gaining a livelihood, as another man does in another profession. The result with me has been comfortable but not splendid, as I think was to have been expected from the combination of such gifts.

I have certainly always had also before my eyes the charms of reputation. Over and above the money view of the question, I wished from the beginning to be something more than a clerk in the Post Office. To be known as somebody,—to be Anthony Trollope if it be no more,—is to me much. The feeling is a very general one, and I think beneficent. It is that which has been called the 'last infirmity of noble mind.' The infirmity is so human that the man who lacks it is either above or below humanity. I own to the infirmity. But I confess that my first object in taking to literature as a profession was that which is common to the barrister when he goes to the Bar, and to the baker when he sets up his oven. I wished to make an income on which I and those belonging to me might live in comfort.

If indeed a man writes his books badly, or paints his pictures badly, because he can make his money faster in that fashion than by doing them well, and at the same time proclaims them to be the best he can do,—if in fact he sells shoddy for broadcloth,—he is dishonest, as is any other fraudulent dealer. So may be the barrister who takes money that he does not earn, or the clergyman who is content to live on a sinecure. No doubt the author or the artist may have a difficulty which will not occur to the seller of cloth, in settling within himself what is good work and what bad,—when labour enough has been given, and when the task has been scamped. It is a danger as to which he is bound to be severe with himself—in which he should feel that his conscience should be set fairly in the balance against the natural bias of his interest. If he do not do so, sooner or later his dishonesty will be discovered, and he will be estimated accordingly. But in this he is to be bound only by the plain rules of honesty which should govern us all. Having said so much, I shall not scruple as I go on to attribute to the pecuniary result of my labours all the importance which I felt them to have at the time.

*Barchester Towers,* for which I had received £100 in advance, sold well enough to bring me further payments—moderate payments—from the publishers. From that day up to this very time in which I am writing, that book and *The Warden* together have given me almost every year some small income. I get the accounts very regularly, and I find that I have received £727, 11s. 3d. for the two. It is more than I got for the three or four works that came afterwards, but the payments have been spread over twenty years.

When I went to Mr. Longman with my next novel, *The Three Clerks,* in my hand, I could not induce him to understand that a lump sum down was more pleasant than a deferred annuity. I wished him to buy it from me at a price which he might think to be a fair value, and I argued with him that as soon as an author has put himself into a position which insures a sufficient sale of his works to give a profit, the publisher is not entitled to expect the half of such proceeds. While there is a pecuniary risk, the whole of which must be borne by the publisher, such division is fair enough; but such a demand on the part of the publisher is monstrous as soon as the article produced is known to be a marketable commodity. I thought that I had now reached that point, but Mr. Longman did not agree with me. And he endeavoured to convince me that I might lose more than I gained, even though I should get more money by going elsewhere. 'It is for you,' said he, 'to think whether our names on your title-page are not worth more to you than the increased payment.' This seemed to me to savour of that high-flown doctrine of the contempt of money which I have never admired. I did think much of Messrs. Longman's name, but I liked it best at the bottom of a cheque. . . .

As I journeyed across France to Marseilles, and made thence a terribly rough voyage to Alexandria, I wrote my allotted number of pages every day. On this occasion more than once I left my paper on the cabin table, rushing away to be sick in the privacy of my state room. It was February, and the weather was miserable; but still I did my work. *Labor omnia vincit improbus.* I do not say that to all men has been given physical strength sufficient for such exertion as this, but I do believe that real exertion will enable most men to work at almost any season. I had previously to this arranged a system of task-work for myself, which I would strongly recommend to those who feel as I have felt, that labour, when not made absolutely obligatory by the circumstances of the hour, should never be allowed to become spasmodic. There was no day on which it was my positive duty to write for the publishers, as it was my duty to write reports for the Post Office. I was free to be idle if I pleased. But as I had made up my mind to undertake this second profession, I found it to be expedient to bind myself by certain self-imposed laws. When I have commenced a new book, I have always prepared a diary, divided into weeks, and carried on for the period which I have allowed myself for the completion of the work. In this I have entered, day by day, the number of pages I have written, so that if at any time I have slipped into idleness for a day or two, the record of idleness has been there, staring me in the face, and demanding of me increased labour, so that the deficiency might be supplied. According to the circumstances of the time,—whether my other business might be then heavy or light, or whether the book which I was writing was or was not wanted with speed,—I have allotted myself so many pages a week. The average number has been about 40. It has been placed as low as 20, and has risen to 112. And as a page is an ambiguous term, page has been made to contain 250 words; and as words, if not watched, will have a tendency to straggle, I have had every word counted as I went. In the bargains I have made with publishers I have,—not, of course, with their knowledge, but in my own mind,—undertaken always to supply them with so many words, and I have never put a book out of hand short of the number by a single word. I may also say that the excess has been very small. I have prided myself in completing it within the proposed time,—and I have always done so. There has ever been the record before me, and a week passed with an insufficient number of pages has been a blister to my eye, and a month so disgraced would have been a sorrow to my heart.

I have been told that such appliances are beneath the notice of a man of genius. I have never fancied myself to be a man of genius, but had I been so I think I might well have subjected myself to these trammels. Nothing surely is so potent as a law that may not be disobeyed. It has the force of the waterdrop that hollows the stone. A small daily task, if it be really daily, will beat the labours of a spasmodic Hercules. It is the tortoise which always catches the hare. The hare has no choice. He loses more time in glorifying himself for a quick spurt than suffices for the tortoise to make half his journey.

I have known authors whose lives have always been troublesome and painful because their tasks have never been done in time. They have ever been as boys struggling to learn their lesson as they entered the school gates. Publishers have distrusted them, and they have failed to write their best because they have seldom written at ease. I have done double their work,—though burdened with another profession,—and have done it almost without an effort. I have not once, through all my literary career, felt myself even in danger of being late with my task. I have known no anxiety as to 'copy'. The needed pages far ahead—very far ahead—have almost always been in the drawer beside me. And that little diary, with its dates and ruled spaces, its record that must be seen, its daily, weekly demand upon my industry, has done all that for me.

There are those who would be ashamed to subject themselves to such a taskmaster, and who think that the man who works with his imagination should allow himself to wait till—inspiration moves him. When I have heard such doctrine preached, I have hardly been able to repress my scorn. To me it would not be more absurd if the shoemaker were to wait for inspiration, or the tallow-chandler for the divine moment of melting. If the man whose business it is to write has eaten too many good things, or has drunk too much, or smoked too many cigars,—as men who write sometimes will do,—then his condition may be unfavourable for work; but so will be the condition of a shoemaker who has been similarly imprudent. I have sometimes thought that the inspiration wanted has been the remedy which time will give to the evil results of such imprudence.—*Mens sana in corpore sano.* The author wants that as does every other workman,—that and a habit of industry. I was once told that the surest aid to the writing of a book was a piece of cobbler's wax on my chair. I certainly believe in the cobbler's wax much more than the inspiration.

It will be said, perhaps, that a man whose work has risen to no higher pitch than mine has attained, has no right to speak of the strains and impulses to which real genius is exposed. I am ready to admit the great variations in brain power which are exhibited by the products of different men, and am not disposed to rank my own very high; but my experience tells me that a man can always do the work for which his brain is fitted if he will give himself the habit of regarding his work as a normal condition of his life. I therefore venture to advise young men who look forward to authorship as the business of their lives, even when they propose that that authorship be of the highest class known, to avoid enthusiastic rushes with their pens, and to seat themselves at their desks day by day as though they were lawyers' clerks;—and so let them sit till the allotted task shall be accomplished.

While I was in Egypt, I finished *Doctor Thorne,* and on the following day began *The Bertrams.* I was moved now by a determination to excel, if not in quality, at any rate in quantity. An ignoble ambition for an author, my readers will no doubt say. But not, I think, altogether ignoble, if an author can bring himself to look at his work as does any other workman. This had become my task, this was the furrow in which my plough was set, this was the thing the doing of which had fallen into my hands, and I was minded to work at it with a will. It is not on my conscience that I have ever scamped my work. My novels, whether good or bad, have been as good as I could make them. Had I taken three months of idleness between each they would have been no better. Feeling convinced of that, I finished *Doctor Thorne* on one day, and began *The Bertrams* on the next.

# George Orwell, *The Road to Wigan Pier*

Our civilisation, *pace* Chesterton, is founded on coal, more completely than one realises until one stops to think about it. The machines that keep us alive, and the machines that make the machines, are all directly or indirectly dependent upon coal. In the metabolism of the Western world the coal-miner is second in importance only to the man who ploughs the soil. He is a sort of grimy caryatid upon whose shoulders nearly everything that is *not* grimy is supported. For this reason the actual process by which coal is extracted is well worth watching, if you get the chance and are willing to take the trouble.

When you go down a coal-mine, it is important to try and get to the coal face when the "fillers" are at work. This is not easy, because when the mine is working visitors are a nuisance and are not encouraged, but if you go at any other time, it is possible to come away with a totally wrong impression. On a Sunday, for instance, a mine seems almost peaceful. The time to go there is when the machines are roaring and the air is black with coal dust, and when you can actually see what the miners have to do. At those times the place is like hell, or at any rate like my own mental picture of hell. Most of the things one imagines in hell are there—heat, noise, confusion, darkness, foul air, and above all, unbearable cramped space. Everything except the fire, for there is no fire down there except the feeble beams of Davy lamps and electric torches which scarcely penetrate the clouds of coal dust.

When you have finally got there—and getting there is a job in itself: I will explain that in a moment—you crawl through the last line of pit props and see opposite you a shiny black wall three or four feet high. This is the coal face. Overhead is the smooth ceiling made by the rock from which the coal has been cut; underneath is the rock again, so that the gallery you are in is only as high as the ledge of coal itself, probably not much more than a yard. The first impression of all, overmastering everything else for a while, is the frightful, deafening din from the conveyor belt which carries the coal away. You cannot see very far, because the fog of coal dust throws back the beam of your lamp, but you can see on either side of you the line of half-naked kneeling men, one to every four or five yards, driving their shovels under the fallen coal and flinging it swiftly over their left shoulders. They are feeding it on to the conveyor belt, a moving rubber belt a couple of feet wide which runs a yard or two behind them. Down this belt a glittering river of coal races constantly. In a big mine it is carrying away several tons of coal every minute. It bears it off to some place in the main roads where it is shot into tubs holding half a ton, and thence dragged to the cages and hoisted to the outer air.

It is impossible to watch the "fillers" at work without feeling a pang of envy for their toughness. It is a dreadful job that they do, an almost superhuman job by the standards of an ordinary person. For they are not only shifting monstrous quantities of coal, they are also doing it in a position that doubles or trebles the work. They have got to remain kneeling all the while—they could hardly rise from their knees without hitting the ceiling—and you can easily see by trying it what a tremendous effort this means. Shovelling is comparatively easy when you are standing up, because you can use your knee and thigh to drive the shovel along; kneeling down, the whole of the strain is thrown upon your arm and belly muscles. And the other conditions do not exactly make things easier. There is the heat—it varies, but in some mines it is suffocating— and the coal dust that snuffs up your throat and nostrils and collects along your eyelids, and the unending rattle of the conveyor belt, which in that confined space is rather like the rattle of a machine gun. But the fillers look and work as though they were made of iron. They really do look like iron— hammered iron statues—under the smooth coat of coal dust which clings to them from head to foot. It is only when you see the miners down the mine and naked that you realise what splendid men they are. Most of them are small (big men are at a disadvantage in that job) but nearly all of them have the most noble bodies; wide shoulders tapering to slender supple waists, and small pronounced buttocks and sinewy thighs, with not an ounce of wasted flesh anywhere. In the hotter mines they wear only a pair of thin drawers, clogs and knee-pads; in the hottest mines of all, only the clogs and knee-pads. You can hardly tell by the look of them whether they are young or old. They may be any age up to sixty or even sixty-five, but when they are black and naked they all look alike. No one could do their work who had not a young man's body, and a figure fit for a guardsman at that; just a few pounds of extra flesh on the waist-line, and the constant bending would be impossible. You can never forget that spectacle once you have seen it—the line of bowed, kneeling figures, sooty black all over, driving their huge shovels under the coal with stupendous force and speed. They are on the job for seven and a half hours, theoretically without a break, for there is no time "off." Actually they catch a quarter of an hour or so some time during the shift to eat the food they have brought with them, usually a hunk of bread and dripping and a bottle of cold tea. The first time I was watching the "fillers" at work I put my hand upon some dreadful slimy thing among the coal dust. It was a chewed quid of tobacco. Nearly all the miners chew tobacco, which is said to be good against thirst.

Probably you have to go down several coal-mines before you can get much grasp of the processes that are going on round you. This is chiefly because the mere effort of getting from place to place makes it difficult to notice anything else. In some ways it is even disappointing, or at least is unlike what you have expected. You get into the cage, which is a steel box about as wide as a telephone box and two or three times as long. It holds ten men, but they pack it like pilchards in a tin, and a tall man cannot stand upright in it. The steel door shuts upon you, and somebody working the winding gear above drops you into the void. You have the usual momentary qualm in your belly and a bursting sensation in the ears, but not much sensation of movement till you get near the bottom, when the cage slows down so abruptly that you could swear it is going upwards again. In the middle of the run the cage probably touches sixty miles an hour; in some of the deeper mines it touches even more. When you crawl out at the bottom you are perhaps four hundred yards under ground. That is to say you have a tolerable-sized mountain on top of you; hundreds of yards of solid rock, bones of extinct beasts, subsoil, flints, roots of growing things, green grass and cows grazing on it—all this suspended over your head and held back only by wooden props as thick as the calf of your leg. But because of the speed at which the cage has brought you down, and the complete blackness through which you have travelled, you hardly feel yourself deeper down than you would at the bottom of the Piccadilly tube.

What *is* surprising, on the other hand, is the immense horizontal distances that have to be travelled underground. Before I had been down a mine I had vaguely imagined the miner stepping out of the cage and getting to work on a ledge of coal a few yards away. I had not realised that before he even gets to his work he may have to creep through passages as long as from London Bridge to Oxford Circus. In the beginning, of course, a mine shaft is sunk somewhere near a seam of coal. But as that seam is worked out and fresh seams are followed up, the workings get further and further from the pit bottom. If it is a mile from the pit bottom to the coal face, that is probably an average distance; three miles is a fairly normal one; there are even said to be a few mines where it is as much as five miles. But these distances bear no relation to distances above ground. For in all that mile or three miles as it may be, there is hardly anywhere outside the main road, and not many places even there, where a man can stand straight.

You do not notice the effect of this till you have gone a few hundred yards. You start off, stooping slightly, down the dim-lit gallery, eight or ten feet wide and about five feet high, with the walls built up with slabs of shale, like the stone walls in Derbyshire. Every yard or two there are wooden props holding up the beams and girders; some of the girders have buckled into fantastic curves under which you have to duck. Usually it is bad going underfoot—thick dust or jagged chunks of shale, and in some mines where there is water it is as mucky as a farmyard. Also there is the rack for the coal tubs, like a miniature railway track with sleepers a foot or two apart, which is tiresome to walk on.

Everything is grey with shale dust; there is a dusty fiery smell which seems to be the same in all mines. You see mysterious machines of which you never learn the purpose, and bundles of tools slung together on wires, and sometimes mice darting away from the beam of the lamps. They are surprisingly common, especially in mines where there are or have been horses. It would be interesting to know how they got there in the first place; possibly by falling down the shaft—for they say a mouse can fall any distance uninjured, owing to its surface area being so large relative to its weight. You press yourself against the wall to make way for lines of tubs jolting slowly towards the shaft, drawn by an endless steel cable operated from the surface. You creep through sacking curtains and thick wooden doors which, when they are opened, let out fierce blasts of air. These doors are an important part of the ventilation system. The exhausted air is sucked out of one shaft by means of fans, and the fresh air enters the other of its own accord. But if left to itself the air will take the shortest way round, leaving the deeper workings unventilated; so all short cuts have to be partitioned off.

At the start to walk stooping is a joke, but it is a joke that soon wears off. I am handicapped by being exceptionally tall, but when the roof falls to four feet or less it is a tough job for anybody except a dwarf or a child. You have not only got to bend double, you have also got to keep your head up all the while so as to see the beams and girders and dodge them when they come. You have, therefore, a constant crick in the neck, but this is nothing to the pain in your knees and thighs. After half a mile it becomes (I am not exaggerating) an unbearable agony. You begin to wonder whether you will ever get to the end—still more, how on earth you are going to get back. Your pace grows slower and slower. You come to a stretch of a couple of hundred yards where it is all exceptionally low and you have to work yourself along in a squatting position. Then suddenly the room opens out to a mysterious height—scene of an old fall of rock, probably—and for twenty whole yards you can stand upright. The relief is overwhelming. But after this there is another low stretch of a hundred yards and then a succession of beams which you have to crawl under. You go down on all fours; even this is a relief after the squatting business. But when you come to the end of the beams and try to get up again, you find that your knees have temporarily struck work and refuse to lift you. You call a halt, ig-nominiously, and say that you would like to rest for a minute or two. Your guide (a miner) is sympathetic. He knows that your muscles are not the same as his. "Only another four hundred yards," he says encouragingly; you feel that he might as well say another four hundred miles. But finally you do somehow creep as far as the coal face. You have gone a mile and taken the best part of an hour; a miner would do it in not much more than twenty minutes. Having got there, you have to sprawl in the coal dust and get your strength back for several minutes before you can even watch the work in progress with any kind of intelligence.

Coming back is worse than going, not only because you are already tired out but because the journey back to the shaft is probably slightly up hill. You get through the low places at the speed of a tortoise, and you have no shame about calling a halt when your knees give way. Even the lamp you are carrying becomes a nuisance and probably when you stumble you drop it; whereupon, if it is a Davy lamp, it goes out. Ducking the beams becomes more and more of an effort, and sometimes you forget to duck. You try walking head down as the miners do, and then you bang your backbone. Even the miners bang their backbones fairly often. This is the reason why in very hot mines, where it is necessary to go about half naked, most of the miners have what they call "buttons down the back"—that is, a permanent scab on each vertebra. When the track is down hill the miners sometimes fit their clogs, which are hollow underneath, on to the trolley rails and slide down. In mines where the "travelling" is very bad all the miners carry sticks about two and a half feet long, hollowed out below the handle. In normal places you keep your hand on top of the stick and in the low places you slide your hand down into the hollow. These sticks are a great help, and the wooden crash-helmets—a comparatively recent invention—are a godsend. They look like a French or Italian steel helmet, but they are made of some kind of pith and very light, and so strong that you can take a violent blow on the head without feeling it. When finally you get back to the surface you have been perhaps three hours underground and travelled two miles, and you are more exhausted than you would be by a twenty-five mile walk above ground. For a week afterwards your thighs are so stiff that coming downstairs is quite a difficult feat; you have to work your way down in a peculiar sidelong manner, without bending the knees. Your miner friends notice the stiffness of your walk and chaff you about it. ("How'd ta like to work down pit, eh?" etc.) Yet even a miner who has been long away from work—from illness, for instance—when he comes back to the pit, suffers badly for the first few days.

It may seem that I am exaggerating, though no one who has been down an old-fashioned pit (most of the pits in England are old-fashioned) and actually gone as far as the coal face, is likely to say so. But what I want to emphasise is this. Here is this frightful business of crawling to and fro, which to any normal person is a hard day's work in itself; and it is not part of the miner's work at all, it is merely an extra, like the City man's daily ride in the Tube. The miner does that journey to and fro, and sandwiched in between there are seven and a half hours of savage work. I have never travelled much more than a mile to the coal face; but often it is three miles, in which case I and most people other than coal-miners would never get there at all. This is the kind of point that one is always liable to miss. When you think of a coal-mine you think of depth, heat, darkness, blackened figures hacking at walls of coal; you don't think, necessarily, of those miles of creeping to and fro. There is the question of time, also. A miner's working shift of seven and a half hours does not sound very long, but one has got to add on to it at least an hour a day for "travelling," more often two hours and sometimes three. Of course, the "travelling" is not technically work and the miner is not paid for it; but it is as like work as makes no difference. It is easy to say that miners don't mind all this. Certainly, it is not the same for them as it would be for you or me. They have done it since childhood, they have the right muscles hardened, and they can move to and fro underground with a startling and rather horrible agility. A miner puts his head down and *runs,* with a long swinging stride, through places where I can only stagger. At the workings you see them on all fours, skipping round the pit props almost like dogs. But it is quite a mistake to think that they enjoy it. I have talked about this to scores of miners and they all admit that the "travelling" is hard work; in any case when you hear them discussing a pit among themselves the "travelling" is always one of the things they discuss. It is said that a shift always returns from work faster than it goes; nevertheless the miners all say that it is the coming away, after a hard day's work, that is especially irksome. It is part of their work and they are equal to it, but certainly it is an effort. It is comparable, perhaps, to climbing a smallish mountain before and after your day's work.

When you have been down two or three pits you begin to get some grasp of the processes that are going on underground. (I ought to say, by the way, that I know nothing whatever about the technical side of mining: I am merely describing what I have seen.) Coal lies in thin seams between enormous layers of rock, so that essentially the process of getting it out is like scooping the central layer from a Neapolitan ice. In the old days the miners used to cut straight into the coal with pick and crowbar—a very slow job because coal, when lying in its virgin state, is almost as hard as rock. Nowadays the preliminary work is done by an electronically-driven coal-cutter, which in principle is an immensely tough and powerful band-saw, running horizontally instead of vertically, with teeth a couple of inches long and half an inch or an inch thick. It can move backwards or forwards on its own power, and the men operating it can rotate it this way and that. Incidentally it makes one of the most awful noises I have ever heard, and sends forth clouds of coal dust which make it impossible to see more than two or three feet and almost impossible to breathe. The machine travels along the coal face cutting into the base of the coal and undermining it to the depth of five feet or five feet and a half; after this it is comparatively easy to extract the coal to the depth to which it has been undermined. Where it is "difficult getting," however, it has also to be loosened with explosives. A man with an electric drill, like a rather smaller version of the drills used in street-mending, bores holes at intervals in the coal, inserts blasting powder, plugs it with clay, goes round the corner if there is one handy (he is supposed to retire to twenty-five yards distance) and touches off the charge with an electric current. This is not intended to bring the coal out, only to loosen it. Occasionally, of course, the charge is too powerful, and then it not only brings the coal out but brings the roof down as well.

After the blasting has been done the "fillers" can tumble the coal out, break it up and shovel it on to the conveyor belt. It comes out at first in monstrous boulders which may weigh anything up to twenty tons. The conveyor belt shoots it on to tubs, and the tubs are shoved into the main road and hitched on to an endlessly revolving steel cable which drags them to the cage. Then they are hoisted, and at the surface the coal is sorted by being run over screens, and if necessary is washed as well. As far as possible the "dirt"—the shale, that is—is used for making the roads below. All that cannot be used is sent to the surface and dumped; hence the monstrous "dirt-heaps," like hideous grey mountains, which are the characteristic scenery of the coal areas. When the coal has been extracted to the depth to which the machine has cut, the coal face has advanced by five feet. Fresh props are put in to hold up the newly exposed roof, and during the next shift the conveyor belt is taken to pieces, moved five feet forward and re-assembled. As far as possible the three operations of cutting, blasting and extraction are done in three separate shifts, the cutting in the afternoon, the blasting at night (there is a law, not always kept, that forbids it being done when there are other men working near by), and the "filling" in the morning shift, which lasts from six in the morning until half past one.

Even when you watch the process of coal-extraction you probably only watch it for a short time, and it is not until you begin making a few calculations that you realise what a stupendous task the "fillers" are performing. Normally each man has to clear a space four or five yards wide. The cutter has undermined the coal the depth of five feet, so that if the seam of coal is three or four feet high, each man has to cut out, break up and load on to the belt something between seven and twelve cubic yards of coal. This is to say, taking a cubic yard as weighing twenty-seven hundredweight, that each man is shifting coal at a speed approaching two tons an hour. I have just enough experience of pick and shovel work to be able to grasp what this means. When I am digging trenches in my garden, if I shift two tons of earth during the afternoon, I feel that I have earned my tea. But earth is tractable stuff compared with coal, and I don't have to work kneeling down, a thousand feet underground, in suffocating heat and swallowing coal dust with every breath I take; nor do I have to walk a mile bent double before I begin. The miner's job would be as much beyond my power as it would be to perform on the flying trapeze or to win the Grand National. I am not a manual labourer and please God I never shall be one, but there are some kinds of manual work that I could do if I had to. At a pitch I could be a tolerable road-sweeper or an inefficient gardener or even a tenth-rate farm hand. But by no conceivable amount of effort or training could I become a coal-miner; the work would kill me in a few weeks.

Watching coal miners at work, you realise momentarily what different universes different people inhabit. Down there where coal is dug it is a sort of world apart which one can quite easily go through life without ever hearing about. Probably a majority of people would even prefer not to hear about it. Yet it is the absolutely necessary counterpart of our world above. Practically everything we do, from eating an ice to crossing the Atlantic, and from baking a loaf to writing a novel, involves the use of coal, directly or indirectly. For all the arts of peace coal is needed; if war breaks out it is needed all the more. In time of revolution the miner must go on working or the revolution must stop, for revolution as much as reaction needs coal. Whatever may be happening on the surface, the hacking and shovelling have got to continue without a pause, or at any rate without pausing for more than a few weeks at the most. In order that Hitler may march the goose-step, that the Pope may denounce Bolshevism, that the cricket crowds may assemble at Lord's, that the Nancy poets may scratch one another's backs, coal has got to be forthcoming. But on the whole we are not aware of it; we all know that we "must have coal," but we seldom or never remember what coal-getting involves. Here am I, sitting writing in front of my comfortable coal fire. It is April but I still need a fire. Once a fortnight the coal cart drives up to the door and men in leather jerkins carry the coal indoors in stout sacks smelling of tar and shoot it clanking into the coal-hole under the stairs. It is only very rarely, when I make a definite mental effort, that I connect this coal with that far-off labour in the mines. It is just "coal"—something that I have got to have; black stuff that arrives mysteriously from nowhere in particular, like manna except that you have to pay for it. You could quite easily drive a car right across the north of England and never once remember that hundreds of feet below the road you are on the miners are hacking at the coal. Yet in a sense it is the miners who are driving your car forward. Their lamp-lit world down there is as necessary to the daylight world above as the root is to the flower.

It is not long since conditions in the mines were worse than they are now. There are still living a few very old women who in their youth have worked underground, with a harness round their waists and a chain that passed between their legs, crawling on all fours and dragging tubs of coal. They used to go on doing this even when they were pregnant. And even now, if coal could not be produced without pregnant women dragging it to and fro, I fancy we should let them do it rather than deprive ourselves of coal. But most of the time, of course, we should prefer to forget that they were doing it. It is so with all types of manual work; it keeps us alive, and we are oblivious of its existence. More than anyone else, perhaps, the miner can stand as the type of the manual worker, not only because his work is so exaggeratedly awful, but also because it is so vitally necessary and yet so remote from our experience, so invisible, as it were, that we are capable of forgetting it as we forget the blood in our veins. In a way it is even humiliating to watch coal-miners working. It raises in you a momentary doubt about your own status as an "intellectual" and a superior person generally. For it is brought home to you, at least while you are watching, that it is only because miners sweat their guts out that superior persons can remain superior. You and I and the editor of the *Times Lit. Supp.,* and the Nancy poets and the Archbishop of Canterbury and Comrade X, author of *Marxism for Infants*—all of us *really* owe the comparative decency of our lives to poor drudges underground, driving their shovels forward with arms and belly muscles of steel.

# Jacques Ellul, *The Ethics of Freedom*

## Freedom and Vocation

Even a cursory study of the Bible soon shows that it contains little that corresponds to our modern ideas of work and vocation. Terms are used which we have to translate by "vocation" or "the call of God," but the context makes it apparent that what is at issue is always a summons to the specific service of God. Thus a man is called to be a prophet or apostle. He is called to be a king, as David was. He is called to serve God by some exceptional act and without even realizing that he is doing it in God's service, e.g., the king of Syria, the king of Assyria, or Cyrus.

Work does not enter into the question apart from the work that Hiram contributed for the building of the temple. Work is a natural exercise of human activity which sets man in a relation to creation that is either positive, as in Eden, or negative, as after the break with God. In the latter case work is laborious and necessary to survival. Either way, however, it is not presented as the service of God. It has to be done, and the Bible is realistic enough not to overlay this necessity with superfluous spiritual ornamentation. Moreover, the Bible displays no essential interest in the situation of work. Work is the painful lot of all men but it is not particularly important. . . .

What must be recalled is that work is a simple necessity. Those who are not prepared to work should not eat. It has no specific value. The Bible never speaks of it as a vocation. If not in the pure sense, at least in the form in which we know it, work is a result of the fall. It forms part of the divided, separated, and alienated condition of man. Work itself is an alienating factor, irrespective of social or economic conditions or of ideology.

In saying this, I am not saying that work is bad. What I am saying is that its value is purely utilitarian and that it is one of the necessities of life. We should simply accept it as such without exalting it and without confusing it with the call of God. How misleading it is to deduce from Genesis 1:28 "Replenish the earth, and subdue it," the idea that work is a divine vocation! We simply have to work—that is all.

Jesus never calls upon anyone to work. On the contrary, he constantly takes the men he calls away from their work, e.g., Peter, James, Levi, the man in the parable who wants to try out his oxen, and so forth. It is possible that Jesus himself worked, but this is by no means certain, and even if he did, it proves nothing. Like others he obeys the necessities of human life.

Finally it should be noted that the Old Testament makes a great deal of the sabbath. It is a sign of liberation. This shows that work is not after all so excellent or desirable a thing as people often tell us. Freedom has to have a place in the pure and simple necessity which is work, since work itself never expresses this freedom. . . .

The idea of work as a curse fades increasingly into the background. From the fifteenth century one begins to find the argument which is often used during the Reformation age and then again in the eighteenth century, namely, that monks, and especially mendicants, are useless because they do not work and do not produce anything. Work begins to become something which it never was up to the thirteenth century—a value and a virtue.

It is against this cultural background, and in the midst of this psycho-economic change in relation to work, that Martin Luther bursts on the scene. He cannot put the clock back. The society to which he belongs is settling down to work as never before. The social group to which he primarily speaks is making of work the aim and meaning of life. The view is still held, however, that everything relates to God and comes from God. Hence work, too, stands in relationship to God. It has its own validity as such, but only because it proceeds from God and is part of the order of God for man.

Luther then, in his well-known statement about the cobbler, can say that by making shoes this man is serving God and following a vocation no less than the preacher of the word of God. In the Reformation period we also find occasionally the idea that work is the service of God mediately through the service of men. By rendering service to other men, the workman obeys the commandment of God.

Another interpretation of vocation also calls for notice. Work can be very laborious, crushing, and mortifying. But this is God's will. The burden and condensation of work have to be accepted because they come from God. This leads on rapidly to an idea which developed in the seventeenth and eighteenth centuries, namely, that work plays a redemptive role. . . .

This can have economic results in the rise of capitalism and the middle class. Another result is the further enhancement of the value of work. We see here a development by reciprocal interaction. The more the value of work is enhanced by the idea of vocation, the greater the increase in economic activity. But the greater the increase in economic activity, the higher the value placed on work.

This has two results in the ideological field. The first is that the middle class carries to an extreme the emphasis on the requirement and concrete value of work. Various truisms express this. Thus we are told that work is prayer—a direct consequence of the confusion between work and divine vocation. Again, work is said to be freedom. The redemptive value of work is also stressed. . . .

We must now turn, however, to the second ideological aspect of work as vocation as we find this in Marx. Marx carries this ideology of work to its ultimate extreme. As he sees it, man is what he does (in his work). Work is that which marks man out in nature as a whole. Hence an exceptional place is given to work and it is viewed as an exceptional virtue.

Work is thus the supreme mediation. As Marx himself says, when others use my product, I have a direct sense of having met a human need, of having been an intermediary between them and the race, of having been recognized by them as complementary to their own being and as a necessary part of themselves, of having been confirmed in their thought as well as their love, of having created in the manifestation of my life a manifestation of theirs, of having confirmed and realized in my activity (or work) my human and social essence.

Now obviously if this is what work is (or ought to be), we are confronted by a contradiction when we look at the work done by the proletariat. This is one of the basic themes in the condemnation of capitalism by Marx. By exploitation, capitalism does not let work play its dominant and constructive role. This extravagant enhancing of the value of work by Marx, for which there is no precedent, results partly from the great growth of work in the west during the nineteenth century and partly from the secularization of the idea of the divine vocation of man in work.

Now it is obvious that with the evolution of our society it is impossible to cling to this kind of ideology of work. Philosophically, of course, we can say anything we like, but it is plain that nothing in any epoch justifies the idealism of work. Since the nineteenth century we can see its degradation in three successive stages. . . .

The first thing to bring this about is capitalism. With salaries work becomes a commodity to be sold and bought. A man trades his working strength and the product of his work for payment which simply enables him to stay alive. This payment does not represent in any sense at all the true, higher, transcendent value of his work. On the contrary, it reduces work to the level of merchandise. The one whose work is sold in this way can have no initiative or joy in work. His work cannot be an expression of his personality, since its only aim is to produce objects which will enter into commercial circulation. In these circumstances it is difficult to maintain the idea of vocation.

The situation is aggravated with the development of mechanization. . . . Work is separated from its product. It becomes a pure and simple obligation without meaning. It is broken up by parcelling out and specialization. The workman does not finally know what he is doing or what is the utility or value of his work. He does not even know what he is making but simply knows the machine on which he is working. The fragmentation and distribution of work on the production line exclude any understanding of the total process. Professional specialization confines the worker in a very narrow sphere of execution. Reflection on the purpose of work is ruled out. A rift develops between action and thought. Everything that is done by the man at the machine is calculated by a third person who is an expert at matching men and machines and at matching machines themselves so as to achieve a smooth flow of production. Thus a man's work is totally subordinated to the machine and to the need to organize the working of the machines. The problem is that of production rhythm. Man is completely dispossessed of his work. It cannot be anything but an alien activity which is imposed from without, corresponds to no inner reality, and in the strict sense no longer forms a true part of the life of man even though it takes up the major part of his time.

In these conditions it is evident that work can no longer be a vocation. It might still be argued that God is able to transform even the worst situation and that he can restore a sense of vocation even in the case of the most absurd work. But this is little more than a convenient refusal to look at the true facts. This type of work can no longer be presented generally as vocation. The most we can say is that God in his grace may miraculously enable a man to live out this kind of work as a gift and calling of God. The theological link between vocation and work, however, is snapped.

The universal technologizing of society has further aggravated the situation. Technology has become a mediation in all actions and for all purposes. The technological path has to be taken to do anything at all in the world. Technology also has its own exclusive efficiency. This is what characterizes it. It thus cuts off all recourse to other types of efficiency. One can no longer say as Ambroise Paré did: "I bandaged him and God healed him." One cannot say: "I pressed down the accelerator and God accelerated the car." The regularity of effects, the exclusiveness of means, and generalized mediation leave no place at all for the concept of vocation.

On the contrary, the concept comes under criticism. When a good technician is needed the man who is full of his vocation or divine calling is of no use. Vocation is a poor substitute for competence. We all know of people who apply for posts as professors, educators, or psychologists because they are following a call from God when in fact they are very poorly qualified. Even in the case of a specialist, vocation may cause him to make foolish mistakes in the use of his skills. The nurse with a vocation can allow emotions to creep into her work when it should be governed by the most rigorous criteria of efficiency. . . .

Work has to be accepted in faith, then, as a sign of our creatureliness and our sinfulness. To this extent it is "normal" even though it is alienating, crushing, and meaningless. We have to accept its stupidity as a mark of the absurdity of our life. Work has no ultimate or transcendent value. Before God it is simply that which makes our survival possible and keeps us in being.

This realism coincides with our thesis and implies the destruction of every romanticizing or idealizing of work, whether bourgeois or Marxist.

On the other hand the recognition that we are in the order of necessity in no way implies contempt for work, rejection of it, or carping criticism. Work is simply part of the order to which we are subject—no more. . . .

When satisfaction is given, e.g., by a successful cure or the production of a work of art, we are not to say that this is the true measure of work by which all other tasks are to be measured, including the worker on the belt or the unfortunate unskilled laborer. No, it is from the latter jobs that we learn the true reality of work. When human work produces joy or what seems to be outside the everyday, we have to realize that this is an exceptional event, a grace, a gift of God for which we must give thanks.

To view work along these lines is to combine realism with biblical insight. It is also to clip the wings of an idealism which projects a marvelous future when everybody will be doing rich and meaningful work. On the other hand, relative work is not completely devoid of value or interest. For it offers the possibility of sustaining life, of upholding the world, and of a continuation of history.

# ID. Work as Vocation

1. 1 Corinthians 7:17–24. Translation is the Revised Standard Version.

2. John Calvin, pp. 724–25 of *Institutes of the Christian Religion,* edited by John T. McNeill and Ford Lewis Battles, vol. 20 of the Library of Christian Classics (Philadelphia: Westminster, 1960). Calvin (1509–1564) was one of the greatest of the sixteenth-century Protestant Reformers. Although a Frenchman, he is especially identified with the Swiss city of Geneva, where his most important work was done.

3. William Perkins, "A Treatise of the Vocations or Callings of Men, with sorts and kinds of them, and the right use thereof," selections from pp. 35–57 in Edmund S. Morgan, ed., *Puritan Political Ideas* (Indianapolis: Bobbs-Merrill, 1965). Perkins (1558–1602), though little known today, was an important Puritan theologian in England. His writings were very influential among Puritan thinkers in sixteenth- and seventeenth-century England and America.

4. George Herbert, "The Elixir," p. 311 in John N. Wall, Jr., ed., *George Herbert: The Country Parson, The Temple* (New York: Paulist Press, 1981). George Herbert (1593–1633) was a priest in the church of England, but he is known chiefly as a great religious poet. Herbert's poem "The Elixir" comes from *The Temple,* his collection of religious poems published posthumously.

5. Charles Wesley, "Forth in thy name, O Lord, I go," p. 213 in Frank Whaling, ed., *John and Charles Wesley: Selected Prayers, Hymns, Journal Notes, Sermons, Letters and Treatises* (New York: Paulist Press, 1981). One of the greatest of English hymn writers, Wesley (1707–1788) worked closely with his brother John, the founder of Methodism in eighteenth-century England.

6. Max Weber, pp. 87–88 of *The Protestant Ethic and the Spirit of Capitalism* (New York: Charles Scribner's Sons, 1958). "The Protestant Ethic and the Spirit of Capitalism" was first published in Germany in 1904–1905. The writings of Weber (1864–1920) on the rise of capitalism and on the nature of bureaucracy have also been very influential in the English-speaking world.

7. Henry Van Dyke, "The Three Best Things—I: Work," p. 166 in *The Poems of Henry Van Dyke* (New York: Charles Scribner's Sons, 1926). Van Dyke

(1852–1933) was a Presbyterian minister whose essays and poems were very popular in early twentieth-century America. Although he is largely unknown today, his story of "The Other Wise Man" is still often read.

8. Charles Taylor, selections from pp. 211–26 of *Sources of the Self: The Making of the Modern Identity* (Cambridge: Harvard University Press, 1989). Charles Taylor (1931–), a Canadian, is a contemporary political philosopher.

9. Michael Novak, pp. 34–36 of *Business as a Calling: Work and the Examined Life* (New York: Free Press, 1996). Michael Novak (1933–) is a contemporary American intellectual who writes on religious, political, and economic topics.

# 1 Corinthians 7:17–24

Only, let every one lead the life which the Lord has assigned to him, and in which God has called him. This is my rule in all the churches. Was any one at the time of his call already circumcised? Let him not seek to remove the marks of circumcision. Was any one at the time of his call uncircumcised? Let him not seek circumcision. For neither circumcision counts for anything nor uncircumcision, but keeping the commandments of God. Every one should remain in the state in which he was called. Were you a slave when called? Never mind. But if you can gain your freedom, avail yourself of the opportunity. [*Alternatively, this verse may be translated:* But if you can gain your freedom, make use of your present condition instead.] For he who was called in the Lord as a slave is a freedman of the Lord. Likewise he who was free when called is a slave of Christ. You were bought with a price; do not become slaves of men. So, brethren, in whatever state each was called, there let him remain with God.

# John Calvin, *Institutes of the Christian Religion*

Finally, this point is to be noted: the Lord bids each one of us in all life's actions to look to his calling. For he knows with what great restlessness human nature flames, with what fickleness it is borne hither and thither, how its ambition longs to embrace various things at once. Therefore, lest through our stupidity and rashness everything be turned topsy-turvy, he has appointed duties for every man in his particular way of life. And that no one may thoughtlessly transgress his limits, he has named these various kinds of living "callings." Therefore each individual has his own kind of living asssigned to him by the Lord as a sort of sentry post so that he may not heedlesssly wander about throughout life. Now, so necessary is this distinction that all our actions are judged in his sight by it, often indeed far otherwise than in the judgment of human and philosophical reason. No deed is considered more noble, even among philosophers, than to free one's country from tyranny. Yet a private citizen who lays his hand upon a tyrant is openly condemned by the heavenly judge [I Sam. 24:7, 11; 26:9].

But I will not delay to list examples. It is enough if we know that the Lord's calling is in everything the beginning and foundation of well-doing. And if there is anyone who will not direct himself to it, he will never hold to the straight path in his duties. Perhaps, sometimes, he could contrive something laudable in appearance; but whatever it may be in the eyes of men, it will be rejected before God's throne. Besides, there will be no harmony among the several parts of his life. Accordingly, your life will then be best ordered when it is directed to this goal. For no one, impelled by his own rashness, will attempt more than his calling will permit, because he will know that it is not lawful to exceed its bounds. A man of obscure station will lead a private life ungrudgingly so as not to leave the rank in which he has been placed by God. Again, it will be no slight relief from cares, labors, troubles, and other burdens for a man to know that God is his guide in all these things. The magistrate will discharge his functions more willingly; the head of the household will confine himself to his duty; each man will bear and swallow the discomforts, vexations, weariness, and anxieties in his way of life, when he has been persuaded that the burden was laid upon him by God. From this will arise also a singular consolation: that no task will be so sordid and base, provided you obey your calling in it, that it will not shine and be reckoned very precious in God's sight.

# William Perkins, "A Treatise of the Vocations or Callings of men, with sorts and kinds of them, and the right use thereof"

I Cor. 7. Verse 20.

*Let every man abide in that calling, wherein hee was called.*

From the 17. verse of this chapt. to the 25. there are two questions handled. First, whether a man beeing called to Christianity uncircumcised, must bee circumcised after his calling. The second is, whether beeing a bondman when he is called, hee must then leave his calling. Now the sum of the Apostles answer to them both, is laid downe in this 20. verse: as if hee should say; let every man continue in that calling, wherein hee was called unto Christ: that is, wherein hee walked and lived when it pleased God by the ministery of his Gospel, to cal him unto the profession of Christian religion. The cause why I have chosen to speake of these words, is, because I meane to intreate of this point of vocation or calling; considering few men rightly know how to live and goe on in their callings, so as they may please God. Therefore to proceede in order, in speaking of this point; First, I will shew what *Vocation* or *Calling is.* Secondly, 1. will set downe the *parts* and *kindes* thereof. Thirdly, the holy & lawfull use of every mans particular calling: all which are in some sort touched in the words of my text.

For the first: *A vocation or calling, is a certain kind of life, ordained and imposed on man by God, for the common good.* First of all I say, it is a *certaine condition or kind of life:* that is, a certaine manner of leading our lives in this world. For example, the life of a king is to spend his time in the governing of his subjects, and that is his calling: and the life of a subject is to live in obedience to the Magistrate, and that is his calling. The state and condition of a Minister is, to leade his life in preaching of the Gospell and word of God, and that is his calling. A master of a family, is to leade his life in the government of his family, and that is his calling, In a word, that particular and honest manner of conversation, whereunto every man is called and set apart, that is (I say) his calling.

Now in every calling we must consider two causes. First, the efficient and author thereof. Secondly, the finall and proper end. The author of every calling, is God himselfe: and therefore *Paul* saith; *As God hath called every man, let him walke,* vers. 17. And for this cause, the order & manner of living in this world, is called a *Vocation;* because every man is to live as he is called of God. For looke as in the campe, the Generall appointeth to every man his place and standing; one place for the horse-man, & another for the foot-man, and to every particular souldier likewise, his office and standing, in which hee is to abide against the enemie, and therein to live and die: even so it is in humane societies: God is the Generall, appointing to every man his particular calling and as it were his standing: and in that calling he assignes unto him his particular office; in performance whereof he is to live & die. And as in a campe, no souldier can depart his standing, without the leave of the Generall; no more may any man leave his calling, except he receive liberty from God. Againe, in a clocke, made by the art and handy-worke of man, there be many wheeles, and every one hath his severall motion, some turne this way, some that way, some goe softly, some apace: and they are all ordered by the motion of the watch. Behold here a notable resemblance of Gods speciall providence over mankinde, which is the watch of the great world, allotting to every man his motion and calling: and in that calling, his particular office and function. Therefore it is true that I say, that God himselfe is the author and beginning of callings. . . .

The finall cause or end of every calling, I note in the last words of the description; *For* the *common good:* that is, for the benefite and good estate of mankinde. In mans body there be sundry parts and members, and every one hath his severall use and office, which it performeth not for it selfe, but for the good of the whole bodie; as the office of the eye, is to see, of the eare to heare, and the foote to goe. Now all societies of men, are bodies, a family is a bodie, and so is every particular Church a bodie, and the common-wealth also: and in these bodies there be severall members which are men walking in severall callings and offices, the execution whereof, must tend to the happy and good estate of the rest; yea of all men every where, as much as possible is. The common good of men stands in this, not onely that they live, but that they live well, in righteousnes and holiness and consequently in true happinesse. And for the attainement hereunto, God hath ordained and disposed all callings, and in his providence designed the persons to beare them. Here then we must in generall know, that he abuseth his calling, whosoever he be that against the end thereof, imployes it for himselfe, seeking wholly his own, and not the common good. And that common saying, *Every man for himselfe, and God for us all,* is wicked, and is directly against the end of every calling or honest kinde of life.

This much of the description of *Vocation* in generall. Now before I come particularly to intreate of the speciall kindes of callings, there are two generall rules to bee learned of all, which belong to every calling.

The first: whatsoever any man enterprizeth or doth, either in word or deede, he must doe it by vertue of his calling, and he must keepe himselfe within the compasse, limits, or precincts thereof. This rule is laid downe in these wordes of the Apostles: *Let every man abide in that calling, wherein he was called:* the drift wherof is, to binde men to their calling, & to teach them to performe all their actions by warrant thereof. It is said, *Hebr. 11. 6. Without faith it is impossible to please God:* and *Whatsoever is not of faith, is sinne.* Whatsoever is not done within the compasse of a calling, is not of faith, because a man must first have some warrant and word of God to assure him of his calling, to do this or that thing, before he can do it in faith. . . .

The second generall rule which must bee remembred, is this: That *Every man must doe the duties of his calling with diligence:* & therfore *Salomon* saith, *Eccl. 9.10. Whatsoever is in thine hand to do, do it with al thy power. S. Paul* bids him that ruleth, rule with diligence; and every man to wait on his office, *Rom. 12.8.* And Jeremy saith, Jer. *48.10 Cursed is he that doth the work of the Lord negligently.* That which Christ saith of the worke of our redemption, *It is meate and drinke for me to do my Fathers will:* the same must every man say in like sort of his particular calling. . . . And on the other side, wee must take heede of two damnable sinnes that are contrary to this diligence. The first is idlenesse, whereby: the duties of our callings, and the occasions of glorifying God, are neglected or omitted. The second is slouthfulnes, whereby they are performed slackly and carelesly. God in the Parable of the husbandman, cals them that are idle into his vineyard, saying, Why *stand ye idle all the day? Mat. 20. 6.* And the servant that had received but one talent, is called an evill servant, because he was slouthfull in the use of it: for so it is said. *Thou evill servant and slouthful, Mat. 25.2 6. S. Paul* gives this rule to the Thessalonians, *He that would not labour, must not eate.* . . .

Thus much of the two general rules. Now follow the parts and kindes of Vocations: and they are of two sorts: Generall, or Particular. The generall calling is the calling of Christianity, which is common to all that live in the Church of God. The particular, is that special calling that belongs to some particular men: as the calling of a Magistrate, the calling of a Minister, the calling of a Master, of a father, of a childe, of a servant, of a subject, or any other calling that is common to all. And *Paul* acknowledging this distinction of *Callings,* when he saith, *Let every man abide in that calling, wherin he is called,* that is, in that particular and personall calling, in which he was called to bee a Christian. Of these two in order.

The generall Calling is that wherby a man is called out of the world to bee a child of God, a member of Christ, & heire of the kingdome of heaven. This calling belongs to every one within the compasse of the Church, not any one accepted. . . .

Thus much of the generall calling common to all men as they are Christians. Now followeth the second kinde of calling, and that is personall. A personall calling is the execution of some particular office; arising of that distinction which God makes betweene man and man in every societie. First I say, it is *the execution of some particular office;* as for example, the calling of a magistrate is to execute the office of government over his subjects, the office of a minister is to execute the duty of teaching his people, the calling of a master, is to execute the office of authority and government over his servants: the office of a Physition, is to put in practice the good means whereby life and health are preserved. In a word, in every estate the practise and execution of that particular office, wherein any man is placed, is his personall calling.

Secondly I adde, that it ariseth from that distinction which God maketh betweene man and man in every society: to shew what is the foundation and ground of all personall callings. And it is a point to bee considered of us, which I thus explaine: God in his word hath ordained the societie of man with man, partly in the Common-wealth, partly in the Church, and partly in the family: and it is not the will of God that man should live and converse alone by himselfe. Now for the maintaining of society, he hath ordained a certaine bond to linke men together, which Saint *Paul* calleth *the bond of peace, and the bond of perfection,* namely, love. And howsoever hee hath ordained societies, and the bond of them all, yet hath he appointed that there should stil remaine a distinction betweene man and man, not onely in regard of person, but also in other respects: for as the whole bodie is not the hand, nor the foote, nor the eye, but the hand one part, the foot another, and the eye another: and howsoever in the bodie one part is linked to another, yet there is a distinction betwixt the members, whereby it commeth to passe, that the hand is the hand, not the foot, and the foote, the foote, not the hand, nor the eye: so it is in societies; there is a distinction in the members thereof, and that in two respects: first, in regard of the inward gifts which God bestowed on every man, giving to severall men severall gifts according to his good pleasure. Of this distinction in regard of inward gifts, *Paul* intreates at large, *1. Cor. 12.* through the whole chapter, where he sheweth the diversity of gifts that God bestowes on his Church, and so proportionally in every society. Now looke as the inward gifts of men are severed, so are the persons distinguished in their societies accordingly. Secondly, persons are distinguished by order, whereby God hath appointed, that in every society one person should bee above or under another; not making all equall, as though the bodie should bee all head and nothing else: but even in degree and order, hee hath set a distinction, that one should be above another. And by reason of this distinction of men, partly in respect of gifts, partly, in respect of order, come personall callings. For if all men had the same gifts, and all were in the same degree and order, then should all have one and the same calling: but in asmuch as God giveth diversitie of gifts inwardly, and distinction of order outwardly, hence proceede diversitie of personal callings, and therefore I added, that personall callings arise from that distinction which God maketh betweene man and man in every societies. And thus wee see what is a personall calling. Now before I come to intreate of the parts thereof, there bee other generall rules to bee learned, which concerne all personall callings whatsoever.

    *1. Rule.* Every person of every degree, state, sexe, or condition without exception, must have some personall and particular calling to walke in. This appeareth plainly by the whole word of God. *Adam* so soone as he was created, even in his integrity had a personall calling assigned him by God: which was, to dresse and keepe the garden. And after *Adams* fall, the Lord giveth a particular commandement to him and all his posterity, which bindeth all men to walke in some calling, either in the Church or Commonwealth, saying, *Gen. 3. 19. In the sweate of thy browes shalt thou eate thy bread.* Againe, in the renewing of the law in mount Sinai, the fourth commaundement doth not onely permit labour on six daies, but also injoynes the same (as I take it) to us all. For Gods example is there propounded for us to follow, that as he rested the seventh day, so must also we: and consequently, as hee spent six dayes in the worke of creation, so should wee in our personall callings. And S. *Paul* giveth this rule, *Eph. 4.2.8. Let him that stole steale no more, but let him rather worke with his hands the thing that is good, that hee may have to give to him. that needeth. . . .*

Hence we may learne sundry points of instruction; first of all, that it is a foule disorder in any Common-wealth, that there should bee suffered rogues, beggars, vagabonds; for such kind of persons commonly are of no civill societie or corporation, nor of any particular Church: and are as rotten legges, and armes that drop from the body. Againe, to wander up and downe from yeere to yeere to this end, to seeke and procure bodily maintenance, is no calling, but the life of a beast: and consequently a condition or state of life flat against the rule; That every one must have a particular calling. And therefore the Statute made the last Parliament for the restraining of beggars and rogues, is an excellent Statute, and being in substance the very law of God, is never to be repealed.

Againe, hereby is otherthrowen the condition of Monkes and Friars: who challenge to themselves that they live in a state of perfection, because they live apart from the societies of men in fasting and prayer: but contrariwise, this Monkish kind of living is damnable; for besides the generall duties of fasting and praier, which appertaine to al Christians, every man must have a particular & personal calling, that he may bee a good and profitable member of some society and body. And the auncient Church condemned all Monkes for theeves and robbers, that besides the generall duties of prayer and fasting, did not withal imploy themselves in some other calling for their better maintenance.

Thirdly, we learne by this, that miserable and damnable is the estate of those that beeing enriched with great livings and revenewes, do spend their daies in eating and drinking, in sports and pastimes, not imploying themselves in service for Church or Common-wealth. It may be haply thought, that such gentlemen have happy lives; but it is farre otherwise: considering every one, rich or poore, man or woman, is bound to have a personall calling, in which they must performe some duties for the common good, according to the measure of the gifts that God hath bestowed upon them.

Fourthly, hereby also it is required that such as we commonly call serving men, should have, beside the office of waiting, some other particular calling, unlesse they tend on men of great place and state: for onely to waite, and give attendance, is not a sufficient calling, as common experience telleth: for waiting servants, by reason they spend the most of their time in eating and drinking, sleeping and gaming after dinner and after supper, do proove the most unprofitable members both in Church and Common-wealth. For when either their good masters die, or they be turned out of their office for some misdemeanour, they are fit for no calling, being unable to labour; and thus they give themselves either to begge or steale. The waiting man of *Cornelius* that Centurion, was also by calling a souldier: and it were to be wished now adaies, that gentlemen would make choice of such servants that might not onely tend on their persons, but also tend upon some other convenient office. It is good for every man to have two strings to his bow.

*II. Rule.* Every man must judge that particular calling, in which God hath placed him, to be the best of all callings for him: I say not simply best, but best for him. This rule is set forth unto us in the example of *Paul, I have learned* (saith he) *in whatsoever state I am, to bee content and well pleased.* The practice of this dutie is the stay & foundation of the good estate both of Church and Commonwealth: for it maketh every man to keepe his owne standing, and to imploy himselfe painefully within his calling; but when we begin to mislike the wise disposition of God, and to thinke other mens callings better for us then our owne, then followes confusion and disorder in every society. . . .

*III. Rule.* Every man must joyne the practice of his personall calling, with the practice of the generall calling of Christianity, before described. More plainely: Every particular calling must be practiced in, & with the generall calling of a Christian. It is not sufficient for a man in the congregation, and in common conversation, to bee a Christian, but in his very personall calling, he must shew himselfe to be so. As for example. A Magistrate must not onely in generall be a Christian, as every man is, but he must be a Christian Magistrate, in executing the office of a Magistrate in bearing the sword. A master of a family, must not onely be a Christian abroad in the towne, and in the congregation, in the sight of strangers, but also in the administration and regiment of his particular family, towards wife, children, and servants. It is not enough for a woman to be vertuous openly to strangers; but her vertue must privately shew it selfe in her subjection and obedience to her owne husband. A Schoole-master must not onely be a Christian in the assembly, when hee heareth the word, and receiveth the Sacraments, but he must also shew himselfe to bee a Christian in the office of teaching. And thus must every man behave himselfe in his particular calling: because the particular calling & practice of the duties thereof, severed from the foresaid generall calling, is nothing else but a practice of injustice and profanenes. And the generall calling of Christianitie, without the practice of some particular calling, is nothing els, but the forme of godlinesse, without the power thereof: And therefore both callings must be joyned, as body and soule are joyned in a living man. And that wee may the better joyne both our callings together, wee must consider the maine end of our lives, and that is, to serve God in the serving of men in the workes of our callings. God, as he made man, so can he preserve man, without the helpe of man: but his pleasure is, that men should be his instruments, for the good of one an-other. For this cause hath he ordained the excellent office of Magistrates & Ministers, and almost an infinite variety of trades of life, all tending to pre-serve the body or soule, or both. Thus God manifests his fatherly care over us, by the imployment of men in his service, according to their severall vocations, for our good: and there is not so much as the vassall or bond-man; but he must serve God by serving his master: as *Paul* teacheth; And by this one point, wee may learne two things. The first, that they profane their lives & callings that imploy them to get honours, pleasures, profits, worldly commodities, &c. for thus wee live to another end then God hath appointed, and thus we serve our selves, & consequently, neither God, nor man. Some man will say perchance; What, must we not labour in our callings, to maintaine our families? I answer; this must be done: but this is not the scope and end of our lives. The true end of our lives is, to do service to God, in serving of man: and for a recompence of this service, God sends his blessings on mens travailes, and he allowes them to take for their labours. Secondly, by this we learne, how men of meane place & calling, may comfort themselves. Let them consider, that in serving of men, by performance of poore and base duties they serve God: and therefore that their service is not base in his sight: & though their reward from men be little, yet the reward at Gods hand, shall not be wanting. For seeing they serve God in serving of men, they may justly looke for reward from both. And thus may we reape marveilous contentation in any kind of calling, though it be but to sweepe the house, or keepe sheepe, if we can thus in practice, unite our callings.

# George Herbert, "The Elixir"

Teach me, my God and King,
   In all things thee to see,
And what I do in anything,
   To do it as for thee:

Not rudely, as a beast,
   To run into an action;
But still to make thee prepossest[1]
   And give it his perfection.

A man that looks on glass,
   On it may stay his eye;
Or if he pleaseth, through it pass,
   And then the heav'n espy.

All may of thee partake:
   Nothing can be so mean,
Which with his tincture (for thy sake)
   Will not grow bright and clean.

A servant with this clause
   Makes drudgery divine:
Who sweeps a room, as for thy laws,
   Makes that and th' action fine.

This is the famous stone
   That turneth all to gold:
For that which God doth touch and own
   Cannot for less be told.

1. Always to give thee a prior claim.

# Charles Wesley, "Forth in thy name, O Lord, I go"

1. Forth in thy name, O Lord, I go,
   My daily labor to pursue,
   Thee, only thee resolved to know
   In all I think, or speak, or do.

2. The task thy wisdom has assigned
   Oh, let me cheerfully fulfill,
   In all my works thy presence find,
   And prove thy acceptable will.

3. Thee may I set at my right hand
   Whose eyes my inmost substance see,
   And labor on at thy command,
   And offer all my works to thee.

4. Give me to bear thy easy yoke,
   And every moment watch and pray,
   And still to things eternal look,
   And hasten to thy glorious day;

5. For thee delightfully employ
   Whate'er thy bounteous grace hath given,
   And run my course with even joy,
   And closely walk with thee to heaven.

# Max Weber, *The Protestant Ethic and the Spirit of Capitalism*

A purely superficial glance shows that there is here [i.e., in Calvinism] a quite different relationship between the religious life and earthly activity than in either Catholicism or Lutheranism. Even in literature motivated purely by religious factors that is evident. Take for instance the end of the *Divine Comedy,* where the poet in Paradise stands speechless in his passive contemplation of the secrets of God, and compare it with the poem which has come to be called the *Divine Comedy of Puritanism.* Milton closes the last song of *Paradise Lost* after describing the *expulsion* from paradise as follows:—

> "They, looking back, all the eastern side beheld
> Of paradise, so late their happy seat,
> Waved over by that flaming brand; the gate
> With dreadful faces thronged and fiery arms.
> Some natural tears they dropped, but wiped them soon:
> The world was all before them, there to choose
> Their place of rest, and Providence their guide."

And only a little before Michael had said to Adam:

> ... "Only add
> Deeds to thy knowledge answerable; add faith;
> Add virtue, patience, temperance; add love,
> By name to come called Charity, the soul
> Of all the rest: then wilt thou not be loth
> To leave this Paradise, but shall possess
> A Paradise within thee, happier far."

One feels at once that this powerful expression of the Puritan's serious attention to this world, his acceptance of his life in the world as a task, could not possibly have come from the pen of a mediaeval writer.

# Henry Van Dyke,
## "The Three Best Things—I: Work"

Let me but do my work from day to day,
   In field or forest, at the desk or loom,
   In roaring market-place or tranquil room;
Let me but find it in my heart to say,
When vagrant wishes beckon me astray,
   "This is my work; my blessing, not my doom;
   "Of all who live, I am the one by whom
"This work can best be done in the right way."

Then shall I see it not too great, nor small,
   To suit my spirit and to prove my powers;
   Then shall I cheerful greet the labouring hours,
And cheerful turn, when the long shadows fall
At eventide, to play and love and rest,
Because I know for me my work is best.

# Charles Taylor, *Sources of the Self*

### Chapter 13: "God Loveth Adverbs"

'Ordinary life' is a term of art I introduce to designate those aspects of human life concerned with production and reproduction, that is, labour, the making of the things needed for life, and our life as sexual beings, including marriage and the family. When Aristotle spoke of the ends of political association being "life and the good life" (*zen kai euzen*), this was the range of things he wanted to encompass in the first of these terms; basically they englobe what we need to do to continue and renew life.

For Aristotle the maintenance of these activities was to be distinguished from the pursuit of the good life. They are, of course, necessary to the good life, but they play an infrastructural role in relation to it. You can't pursue the good life without pursuing life. But an existence dedicated to this latter goal alone is not a fully human one. Slaves and animals are concerned exclusively with life. Aristotle argues in the *Politics* that a mere association of families for economic and defence purposes is not a true polis, because it is designed only for this narrow purpose. The proper life for humans builds on this infrastructure a series of activities which are concerned with the good life: men deliberate about moral excellence, they contemplate the order of things; of supreme importance for politics, they deliberate together about the common good, and decide how to shape and apply the laws.

Aristotle manages to combine in his 'good life' two of the activities which were most commonly adduced by later ethical traditions as outranking ordinary life: theoretical contemplation and the participation as a citizen in the polity. These were not unanimously favoured. Plato looked with a jaundiced eye on the second (at least in its normal form of competing for office). And the Stoics challenged both. But these authors still gave ordinary life a lesser status in the order of ends. For the Stoics, the sage should be *detached* from the fulfilment of his vital and sexual needs. These might indeed be "preferred" (*proegmena*), in the sense that when other things are equal they should be selected, but fundamentally their status was that of "*adiaphora*", things ultimately indifferent. One must be detached from them in a way that one was not from wisdom and the whole order of things which the wise love. One gladly gives them up because one is following this order.

But the influential ideas of ethical hierarchy exalted the lives of contemplation and participation. We can see a manifestation of the first in the notion that philosophers should not busy themselves with the mere manipulation of things, and hence with the crafts. This was one source of resistance to the new experimental science which Bacon advocated. Scholarly humanism was imbued with this hierarchical notion, which was also linked to a distinction between the true sciences, which admitted of demonstration, and lower forms of knowledge, which could only hope to attain to the 'probable', in the sense the word had then, e.g., the forms of knowledge practiced by alchemists, astrologers, miners, and some physicians.

We see the second idea returning in early modern times with the various doctrines of civic humanism, first in Italy and later in northern Europe. Life as a mere householder is inferior to one which also involves participation as a citizen. There is a kind of freedom citizens enjoy which others are deprived of. And in most variants, too great a striving for or possession of riches was felt to be a danger to the free life of the republic. If the means of mere life bulk too big, they endanger the good life. . . .

The transition I am talking about here is one which upsets these hierarchies, which displaces the locus of the good life from some special range of higher activities and places it within 'life' itself. The full human life is now defined in terms of labour and production, on one hand, and marriage and family life, on the other. At the same time, the previous 'higher' activities come under vigorous criticism.

Under the impact of the scientific revolution, the ideal of *theoria*, of grasping the order of the cosmos through contemplation, came to be seen as being vain and misguided, as a presumptuous attempt to escape the hard work of detailed discovery. . . .

The Baconian revolution involved a transvaluation of values, which is also the reversal of a previous hierarchy. What was previously stigmatized as lower is now exalted as the standard, and the previously higher is convicted of presumption and vanity. And this involved a revaluation of professions as well. The lowly artisan and artificer turn out to have contributed more to the advance of science than the leisured philosopher.

And indeed, an inherent bent towards social levelling is implicit in the affirmation of ordinary life. The centre of the good life lies now in something which everyone can have a part in, rather than in ranges of activity which only a leisured few can do justice to. The scope of this social reversal can be better measured if we look at the critique launched against the other main variant of the traditional hierarchical view, the honour ethic, which had its original roots in the citizen life. . . .

In the latter part of the century, the critique is taken up and becomes a commonplace of a new ideal of life, in which sober and disciplined production was given the central place, and the search for honour condemned as fractious and undisciplined self-indulgence, gratuitously endangering the really valuable things in life. A new model of civility emerges in the eighteenth century, in which the life of commerce and acquisition gains an unprecedentedly positive place. . . .

The transition I have been talking about is easy to identify negatively, in terms of the ethics it (partly) displaced. But for my purposes here, it is important to understand the positive new valuation it put on ordinary life. The displaced traditional views were connected with conceptions of moral sources. The idea that our highest activity was contemplation was contingent on a view of the world order as structured by the Good; the ethic of honour saw the love of fame and immortality as the source of great deeds and exemplary courage. Both could offer a positive account of what made their favoured version of the good life really a higher form of existence for man. What was the corresponding account for the various ethics of ordinary life?

To see this aright we have to return to a theological point of origin. The affirmation of ordinary life finds its origin in Judaeo-Christian spirituality, and the particular impetus it receives in the modern era comes first of all from the Reformation. One of the central points common to all Reformers was their rejection of mediation. The mediaeval church as they understood it, a corporate body in which some, more dedicated, members could win merit and salvation for others who were less so, was anathema to them. . . .

If the church is the locus and vehicle of the sacred, then we are brought closer to God by the very fact of belonging and participating in its sacramental life. Grace can come to us mediately through the church, and we can mediate grace to each other, as the lives of the saints enrich the common life on which we all draw. Once the sacred is rejected, then this kind of mediation is also. Each person stands alone in relation to God: his or her fate—salvation or damnation—is separately decided.

The rejection of the sacred and of mediation together led to an enhanced status for (what had formerly been described as) profane life. This came out in the repudiation of the special monastic vocations which had been an integral part of mediaeval Catholicism. . . .

Thus by the same movement through which the Protestant churches rejected a special order of priesthood in favour of the doctrine of the priesthood of all believers, they also rejected the special vocation to the monastic life and affirmed the spiritual value of lay life. By denying any special form of life as a privileged locus of the sacred, they were denying the very distinction between sacred and profane and hence affirming their interpenetration. The denial of a special status to the monk was also an affirmation of ordinary life as more than profane, as itself hallowed and in no way second class. The institution of the monastic life was seen as a slur on the spiritual standing of productive labour and family life, their stigmatization as zones of spiritual underdevelopment. The repudiation of monasticism was a reaffirmation of lay life as a central locus for the fulfilment of God's purpose. Luther marks their break in his own life by ceasing to be such a monk and by marrying a former nun.

What is important for my purpose is this positive side, the affirmation that the fulness of Christian existence was to be found within the activities of this life, in one's calling and in marriage and the family. The entire modern development of the affirmation of ordinary life was, I believe, foreshadowed and initiated, in all its facets, in the spirituality of the Reformers. . . .

The foundation for this new radical revaluation of ordinary life was, of course, one of the most fundamental insights of the Jewish-Christian-Islamic religious tradition, that God as creator himself affirms life and being, expressed in the very first chapter of Genesis in the repeated phrase: "and God saw that it was good". Life in a calling could be a fully Christian life, because it could be seen as participating in this affirmation of God's. In this sense, of course, the Reformers were only drawing the radical consequences from a very old theme in Christendom. . . .

Thus ordinary life is to be hallowed. But this doesn't come about in the manner of the Catholic tradition, by connecting it to the sacramental life of the church; rather it comes about within this life itself, which has to be lived in a way which is both earnest and detached. Marriage and a calling are not optional extras; they are the substance of life, and we should throw ourselves into them purposefully. But all the while our hearts should be elsewhere. . . .

And so we can appreciate the full seriousness of the Puritan idea of the calling. In addition to the general calling to be a believing Christian, everyone had a particular calling, the specific form of labour to which God summoned him or her. Whereas in Catholic cultures, the term 'vocation' usually arises in connection with the priesthood or monastic life, the meanest employment was a calling for the Puritans, provided it was useful to mankind and imputed to use by God. In this sense, all callings were equal, whatever their place in the social hierarchy, or in what we think of as the hierarchy of human capacities. As John Dod says:

> Whatsoever our callings be, we serve the Lord Christ in them . . . Though your worke be base, yet it is not a base thing to serve such a master in it. They are the most worthy servants, whatsoever their imploiment bee, that do with most conscionable, and dutifull hearts and minds, serve the Lord, where hee hath placed them, in those works, which hee hath allotted unto them.

Joseph Hall makes substantially the same point:

> The homeliest service that we doe in an honest calling, though it be but to plow, or digge, if done in obedience, and conscience of God's Commandement, is crowned with an ample reward; whereas the best workes for their kinde (preaching, praying, offering Evangelicall sacrifices) if without respect of God's injunction and glory, are loaded with curses. God loveth adverbs; and cares not how good, but how well.

Hall captures the essence of the transvaluation implicit in affirming the ordinary. The highest can no longer be defined by an exalted *kind* of activity; it all turns on the *spirit* in which one lives whatever one lives, even the most mundane existence. . . .

Thus labour in a calling was a spiritually serious business, something we should give ourselves to not just intermittently but earnestly and unremittingly. Puritans exhorted their hearers to shun idleness. This was partly because it bred temptation. "A heart not exercised in some honest labour works trouble out of itself". "An idle man's brain becometh quickly the shop of the devil." But this was not the only reason. Or rather, this was the negative side of a positive reason, which was that it was largely through such work that sanctification took place. . . .

We see here the basis for one strand of Weber's thesis about Protestantism as the nurturing ground of capitalism. Weber thought that the Puritan notion of the calling helped to foster a way of life focussed on disciplined and rationalized and regular work, coupled with frugal habits of consumption, and that this form of life greatly facilitated the implantation of industrial capitalism. There may be some quarrel on the latter half of this thesis, that is, concerning the degree to which this new work culture was widespread among capitalists and their workers, or whether it was or was not essential to capitalism's development. But the first half of the claim seems well founded. A spiritual outlook which stressed the necessity of continuous disciplined work, work which should be of benefit to people and hence ought to be efficacious, and which encouraged sobriety and restraint in the enjoyment of its fruits surely must be recognized as one of the formative influences of the work ethic of modern capitalist culture, at least in the Anglo-Saxon world.

# Michael Novak, *Business as a Calling*

## Four Characteristics of a Calling

What have we learned about callings from these examples? At least four points should now be clear, about callings in general and those in business in particular.

First, each calling is unique to each individual. Not everyone wants to be a psychiatrist. . . . Nor, for that matter, does everyone want to work in business. Each of us is as unique in our calling as we are in being made in the image of God. (It would take an infinite number of human beings, St. Thomas Aquinas once wrote, to mirror back the infinite facets of the Godhead. Each person reflects only a small—but beautiful—part of the whole.)

Second, a calling requires certain preconditions. It requires more than desires; it requires talent. Not everyone can be, simply by desiring it, an opera singer, or professional athlete, or leader of a large enterprise. For a calling to be right, it must fit our abilities. Another precondition is love—not just love of the final product but, as the essayist Logan Pearsall Smith once put it, "The test of a vocation is love of drudgery it involves." Long hours, frustrations, small steps forward, struggles; unless these too are welcomed with a certain joy, the claim to being called has a hollow ring.

Third, a true calling reveals its presence by the enjoyment and sense of renewed energies its practice yields us. This does not mean that sometimes we do not groan inwardly at the weight of the burdens imposed on us or that we never feel reluctance about reentering bloody combat. Facing hard tasks necessarily exacts dread. Indeed, there are times when we wish we did not have to face every burden our calling imposes on us. Still, finding ourselves where we are and with the responsibilities we bear, we know it is our duty—part of what we were meant to do—to soldier on.

Enjoying what we do is not always a feeling of enjoyment; it is sometimes the gritty resolution a man or woman shows in doing what must be done—perhaps with inner dread and yet without whimpering self-pity. These are things a grown man or woman must do. There is an odd satisfaction in bearing certain pains. The young men who died defending the pass at Thermopylae, Aristotle intimates, died happy. But he was not describing their feelings, only their knowledge that they did what brave young Spartans ought to do to protect their city, no matter the taste of ashes in their mouths.

A fourth truth about callings is also apparent: they are not usually easy to discover. Frequently, many false paths are taken before the satisfying path is at last uncovered. Experiments, painful setbacks, false hopes, discernment, prayer, and much patience are often required before the light goes on.

Business people who have found their calling will recognize all of these things, if only tacitly. Against sometimes dreary opposition, they know their calling to be morally legitimate, even noble. Listen again to the testimony heard in this chapter. The point of business is "to accomplish something collectively," "to make a contribution to society," "to do something which is of value," "to provide something that is unique," "to test a person's talents and character," "to build community." This is unambiguously moral language that reflects moral reality.

# II. THE LIMITS OF WORK

# IIA. Rhythms of Life

1. Ecclesiastes 3:1–9. Translation is the Revised Standard Version.

2. Seneca, "On the Shortness of Life," pp. 333, 335, 337 in *Moral Essays,*
vol. 2, translated by John W. Basore ((London: William Heinemann, 1951). Lu-
cius Annaeus Seneca (4 B.C.–65 A.D.) was one of the greatest of Roman Stoic
philosophers. He was also for some time tutor and then counselor to the Emperor Nero.

3. Augustine, Book XIX, chapter 19 (p. 880) in *The City of God,* translated
by Henry Bettenson (Penguin Books, 1971). Aurelius Augustinus (354–430) is
known to us as St. Augustine of Hippo (in North Africa). His *City of God,*
written to defend Christians against charges that their faith had weakened the
Roman Empire, is one of the greatest works of Christian thought.

4. Karl Barth, selections from pp. 607–617 of *Church Dogmatics,* vol. 3,
part 4 (Edinburgh: T. & T. Clark, 1961). Karl Barth (1886–1968) is regarded by
many as the greatest Christian theologian of the twentieth century. His multi-
volume *Church Dogmatics,* from which this short selection is taken, was
unfinished at his death.

5. Oliver Wendell Holmes, Radio Address, p. 541 in Sheldon M. Novick, ed.,
*The Collected Works of Justice Holmes,* vol. 1 (Chicago: University of Chicago
Press, 1995). Oliver Wendell Holmes (1841–1935) served as Justice on the U.S.
Supreme Court from 1902 until his resignation, due to ill health, in 1932. The
short selection here is from a comment made on the occasion of his ninetieth
birthday.

6. Anne Morrow Lindbergh, pp. 99–103 of *Gift from the Sea* (New York: Pantheon Books, 1955). Although Anne Morrow Lindbergh (1906–) is a widely published author, the book from which this selection is taken continues to be her most well known work.

7. Mickey Kaus, "Getting Sleepy," *The New Republic* (July 5, 1993), p. 6.

8. Sidney Callahan, pp. 88–90 of *Parents Forever: You and Your Adult Children* (New York: Crossroad, 1992). Callahan (1933–) is a psychologist who has written on a wide range of moral and religious topics.

# Ecclesiastes 3:1–9

For everything there is a season, and a time for every matter under heaven;
a time to be born, and a time to die;
a time to plant, and a time to pluck up what is planted;
a time to kill, and a time to heal;
a time to break down, and a time to build up;
a time to weep, and a time to laugh;
a time to mourn, and a time to dance;
a time to cast away stones, and a time to gather stones together;
a time to embrace, and a time to refrain from embracing;
a time to seek, and a time to lose;
a time to keep, and a time to cast away;
a time to rend, and a time to sew;
a time to keep silence, and a time to speak;
a time to love, and a time to hate;
a time for war, and a time for peace.
What gain has the worker from his toil?

# Seneca, "On the Shortness of Life"

Of all men, they alone are at leisure who take time for philosophy, they alone really live; for they are not content to be good guardians of their own life-time only. They annex every age to their own; all the years that have gone before them are an addition to their store. Unless we are most ungrateful, all those men, glorious fashioners of holy thoughts, were born for us; for us they have prepared a way of life. By other men's labours we are led to the sight of things most beautiful that have been wrested from darkness and brought into light; from no age are we shut out, we have access to all ages, and if it is our wish, by greatness of mind, to pass beyond the narrow limits of human weakness, there is a great stretch of time through which we may roam. We may argue with Socrates, we may doubt with Carneades, find peace with Epicurus, overcome human nature with the Stoics, exceed it with the Cynics. Since Nature allows us to enter into fellowship with every age, why should we not turn from this paltry and fleeting span of time and surrender ourselves with all our soul to the past, which is boundless, which is eternal, which we share with our betters?

Those who rush about in the performance of social duties, who give themselves and others no rest, when they have fully indulged their madness, when they have every day crossed everybody's threshold, and have left no open door unvisited, when they have carried around their venal greeting to houses that are very far apart—out of a city so huge and torn by such varied desires, how few will they be able to see? How many will there be who either from sleep or self-indulgence or rudeness will keep them out! How many who, when they have tortured them with long waiting, will rush by, pretending to be in a hurry! How many will avoid passing out through a hall that is crowded with clients, and will make their escape through some concealed door—as if it were not more discourteous to deceive than to exclude. How many, still half asleep and sluggish from last night's debauch, scarcely lifting their lips in the midst of a most insolent yawn, manage to bestow on yonder poor wretches, who break their own slumber in order to wait on that of another, the right name only after it has been whispered to them a thousand times!

But we may fairly say that they alone are engaged in the true duties of life who shall wish to have Zeno, Pythagoras, Democritus, and all the other high priests of liberal studies, and Aristotle and Theophrastus as their most intimate friends every day. No one of these will be "not at home," no one of these will fail to have his visitor leave more happy and more devoted to himself than when he came, no one of these will allow anyone to leave him with empty hands; all mortals can meet with them by night or by day.

No one of these will force you to die, but all will teach you how to die; no one of these will wear out your years, but each will add his own years to yours; conversations with no one of these will bring you peril, the friendship of none will endanger your life, the courting of none will tax your purse. From them you will take whatever you wish; it will be no fault of theirs if you do not draw the utmost that you can desire. What happinesss, what a fair old age awaits him who has offered himself as a client to these! He will have friends from whom he may seek counsel on matters great and small, whom he may consult every day about himself, from whom he may hear truth without insult, praise without flattery, and after whose likeness he may fashion himself.

# St. Augustine, *City of God*

As for the three kinds of life, the life of leisure, the life of action, and the combination of the two, anyone, to be sure, might spend his life in any of these ways without detriment to his faith, and might thus attain to the everlasting rewards. What does matter is the answers to those questions: What does a man possess as a result of his love of truth? And what does he pay out in response to the obligations of Christian love? For no one ought to be so leisured as to take no thought in that leisure for the interest of his neighbour, nor so active as to feel no need for the contemplation of God. The attraction of a life of leisure ought not to be the prospect of lazy inactivity, but the chance for the investigation and discovery of truth, on the understanding that each person makes some progress in this, and does not grudgingly withhold his discoveries from another.

In the life of action, on the other hand, what is to be treasured is not a place of honour or power in this life, since 'everything under the sun is vanity' but the task itself that is achieved by means of that place of honour and that power—if that achievement is right and helpful, that is, if it serves to promote the well-being of the common people, for, as we have already argued, this well-being is according to God's intention. . . . Hence, a 'bishop' who has set his heart on a position of eminence rather than an opportunity for service should realize that he is no bishop. So then, no one is debarred from devoting himself to the pursuit of truth, for that involves a praiseworthy kind of leisure. But high position, although without it a people cannot be ruled, is not in itself a respectable object of ambition, even if that position be held and exercised in a manner worthy of respect. We see then that it is love of truth that looks for sanctified leisure, while it is the compulsion of love that undertakes righteous engagement in affairs. If this latter burden is not imposed on us, we should employ our freedom from business in the quest for truth and in its contemplation, while if it is laid upon us, it is to be undertaken because of the compulsion of love. Yet even in this case the delight in truth should not be utterly abandoned, for fear that we should lose this enjoyment and that compulsion should overwhelm us.

# Karl Barth, *Church Dogmatics*

To the concept of the vocation in which the calling of God already finds man there belongs the clear and definite element of his age. . . . As the one he is, as he has developed up to this moment in the whole series of the moments of his life, he is to proceed into the future of his being and action in the moment which follows according to the direction of the command as it now meets him. And he is to do so as if he were just setting out. As if! It is seriously the case that every meeting with the command of God and every act of obedience demanded by Him, whatever similar events may have preceded this present, is also a beginning at the beginning. . . . The particular seriousness of every age does not consist, therefore, in a special attitude which one has to assume to life in youth, maturity or old age, but in the seriousness with which at every age one has to go from the Lord of life to meet the Lord of life and therefore to try to live as though for the first time or as though this were the only age. . . .

Youth is the capacity and will to devote oneself to an object without considering or intending that the manner of this devotion should be specifically youthful. . . . He who wants to be a child is not a child; he is merely childish. He who is a child does not want to be a child; he takes his play, his study, his first attempts at accomplishment, his first wrestlings with his environment, in bitter earnest, as though he were already an adult. In so doing he is genuinely childlike. This is what it means to accept the command of the particular hour in true loyalty to its specific determination, to be free in its distinctive limitation. . . .

An act is youthful in the true sense when it is evident that a man has only relatively little time behind him and obedience to the command of God is seen particularly as a step into freedom from the past. . . . That the young person is still relatively without experience means that he is not in such danger of already being the slave of habit, chained to a routine and therefore traditionalistic, sophisticated, relativistic or sceptical. He should be capable of a certain independence, of a fruitful astonishment, of a measure of faith. . . . He should not be the victim of boredom because everything is so familiar. The thought of impotence in face of a blind fate should be far from him. He is also lacking in materials to make a picture of himself, to think out his particular role and to learn it off—notions which he might be tempted to make normative for his future. . . . Will he see and grasp his opportunity? If so, his obedience will be characterised by the fact that he does actually make with particular resolution and joy the step into freedom to which he is particularly invited. . . .

"Maturity is everything." This is true enough. And the middle years of life—just because they are the middle years—present us with a particular opportunity to attain it. . . . The sowing is behind; now is the time to reap. The run has been taken; now is the time to leap. Preparation has been made; now is the time for the venture of the work itself. The young and the old must also venture and work. The middle-aged man, however, is the one upon whom the venture and work are particularly imposed in virtue of his age. . . . He has had just enough real experience to be impelled, encouraged and stimulated for the decision now before him. He can also see at a distance the end, "the night when no man can work." But he sees it at such a distance that the thought of it does not tempt him either to resignation or to the attitudes and acts of anxious panic lest the door should close. On the contrary, it stirs him to measured haste. At this stage the limitation in which he is summoned to be free consists rather oddly in a certain relative limitlessness of development which he did not yet enjoy as a young man and which he will no longer have as an old. He can still be open and yet already resolute. His watch need be neither fast nor slow. . . . Will he see and grasp his opportunity? If his thinking, decision and action are an expression and confession of this acceptance, he will act as a mature person in the true sense. . . .

Finally, our criterion teaches us to describe the being and action of the old man as unwise in so far as it may bear the character of an automatic repetition of earlier answers in easy disposal of the question of the command, thus claiming a supposed right of age to undisturbed tranquillity. . . . As if there were only the calm of a holiday evening! As if he were no longer alive but already dead!. . . . The special opportunity offered to man at this stage obviously consists in his actual proximity to the future which will no longer be the future of his own free decisions and deeds, but which belongs to him, if at all, only as the gift of the free, omnipotent grace of God which alone can be his pure future. . . . This is, of course, true even for the younger and youngest of men. . . . The drama of age, however, is that this pure future obtrudes with increasing concreteness. . . . The decisive moment is at hand. There is the obvious difference that when man was younger he could imagine that it was a matter of his own going to meet his Sovereign on his own initiative. When he grows old it can be his special opportunity to discover that the Sovereign comes to meet him. . . . Yet now his chance has come to realise in practice as well as theory—and thus to become truly wise—that even in the fire of youth and the strength of maturity he really lived only by the free and unmerited mercy of God. . . . Hence the time has come, not to become Olympian like the old Goethe, but open on all sides, a little milder as well as more resolute, and therefore more helpful. This is the special opportunity of the old man to become wise. He should take it seriously. And in this form of obedience he should set an example to those who follow him."

# Oliver Wendell Holmes, Radio Address

In this symposium my part is only to sit in silence. To express one's feelings as the end draws near is too intimate a task. But I may mention one thought that comes to me as a listener in. The riders in a race do not stop short when they reach the goal. There is a little finishing canter before coming to a stand still. There is time to hear the kind voice of friends and to say to oneself: The work is done. But just as one says that, the answer comes: The race is over, but the work never is done while the power to work remains. The canter that brings you to a stand still need not be only coming to rest. It cannot be, while you still live. For to live is to function. That is all there is in living. And so I end with a line from a Latin poet who uttered the message more than fifteen hundred years ago—"Death plucks my ear and says, 'Live—I am coming.'"

# Anne Morrow Lindbergh, *Gift from the Sea*

We wake in the same small room from the deep sleep of good children, to the soft sound of wind through the casuarina trees and the gentle sleep-breathing rhythm of waves on the shore. We run bare-legged to the beach, which lies smooth, flat, and glistening with fresh wet shells after the night's tides. The morning swim has the nature of a blessing to me, a baptism, a rebirth to the beauty and wonder of the world. We run back tingling to hot coffee on our small back porch. Two kitchen chairs and a child's table between us fill the stoop on which we sit. With legs in the sun we laugh and plan our day.

We wash the dishes lightly to no system, for there are not enough to matter. We work easily and instinctively together, not bumping into each other as we go back and forth about our tasks. We talk as we sweep, as we dry, as we put away, discussing a person or a poem or a memory. And since our communication seems more important to us than our chores, the chores are done without thinking.

And then to work behind closed doors neither of us would want to invade. What release to write so that one forgets oneself, forgets one's companion, forgets where one is or what one is going to do next—to be drenched in work as one is drenched in sleep or in the sea. Pencils and pads and curling blue sheets alive with letters heap up on the desk. And then, pricked by hunger, we rise at last in a daze, for a late lunch. Reeling a little from our intense absorption, we come back with relief to the small chores of getting lunch, as if they were life-lines to reality—as if we had indeed almost drowned in the sea of intellectual work and welcomed the firm ground of physical action under our feet.

After an hour or so of practical jobs and errands we are ready to leave them again. Out onto the beach for the afternoon where we are swept clean of duties, of the particular, of the practical. We walk up the beach in silence, but in harmony, as the sandpipers ahead of us move like a corps of ballet dancers keeping time to some interior rhythm inaudible to us. Intimacy is blown away. Emotions are carried out to sea. We are even free of thoughts, at least of their articulation; clean and bare as whitened driftwood; empty as shells, ready to be filled up again with the impersonal sea and sky and wind. A long afternoon soaking up the outer world.

And when we are heavy and relaxed as the seaweed under our feet, we return at dusk to the warmth and intimacy of our cottage. We sip sherry at leisure in front of a fire. We start supper and we talk. Evening is the time for conversation. Morning is for mental work, I feel, the habit of school-days persisting in me. Afternoon is for physical tasks, the out-of-door jobs. But evening is for sharing, for communication. Is it the uninterrupted dark expanse of the night after the bright segmented day, that frees us to each other? Or does the infinite space and infinite darkness dwarf and chill us, turning us to seek small human sparks?

Communication—but not for too long. Because good communication is stimulating as black coffee, and just as hard to sleep after. Before we sleep we go out again into the night. We walk up the beach under the stars. And when we are tired of walking, we lie flat on the sand under a bowl of stars. We feel stretched, expanded to take in their compass. They pour into us until we are filled with stars, up to the brim.

This is what one thirsts for, I realize, after the smallness of the day, of work, of details, of intimacy—even of communication, one thirsts for the magnitude and universality of a night full of stars, pouring into one like a fresh tide.

And then at last, from the immensity of interstellar space, we swing down to a particular beach. We walk back to the lights of the cottage glowing from the dark mist of trees. Small, safe, warm and welcoming, we recognize our pin-point human match-light against the mammoth chaos of the dark. Back again to our good child's sleep.

What a wonderful day, I think, turning it around in my hand to its starting point again. What has made it so perfect? Is there not some clue here in the pattern of this day? To begin with, it is a pattern of freedom. Its setting has not been cramped in space or time. An island, curiously enough, gives us a limitless feeling of both. Nor has the day been limited in kinds of activity. It has a natural balance of physical, intellectual and social life. It has an easy un-forced rhythm.

# Mickey Kaus, "Getting Sleepy"

I'm really too tired to write this column. To be honest, I'd rather be puttering around my house. I'm 41, yet my boss seems to expect me to work like a 25-year-old. This isn't how I'd imagined my life turning out. I mean, I've been working fairly steadily for about seventeen years. I just don't want to work so hard anymore. I need a vacation. Actually, I need more than a vacation.

There's a Trend here. I'm not such an unusual person. Recently, I received my college class's "Twentieth Anniversary Report" and began flipping through my classmates' self-descriptions. There they were, the unmistakable signs of revolutionary fatigue:

> "For the first time in my life, I want to slow things down. . . . "
> "At present I am on semi-sabbatical. . . . I quit private practice in October of 1988 and have been scaling down professional activities ever since."
> "I am in the middle of an extended life change, which began in 1989. Joy and I spent three months in 1990 on sabbatical. . . . "
> "After ten years in the computer software business I decided to get out of the fast lane. . . . Now, I'm theoretically working on a novel, getting in shape and leading a stress-free existence."
> "I resigned my partnership. . . . "

These are alumni who bothered to send reports—a self-selected, typically sunny group given to boasting about their kids' soccer skills. The real burnout cases were presumably too exhausted to write in at all.

Nor will things be better in five years, at least if the Twenty-*fifth* Reunion Class Book of Yale University is any indication. If anything, the older Yalies are more flamboyantly enervated. For example:

> "As the commitment to achieve fades . . . [the] forward momentum fueled by the desire to advance one's position has come slowly to a halt. . . . I am beginning to discover the beauty of and the satisfaction in standing still."

Of course, neither the class of '68 nor the class of '73 are the first middle-aged Americans to get tired. But we're baby boomers, and anything baby boomers do, no matter how predictable, seems to get dramatized in a way that colors the entire national culture. When boomers first began to take well-paying jobs there were anguished discussions about selling out. When they started having kids they made a huge to-do about the joys of parenting. Now that they're starting to poop out we can expect a fuss about that.

Since trends are susceptible to abuse, especially by magazine writers, it's important to be precise about this one. The phenomenon I'm talking about—let's call it Baby-Boomer Burnout (BBB)—is not the traditional "midlife crisis." A midlife crisis (there are plenty of them, too, in the college reunion books) implies some sort of anguished reassessment of one's life course. But even people quite happy with their life course often lose the energy needed to pursue it at anywhere near their previous pace. That's BBB.

Nor does BBB depend on the general tendency of Americans to work excessive hours, a tendency described in Juliet B. Schor's *The Overworked American* (though BBB does help explain why Schor's fairly sober volume became a best seller). Working hours may well have risen over the past two decades. And when wives as well as husbands work, the result is a time squeeze for young parents. Complaints about lack of time to "balance" work and family are repeated to the point of tedium in the reunion reports. In fact, as Gary Burtless of the Brookings Institution notes, Americans are retiring earlier—so if overall hours of labor have risen, the increase must be heavily concentrated in the 25- to 45-year-old age bracket.

All this undoubtedly aggravates the tendency of boomers to wilt. But it's not a necessary condition for BBB. Again, burning out is part of the natural human life cycle. What's different is that those doing the burning-out are now the most populous group in America—and that the economy doesn't seem prepared to handle them. Just when millions of boomers are yearning to find secure niches where they can slow down and coast for a while, those niches are disappearing. The nation's economy and its demography are heading in different directions.

What is supposed to happen, after all, when middle-aged fatigue sets in? In previous eras, the answer—especially for many white-collar workers—was that they were accommodated by large, paternalistic employees. If you went to work for IBM, or even GM, there was an implicit deal: You might work like mad in your 20s and 30s. The payoff was that in your 40s and 50s you could throttle back—in a full-time, full-pay position. You might be supervising the hard-working 20- and 30-year-olds. Or, even if you dropped out of the management race, you could be valued for your expertise (and go home at 5:00). As Harvard economists James Medoff and Richard Freeman pointed out in *What Do Unions Do?*, one of the things unions do, when they get the chance, is to enforce this deal. The deal even has an economic payoff, since older workers are more likely to share their knowledge with younger workers if they know the younger workers aren't then going to take their jobs.

The problem is that large, paternalistic organizations are becoming a smaller part of the economy. So are unions. As corporations get "lean," they can no longer offer anything like tenure to aging white-collar workers. Quite the contrary. Those who don't produce get pruned. Economist Paul Osterman notes that in 1979 about 57 percent of 45- to 60-year-old men had worked for their employers for more than ten years. Just nine years later, that figure had fallen to 51 percent. Even IBM is laying off older workers who probably thought they had lifetime jobs. In the new economy, it seems, everybody is expected to work like a 30-year-old. Those who can't keep up—well, to judge from the alumni reports, they wind up trying to start consulting firms out of their basements.

This isn't a "crisis." The market will adjust to whatever mix of workers' skills and desires is out there. But that will involve changes. Younger workers may start demanding higher pay to go along with their long hours (since employers can't promise to take care of them later on). Middle-aged workers may wind up trading away income for job tenure. Nothing terribly wrong with this—except that the baby boomers, as is often the case, get screwed at both ends. They made relatively low wages when they were young, and now they may wind up making relatively low wages when they are old.

The more profound effects will be cultural. Not only are there a lot of baby boomers, but BBB will be concentrated in the precise class of boomers (white-collar professionals) who both generate and consume cultural products. Before boomer writers and moviemakers collapse completely, expect to see the emergence of burnout lit and cinema fatigue. I would also invest heavily in high-quality gardening-equipment stocks.

There are other vitally significant ramifications, of course. But I'm not up to figuring them all out. Take it away, *Newsweek*. I'm going to lie down for a bit.

# Sidney Callahan, *Parents Forever*

One of the greatest happinesses in a parent's life can be to work with an adult child in a cooperative enterprise. In the past many children worked with a parent in the family's farm or business, but today the satisfactions of working together are more infrequent and thereby more gratifying. How few firms and businesses can add the "& Sons" to the stationery! Nor do we see "& Daughter" on the office door. Mothers and daughters have had more chance to work together in the home, at least during the cooking involved in family celebrations or when new babies arrive. What may be new is that today mothers and daughters may share experiences as they both work outside the home in jobs and in professions.

Professional mother-daughter collaboration is more unique. One mother who is a professor of philosophy expressed her joy in going to a professional conference and giving a paper with her daughter, a lawyer working in the same field. This experience of being a professional colleague with her daughter was an unexpected pleasure of mid-life. Another professional mother who is a theater director spoke of her delight in working with her daughter, a fine actress. Women who can now more easily enter new fields of work can enjoy seeing their daughters accompany them in their own achievements.

Of course the sharing of professional work can also induce new arenas of conflict. The mother who is a theater director faced a conflict, for instance, when auditioning her daughter for a part in a play she was directing. The mother regretfully had to reject her actress daughter whom she deemed inappropriate for the part. Once this mother had made her professional commitment to direct, the commitment had to supersede her maternal interests in furthering her child's career—but it was a difficult moment. Women, unlike men, are not so inured to keeping their roles as professionals separate from their private lives. The role of father has traditionally been imbued with the aura of impartial judge, but the role of mother traditionally promises unconditional support whenever and whatever. New roles take some getting used to.

The challenge to the parent-child relationship presented by the world of work is not easy. Parents struggle to give nurturing love and unstinting care to their sons and daughters, while at the same time raising them to be hardy enough to meet the outside world's impersonal and critical standards. Partiality must not allow a parent to forget the fact that impartial scrutiny is coming in the larger world of work and achievement.

When all goes well a child becomes a good worker and finds good work that suits his or her capacities and talents. Watching a child have a happy productive work life is one of the great delights of parenthood. If a parent is always to some extent empathetically reliving the stages in the life cycle as their children age, a child finding good work renews a parent's own sense of achievement. Their success is our success. One part of the American dream has come true.

# IIB. Play

1. William Shakespeare, *Henry IV,* Part I, lines 202–220. Shakespeare lived from 1564 to 1616. The context of these lines is as follows: Prince Hal is spending time in the company of Falstaff, who, together with Poins and several other rogues, plans to rob a group of travelers. But Poins persuades Prince Hal that the two of them should let the others rob the travelers, and then they, in turn, will rob the robbers. The fun will come later when they listen to Falstaff tell stories of how they were set upon by a large band of thieves, and how much valor he displayed in an unequal struggle. Hal agrees to do this, and then, in a soliloquy, explains why: He is doing this in order to seem to be much more frivolous than he is. When the time comes for him to act, he will cast the mask aside and show his true seriousness, which will be all the more impressive because it is unexpected.

2. John Ruskin, pp. 35–36, 41–42 of *The Crown of Wild Olive* (New York: F. M. Lupton, n.d.). Ruskin (1819–1900), considered an influential Victorian thinker, first made his reputation as an art critic. Later in life he turned to topics more political and economic in character.

3. Mark Twain, chapter 2 of *The Adventures of Tom Sawyer* (New York: P. F. Collier & Son, 1920). Mark Twain was the pseudonym of Samuel Clemens (1835–1910), one of America's greatest humorists.

4. Adriano Tilgher, chapter 23 of *Homo Faber: Work through the Ages* (Chicago: Henry Regnery Co., 1958). Tilgher (1887–1941) was an Italian social and literary critic. *Homo Faber* was first published in 1929.

5. George F. Will, pp. 4–6, 329–30 of *Men at Work: The Craft of Baseball* (New York: Macmillan, 1990). George Will (1941–) is a nationally syndicated political columnist who, on occasion, has also written about baseball.

6. Roger Angell, "Goodbye Tom," p. 36 of *Late Innings* (New York: Ballantine Books, 1982). Roger Angell has written for years about baseball in the pages of the *New Yorker*. This short selection evokes the style of one of the great pitchers, who was also a hard-working student of the craft of pitching.

7. Roger Angell, "One Hard Way to Make a Living," pp. 350–51 of *Late Innings* (New York: Ballantine Books, 1982).

8. Witold Rybczynski, "Waiting for the Weekend," pp. 50–51 in *The Atlantic Monthly* (August 1991). Rybczynski (1943–) is a professor of architecture who, as is clear from this selection, writes on a wide range of topics.

# William Shakespeare, *Henry IV,* Part I

Yet herein will I imitate the sun,
Who doth permit the base contagious clouds
To smother up his beauty from the world,
That, when he please again to be himself,
Being wanted, he may be more wond'red at
By breaking through the foul and ugly mists
Of vapors that did seem to strangle him.
If all the year were playing holidays,
To sport would be as tedious as to work;
But when they seldom come, they wished-for come,
And nothing pleaseth but rare accidents.
So, when this loose behavior I throw off
And pay the debt I never promised,
By how much better than my word I am,
By so much shall I falsify men's hopes;
And, like bright metal on a sullen ground,
My reformation, glitt'ring o'er my fault,
Shall show more goodly and attract more eyes
Than that which hath no foil to set it off.

# John Ruskin, *The Crown of Wild Olive*

First, then, of the distinction between the classes who work and the classes who play. Of course we must agree upon a definition of these terms,—work and play,—before going farther. Now, roughly, not with vain subtlety of definition, but for plain use of the words, "play" is an exertion of body or mind, made to please ourselves, and with no determined end; and work is a thing done because it ought to be done, and with a determined end. You play, as you call it, at cricket, for instance. That is as hard work as anything else; but it amuses you, and it has no result but the amusement. If it were done as an ordered form of exercise, for health's sake, it would become work directly. So, in like manner, whatever we do to please ourselves, and only for the sake of the pleasure, not for an ultimate object, is "play," the "pleasing thing," not the useful thing. Play may be useful in a secondary sense (nothing is indeed more useful or necessary); but the use of it depends on its being spontaneous. . . .

This, then, is the first distinction between the "upper and lower" classes. And this is one which is by no means necessary; which indeed must, in process of good time, be by all honest men's consent abolished. Men will be taught that an existence of play, sustained by the blood of other creatures, is a good existence for gnats and sucking fish; but not for men: that neither days, nor lives, can be made holy by doing nothing in them: that the best prayer at the beginning of a day is that we may not lose its moments; and the best grace before meat, the consciousnesss that we have justly earned our dinner. And when we have this much of plain Christianity preached to us again; and enough respect what we regard as inspiration, as not to think that "Son, go work to-day in my vineyard," means "Fool, go play to-day in my vineyard," we shall all be workers, in one way or another; and this much at least of the distinction between "upper" and "lower" forgotten.

# Mark Twain, *The Adventures of Tom Sawyer*

### Chapter Two

Saturday morning was come, and all the summer world was bright and fresh, and brimming with life. There was a song in every heart; and if the heart was young the music issued at the lips. There was cheer in every face and a spring in every step. The locust trees were in bloom and the fragrance of the blossoms filled the air. Cardiff Hill, beyond the village and above it, was green with vegetation, and it lay just far enough away to seem a Delectable Land, dreamy, reposeful, and inviting.

Tom appeared on the sidewalk with a bucket of whitewash and a long-handled brush. He surveyed the fence, and all gladness left him and a deep melancholy settled down upon his spirit. Thirty yards of board fence nine feet high. Life to him seemed hollow, and existence but a burden. Sighing he dipped his brush and passed it along the topmost plank; repeated the operation; did it again; compared the insignificant whitewashed streak with the far-reaching continent of unwhitewashed fence, and sat down on a tree-box discouraged. Jim came skipping out at the gate with a tin pail, and singing "Buffalo Gals." Bringing water from the town pump had always been hateful work in Tom's eyes, before, but now it did not strike him so. He remembered that there was company at the pump. White, mulatto, and negro boys and girls were always there waiting their turns, resting, trading playthings, quarreling, fighting, sky-larking. And he remembered that although the pump was only a hundred and fifty yards off, Jim never got back with a bucket of water under an hour—and even then somebody generally had to go after him. Tom said:

"Say, Jim, I'll fetch the water if you whitewash some."

Jim shook his head and said:

"Can't, Mars Tom. Ole missis, she tole me I got to go an' git dis water an' not stop foolin' roun' wid anybody. She say she spec' Mars Tom gwine to ax me to whitewash, an' so she tole me go 'long an' 'tend to my own business—she 'lowed *she'd* 'tend to de whitewashing'."

"Oh, never you mind what she said, Jim. That's the way she always talks. Gimme the bucket.—I won't be gone only a minute. *She* won't ever know."

"Oh, I dasn't, Mars Tom. Ole missis she'd take an' tar de head off'n me. 'Deed she would."

"*She!* She never licks anybody—whacks 'em over the head with her thimble—and who cares for that, I'd like to know. She talks awful, but talk don't hurt—anyways it don't if she don't cry. Jim, I'll give you a marvel. I'll give you a white alley!"

Jim began to waver.

"White alley, Jim! And it's a bully taw."

"My! Dat's a mighty gay marvel, I tell you! But Mars Tom I's powerful 'fraid ole missis—"

"And besides, if you will I'll show you my sore toe."

Jim was only human—this attraction was too much for him. He put down his pail, took the white alley, and bent over the toe with absorbing interest while the bandage was being unwound. In another moment he was flying down the street with his pail and a tingling rear, Tom was whitewashing with vigor, and Aunt Polly was retiring from the field with a slipper in her hand and triumph in her eye.

But Tom's energy did not last. He began to think of the fun he had planned for this day, and his sorrows multiplied. Soon the free boys would come tripping along on all sorts of delicious expeditions, and they would make a world of fun of him for having to work—the very thought of it burnt him like fire. He got out his worldly wealth and examined it—bits of toys, marbles, and trash; enough to buy an exchange of *work*, maybe, but not half enough to buy so much as half an hour of pure freedom. So he returned his straitened means to his pocket, and gave up the idea of trying to buy the boys. At this dark and hopeless moment an inspiration burst upon him! Nothing less than a great, magnificent inspiration.

He took up his brush and went tranquilly to work. Ben Rogers hove in sight presently—the very boy, of all boys, whose ridicule he had been dreading. Ben's gait was the hop-skip-and-jump—proof enough that his heart was light and his anticipations high. He was eating an apple, and giving a long, melodious whoop, at intervals, followed by a deep-toned ding-dong-dong, ding-dong-dong, for he was personating a steamboat. As he drew near, he slackened speed, took the middle of the street, leaned far over to starboard and rounded to ponderously and with laborious pomp and circumstance—for he was personating the *Big Missouri*, and considered himself to be drawing nine feet of water. He was boat and captain and engine-bells combined, so he had to imagine himself standing on his own hurricane-deck giving the orders and executing them:

"Stop her, sir! Ting-a-ling-ling!" The headway ran almost out and he drew up slowly toward the sidewalk.

"Ship up to back! Ting-a-ling-ling!" His arms straightened and stiffened down his sides.

"Set her back on the stabboard! Ting-a-ling-ling! Chow! ch-chow-wow! Chow!" His right hand, meantime, describing stately circles—for it was representing a forty-foot wheel.

"Let her go back on the labboard! Ting-a-ling-ling! Chow-ch-chow-chow!" The left hand began to describe circles.

"Stop the stabboard! Ting-a-ling-ling! Stop the labboard! Come ahead on the stabboard! Stop her! Let your outside turn over slow! Ting-a-ling-ling! Chow-ow-ow! Get out that head-line! *Lively* now! Come—out with your spring-line—what 're you about there! Take a turn round that stump with the bight of it! Stand by that stage, now—let her go! Done with the engines, sir! Ting-a-ling-ling! *Sh't! s'h't! sh't!*" (trying the gaugecocks).

Tom went on whitewashing—paid no attention to the steamboat. Ben stared-a moment and then said:

"Hi-*yi!* You're up a stump, ain't you!"

No answer. Tom surveyed his last touch with the eye of an artist, then he gave his brush another gentle sweep and surveyed the result, as before. Ben ranged up alongside of him. Tom's mouth watered for the apple, but he stuck to his work.

"Hello, old chap, you got to work, hey?"

Tom wheeled suddenly and said:

"Why, it's you, Ben! I warn't noticing."

"Say—I'm going in a-swimming, I am. Don't you wish you could? But of course you'd druther *work*—wouldn't you? Course you would!"

Tom contemplated the boy a bit, and said:

"What do you call work?"

"Why, ain't *that* work?"

Tom resumed his whitewashing, and answered carelessly:

"Well, maybe it is, and maybe it ain't. All I know, is, it suits Tom Sawyer."

Oh come, now, you don't mean to let on that you *like* it?"

The brush continued to move.

"Like it? Well, I don't see why I oughtn't like it. Does a boy get a chance to whitewash a fence every day?"

That put the thing in a new light. Ben stopped nibbling his apple. Tom swept his brush daintily back and forth—stepped back to note the effect—added a touch here and there—criticized the effect again—Ben watching every move and getting more and more interested, more and more absorbed. Presently he said:

"Say, Tom, let *me* whitewash a little."

Tom considered, was about to consent; but he altered his mind:

"No—no—I reckon it wouldn't hardly do, Ben. You see, Aunt Polly's awful particular about this fence—right here on the street, you know—but if it was the back fence I wouldn't mind and *she* wouldn't. Yes, she's awful particular about this fence; it's got to be done very careful; I reckon there ain't one boy in a thousand, maybe two thousand, that can do it the way it's got to be done."

"No—is that so? Oh come, now—lemme just try. Only just a little—I'd let *you,* if you was me, Tom."

"Ben, I'd like to, honest injun; but Aunt Polly—well, Jim wanted to do it, but she wouldn't let him; Sid wanted to do it, and she wouldn't let Sid. Now don't you see how I'm fixed? If you was to tackle this fence and anything was to happen to it—"

"Oh, shucks, I'll be just as careful. Now lemme. Say—I'll give you the core of my apple."

"Well, here—No, Ben, now don't. I'm afeard—"

"I'll give you all of it!"

Tom gave up the brush with reluctance in his face, but alacrity in his heart. And while the late steamer *Big Missouri* worked and sweated in the sun the retired artist sat on a barrel in the shade close by, dangled his legs, munched his apple, and planned the slaughter of more innocents. There was no lack of material; boys happened along every little while; they came to jeer, but remained to whitewash. By the time Ben was fagged out, Tom had traded the next chance to Billy Fisher for a kite, in good repair; and when *he* played out, Johnny Miller bought in for a dead rat and a string to swing it with—and so on, and so on, hour after hour. And when the middle of the afternoon came, from being a poor poverty-stricken boy in the morning, Tom was literally rolling in wealth. He had, beside the things before mentioned, twelve marbles, part of a jews '-harp, a piece of blue bottle-glass to look through, a spool cannon, a key that wouldn't unlock anything, a fragment of chalk, a glass stopper of a decanter, a tin soldier, a couple of tadpoles, six firecrackers, a kitten with only one eye, a brass door-knob, a dog-collar—but no dog—the handle of a knife, four pieces of orange-peel, and a dilapidated old window-sash.

He had had a nice, good, idle time all the while—plenty of company—and the fence had three coats of whitewash on it! If he hadn't run out of whitewash, he would have bankrupted every boy in the village.

Tom said to himself that it was not such a hollow world, after all. He had discovered a great law of human action, without knowing it—namely, that in order to make a man or a boy covet a thing, it is only necessary to make the thing difficult to attain. If he had been a great and wise philosopher, like the writer of this book, he would now have comprehended that Work consists of whatever a body is *obliged* to do, and that Play consists of whatever a body is not obliged to do. And this would help him to understand why constructing artificial flowers or performing on a treadmill is work, while rolling tenpins or climbing Mont Blanc is only amusement. There are wealthy gentlemen in England who drive four-horse passenger-coaches twenty or thirty miles on a daily line, in the summer, because the privilege costs them considerable money; but if they were offered wages for the service, that would turn it into work and then they would resign.

The boy mused awhile over the substantial change which had taken place in his worldly circumstances and then wended toward headquarters to report.

# Adriano Tilgher, *Homo Faber*

What is play? Professor Giuseppe Rensi has put his keen and pregnant mind to work on that question and has defined play as any activity exercised "for itself because of the pleasure or interest which it inspires in us intrinsically considered in itself, as an end in itself, with no ulterior views." This is as much as to say that we are playing whenever we act, not to bring about a result, but for the pure and simple joy of acting, or, in Rensi's academically accurate definition, "for the pleasure (which, inclosed and circumscribed in itself, independent of any need of ulterior effects) given by us by the action of play." He defines work as each and every action performed not for the pleasure of acting, but with the interest so intent on a result outside of the action that if we did not expect the result to follow, we would not act. Having thus defined his position, Professor Rensi goes on with great logical ingenuity to develop from it the consequence that every sort of work necessarily has in it a trace of the disagreeable, something against which our spontaneous impulse rebels. He feels that only willpower can drive us to work. Since work is in itself not a pleasure, since man conquers his native dislike of work only because necessity makes him work to possess the things he desires—economic rewards, profits, advancement, fame, honor, and the like—it follows that when he works, he is always in combat with his deep natural inclinations, is always more or less in a state of subjection and slavery. Rensi considers that man is truly himself only when he acts from the intrinsic pleasure of the action—in a word, when he plays. Not work but play ennobles man.

With a characteristic display of logic, Rensi goes on to draw from these definitions of work and play other conclusions equally logical, equally paradoxical. I pass over them. Let us rather examine the soundness of his definitions themselves.

If it were true that the word "play" means any activity performed solely for the pleasure of the activity itself, then it would follow that not only the boy kicking a football, a man playing poker, but the artist expressing the fancies of his imagination (so long as he is not thinking of pay or glory), the philosopher wearing himself out in meditation for the satisfaction of solving a difficult problem, the scientist bent over his microscope, the mathematician puzzling over a difficult equation—all are not working but playing. Rensi would not deny this. In fact he clearly affirms that the artist, the philosopher, mathematician, man of science, in so far as they act from the pleasure and passion which they draw from the action itself, are not working but playing. I admit that this

all follows logically enough from his premises, but I find it so absurdly paradoxical that I suspect there must be something absurd about the premises.

The trouble lies in the premise from which Rensi starts. There is something
else in play than action for the mere pleasure of action. Play—if it is real play—
always has something of triviality in it. Play is not serious, there can be no
passion about it. If you can imagine a philosopher putting together a system
for the fun of the thing as light-heartedly as he might pass his time over a
cross-word puzzle, you might fairly say that he was playing, just as you could
fairly say that the athlete who loses his temper and slugs his opponent in a
football match has passed beyond the spirit of play. Seriousness to the point
of passion marks the difference, and it is exactly because art, science, love,
and politics—all the intellectual, emotional, and spiritual activities, in short—
arouse men's deep interest and passionate love that it is preposterous to think
of them as forms of play. If you cut the passion out of them you change their
very nature, reduce them to the mere superficial shadows and masks of themselves. Love, taken lightly, for instance, is mere flirtation. Happy are those
whose passionate interest centers naturally in a worthy object; when it finds
expression only in a field essentially trivial, the result is monstrous, passion and
play mingled—mad play, frenzied play, play that is no longer play at all but
something frighteningly grave and serious.

The other side of Rensi's picture is equally distorted. It is not true that
work is merely something that has to be gone through with in order to get
something else, something different. It is only juggling with words to say that
the artist, the scientist, the philosopher, the mathematician, who pass their
nights in hand-to-hand struggles with a rebellious angel, toiling in the effort
to give form to their imagination, to solve problems which exhaust their minds,
are playing and not working. Who could be found to agree with that definition? It is far too narrow. Work is something more than the pursuit of an object
resulting from (but essentially different from) the effort necessary to gain it.
This is true only of work in its lowest terms. Work at its fullest is every process,
every activity, by which man masters rebellious matter and subjects it to his
will, to his personality. The essential spirit of man is activity which demands
the opportunity to expend itself, to strengthen itself, in struggle. That is why
inaction is of all things the most irksome, the hardest to endure. That is why
work which enables man to triumph little by little over the opposition both of
the external world and of his inner life is a source of joy, deep in proportion
to the passionate interest felt in his task by the worker. No play, no sport, can
bring such joy as loving labor. Obviously; for play remains upon the surface of
the soul while work rouses its depths, gives it a measure of what it is and what
it is worth. Any one who has ever put his heart into work knows that there is

no joy on earth like feeling the obstacles one by one fall under the blows of one's labor, and at the day's end, of looking back over the field of victory, retracing in one's mind the road conquered step by weary step. The "joy of work" is no rhetorical phrase. It is a psychological reality experienced by every worker. There can be no doubt that Professor Rensi felt it keenly while writing his fine essay denying the joy of work.

Precisely because it has not and cannot have profound roots of passion and interest, play cannot satisfy the soul as fully as work. All the available first-hand testimony as to the inner life of the modern sport-crazy youth shows it to be arid, unsatisfied, sad. Consider also the matter of games of chance. Because play is an activity pursued for itself but without deep seriousness, the most typical kind of play, play par excellence, is that which frees the player from the need of any sort of activity and puts its outcome wholly in the hands of brute Fate. If Rensi were right in saying that man is truly man only when he plays, it would follow that he is most of all man when he plays games of chance. But Rensi is wrong. For man is never occupied to the bottom of his soul by play—or if he is, then for him it has ceased to be play.

A life all work is far too heavy and serious, lacks light and cheerfulness. A life all play is trivial and empty, lacks weight and consistency. Wisdom lies in alternating the two. Human activity enjoys amusing itself in the void with play; but afterward, to feel sure of its strength, it needs to grapple with obstinate, dense-fibered raw material, shaping it to human ends. Yet it cannot always struggle tensely with rebellious matter; sometimes it needs to scatter its energy freely, enjoying the sensation of fresh, full, free life, rejoicing in itself and nothing but itself. But if play is to bring lightness and freshness to the soul, it must remain what it really is—a pause in the difficult serious affair which is human life. When any one pretends to fill his life with play, either his life is empty and dissatisfied, or play has become a madness, a passion—has stopped being play at all.

# George F. Will, *Men at Work*

Winning is not everything. Baseball—its beauty, its craftsmanship, its exact-ingness—is an activity to be loved, as much as ballet or fishing or politics, and loving it is a form of participation. But this book is not about romance. Indeed, it is an antiromantic look at a game that brings out the romantic in the best of its fans.

A. Bartlett Giamatti was to the Commissioner's office what Sandy Koufax was to the pitcher's mound: Giamatti's career had the highest ratio of excellence to longevity. If his heart had been as healthy as his soul—if his heart had been as strong as it was warm—Giamatti would one day have been ranked among commissioners the way Walter Johnson is ranked (by correct thinkers) among pitchers: as the best, period. Baseball's seventh commissioner, who was the first to have taught Renaissance literature at Yale, was fond of noting the etymological fact that the root of the word "paradise" is an ancient Persian word meaning "enclosed park of green." Ballparks exist, he said, because there is in humanity "a vestigial memory of an enclosed green space as a place of freedom or play." Perhaps. Certainly ballparks are pleasant places for the multitudes. But for the men who work there, ballparks are for hard, sometimes dangerous, invariably exacting business. Physically strong and fiercely competitive men make their living in those arenas. Most of these men have achieved, at least intermittently, the happy condition of the fusion of work and play. They get physical pleasure and emotional release and fulfillment from their vocation. However, Roy Campanella's celebrated aphorism—that there has to be a lot of little boy in a man who plays baseball—needs a corollary. There has to be a lot of hardness in a man who plays—who works at—this boys' game.

Success in life has been described as the maintained ecstasy of burning with a hard, gemlike flame. The image recurs. In his famous essay on Ted Williams's final game, "Hub Fans Bid Kid Adieu," John Updike wrote of Williams radiating "the hard blue glow of high purpose." Updike said, "For me, Williams is the classic ballplayer of the game on a hot August weekday before a small crowd, when the only thing at stake is the tissue-thin difference between a thing done well and a thing done ill." Baseball, played on a field thinly populated with men rhythmically shifting from languor to tension, is, to Updike's eyes, an essentially lonely game. The cool mathematics of individual performances are the pigments coloring the long season of averaging out. Baseball heroism comes not from flashes of brilliance but rather, Updike says, from "the players who always *care*," about themselves and their craft.

The connection between character and achievement is one of the fundamental fascinations of sport. Some say that sport builds character. Others say that sport reveals character. But baseball at its best puts good character on display in a context of cheerfulness. Willie Stargell, the heart of the order during the Pirates' salad days in the 1970s, insisted that baseball is, or at any rate ought to be, fun. Walking wearily through the Montreal airport after a night game, he said, "I ain't complaining. I asked to be a ball player." Indeed, it is likely that a higher percentage of ball players than of plumbers or lawyers or dentists or almost any other group are doing what they passionately enjoy doing. On another occasion Stargell said, "The umpire says 'Play ball,' not 'Work ball.'" (Actually, the rule book requires the umpire to call out only the word "play.") But professional baseball is work.

---

America has been called the only nation founded on a good idea. That idea has been given many and elaborate explanations, but the most concise and familiar formulation is the pursuit of happiness. For a fortunate few people, happiness is the pursuit of excellence in a vocation. The vocation can be a profession or a craft, elite or common, poetry or carpentry. What matters most is an idea of excellence against which to measure achievement. The men whose careers are considered here exemplify the pursuit of happiness through excellence in a vocation. Fortunate people have a talent for happiness. Possession of any talent can help a person toward happiness. As Aristotle said, happiness is not a condition that is produced or stands on its own; rather, it is a frame of mind that accompanies an activity. But another frame of mind comes first. It is a steely determination to do well.

When Ted Williams, the last .400 hitter, arrived in Boston for his first season he said, with the openness of a Westerner and the innocence of a 20-year-old, "All I want out of life is that when I walk down the street folks will say, 'There goes the greatest hitter who ever lived.'" Today, if you see Williams walking down the street and you say, "There goes the greatest hitter who ever lived," you may get an argument but you will not get derision. He won 6 batting titles and lost another by one hit. (In 1949 George Kell batted .3429, Williams .3427.) He batted .406 in 1941 and .388 in 1957, when his 38-year-old legs surely cost him at least the 3 hits that would have given him his second .400 season.

The hard blue glow from people like Williams lights the path of progress in any field. I said at the outset that this was to be an antiromantic look at baseball. I meant that baseball is work. Baseball is hard and demands much drudgery. But it is neither romantic nor sentimental to say that those who pay the price of excellence in any demanding discipline are heroes. Cool realism recognizes that they are necessary. As a character says in Bernard Malamud's baseball novel *The Natural,* when we are without heroes we "don't know how far we can go."

# Roger Angell, "Goodbye Tom"

One of the images I have before me now is that of Tom Seaver pitching; the motionless assessing pause on the hill while the sign is delivered, the easy, rocking shift of weight onto the back leg, the upraised arms, and then the left shoulder coming forward as the whole body drives forward and drops suddenly downward—down so low that the right knee scrapes the sloping dirt of the mound—in an immense thrusting stride, and the right arm coming over blurrily and still flailing, even as the ball, the famous fastball, flashes across the plate, chest-high on the batter and already past his low, late swing.

# Roger Angell, "One Hard Way to Make a Living"

"Well, hitting is a physical art, and that's never easy to explain," he [Ted Simmons] said. "And it's hard. It's one hard way to make a living if you're not good at it. Hitting is mostly a matter of feel, and it's abstract as hell. If I'm in a slump, it's because I've lost the feel of making solid contact with the ball on the thick part of the bat, and I get a pitcher and go out and take extra batting practice until that feeling comes back—maybe ten minutes, maybe half an hour: for as long as it takes." . . .

I asked Simmons about batters' picking up the spin on the pitch—the part of hitting that most startled me when I first heard batters mention it. Simmons said that Carl Yastrzemski had once told him that the players who hit the ball hardest and most often are simply the ones who are quickest to see the spin and identify it. Some pitches can be read before they leave the pitcher's hand, Simmons said—the curveball, much of the time, because it is delivered from a wider angle . . . —but most pitches are identified by the precise appearance of the ball in mid-flight. The fastball has a blurry, near-vertical spin. The curveball spins on a slight axis. The slider—well, there is more than one kind of slider.

"If a pitcher holds the ball with his forefinger and middle finger between the wide part of the seams, out at that horseshoe-shaped part of the ball, you see a big, wide white spot when it's pitched—sort of a flicker," Simmons said. "The better slider comes when he grabs the ball where the seams are close together. Then the red laces on the ball make a little red spot out there. That's because the ball is spiraling so hard that it's like the tip of a football that's just been passed. The seams make a little circle—that red dot—and you think, *Slider!* The red-dot sliders are the hard ones to hit—like J. R. Richard's. The white ones tend to hang. You can read the white one when it's about three feet out of the pitcher's hand. The red dot I can pick up about five feet from his hand."

# Witold Rybczynski, "Waiting for the Weekend"

Recreations like tennis and sailing are hardly new, but before the arrival of the weekend they were for most people chiefly seasonal activities. Once a year, when vacation time came around, tennis rackets were removed from the back of the cupboard, swimwear was taken out of mothballs, or skis were dusted off. The accent was less on technique than on having a good time. It was like playing Monopoly at the summer cottage: no one remembered all the rules, but everyone could still enjoy the game. Now the availability of free time every weekend has changed this casual attitude. The very frequency of weekend recreations allows continual participation and improvement, which encourages the development of proficiency and skill.

The desire to do something well, whether it is sailing a boat or building a boat, reflects a need that was previously met in the workplace. Competence was shown on the job—holidays were for messing around. Now the situation is reversed. Technology has removed craft from most occupations. This is true in assembly-line jobs, where almost no training or experience, hence no skill, is required, as well as in most service positions (store clerks, fast-food attendants), where the only talent required is to smile and say "Have a good day." But it's also true in such skill-dependent work as house construction, where the majority of parts come ready-made from the factory and the carpenter merely assembles them, or automobile repair, which consists largely in replacing one throwaway part with another. Nor is the reduction of skills limited to manual work. Memory, once the prerequisite skill of the white-collar worker, has been rendered superfluous by computers; teachers, who once needed dramatic skills, now depend on mechanical aids; in politics, oratory has been killed by the thirty-second sound bite.

Hence an unexpected development in the history of leisure: for many people weekend free time has become not a chance to escape work but a chance to create work that is more meaningful—to work at recreation—in order to realize the personal satisfactions that the workplace no longer offers.

# IIC. Personal Bonds

1. Arlie Russell Hochschild, selections from pp. 50–55, 81, 84 of "Work: The Great Escape," *New York Times Magazine* (April 20, 1997). Hochschild's article is based on interviews with 130 respondents over a recent three-year period. Hochschild is a professor of sociology at the University of California at Berkeley.

2. Leo Tolstoy, chapter 2 of *The Death of Ivan Ilyich* (New York: Bantam Books, 1981). Tolstoy (1828–1910) is generally regarded as one of the greatest novelists. *The Death of Ivan Ilyich* is among the best of his shorter works.

3. Judith Martin, selections from pp. 36–53 of *Common Courtesy* (New York: Atheneum, 1985). Judith Martin (1938–) is better known to her readers as "Miss Manners."

4. William F. May, pp. 182–86 of *The Physician's Covenant* (Philadelphia: Westminster, 1983). May is a Christian theologian and the author of a number of widely read works in professional ethics. He is Cary M. Maguire Professor of Ethics at Southern Methodist University.

5. Sidney Callahan, selections from pp. 73–84 of *Parents Forever: You and Your Adult Children* (New York: Crossroad, 1992). Callahan (1933–) is a psychologist and has written on a wide range of moral and religious topics.

6. Barbara Dafoe Whitehead, "Lost in Work," *The American Enterprise* 6 (September/October 1995), pp. 39–40. Whitehead (1944–) is well known as a contemporary social critic for her writings on marriage and family life.

# Arlie Russell Hochschild, "Work: The Great Escape"

We are used to thinking that work is where most people feel like "just a number" or "a cog in a machine." It is where they have to be "on," have to "act," where they are least secure and most harried.

But new management techniques so pervasive in corporate life have helped transform the workplace into a more appreciative, personal sort of social world. Meanwhile, at home the divorce rate has risen, and the emotional demands have become more baffling and complex. In addition to teething, tantrums and the normal developments of growing children, the needs of elderly parents are creating more tasks for the modern family—as are the blending, unblending, reblending of new stepparents, stepchildren, exes and former in-laws.

This idea began to dawn on me during one of my first interviews with an Amerco worker. Linda Avery, a friendly, 38-year-old mother, is a shift supervisor at an Amerco plant. When I meet her in the factory's coffee-break room over a couple of Cokes, she is wearing blue jeans and a pink jersey, her hair pulled back in a long, blond ponytail. Linda's husband, Bill, is a technician in the same plant. By working different shifts, they manage to share the care of their 2-year-old son and Linda's 16-year-old daughter from a previous marriage. "Bill works the 7 A.M. to 3 P.M. shift while I watch the baby," she explains. "Then I work the 3 P.M. to 11 P.M. shift and he watches the baby. My daughter works at Walgreen's after school."

Linda is working overtime, and so I begin by asking whether Amerco required the overtime, or whether she volunteered for it. "Oh, I put in for it," she replies. I ask her whether, if finances and company policy permitted, she'd be interested in cutting back on the overtime. She takes off her safety glasses, rubs her face and, without answering my question explains: "I get home, and the minute I turn the key, my daughter is right there. Granted, she needs somebody to talk to about her day. . . . The baby is still up. He should have been in bed two hours ago, and that upsets me. The dishes are piled in the sink. My daughter comes right up to the door and complains about anything her stepfather said or did, and she wants to talk about her job. My husband is in the other room hollering to my daughter, 'Tracy, I don't ever get any time to talk to your mother, because you're always monopolizing her time before I even get a chance!' They all come at me at once."

Linda's description of the urgency of demands and the unarbitrated quarrels that await her homecoming contrast with her account of arriving at her job as a shift supervisor: "I usually come to work early, just to get away from the house. When I arrive, people are there waiting. We sit, we talk, we joke. I let them know what's going on, who has to be where, what changes I've made for the shift that day. We sit and chitchat for 5 or 10 minutes. There's laughing, joking, fun."

For Linda, home has come to feel like work and work has come to feel a bit like home. Indeed, she feels she can get relief from the "work" of being at home only by going to the "home" of work. . . .

Forces at work and at home are simultaneously reinforcing this "reversal." The lure of work has been enhanced in recent years by the rise of company cultural engineering—in particular, the shift from Frederick Taylor's principles of scientific management to the Total Quality principles originally set out by W. Edwards Deming. Under the influence of a Taylorist world view, the manager's job was to coerce the worker's mind and body, not to appeal to the worker's heart. The Taylorized worker was de-skilled, replaceable and cheap, and as a consequence felt bored, demeaned and unappreciated.

Using modern participative management techniques, many companies now train workers to make their own work decisions, and then set before their newly "empowered" employees moral as well as financial incentives. At Amerco, the Total Quality worker is invited to feel recognized for job accomplishments. Amerco regularly strengthens the familylike ties of co-workers by holding "recognition ceremonies" honoring particular workers or self-management production teams. Amerco employees speak of "belonging to the Amerco family," and proudly wear their "Total Quality" pins or "High Performance Team" T-shirts, symbols of their loyalty to the company and of its loyalty to them. . . .

If Total Quality calls for "re-skilling" the worker in an "enriched" job environment, technological developments have long been de-skilling parents at home. Over the centuries, store-bought goods have replaced homespun cloth, homemade soap and home-baked foods. Day care for children, retirement homes for the elderly, even psychotherapy are, in a way, commercial substitutes for jobs that a mother once did at home. Even family-generated entertainment has, to some extent, been replaced by television, video games and the VCR. I sometimes watched Amerco families sitting together after their dinners, mute but cozy, watching sitcoms in which television mothers, fathers and children related in an animated way to one another while the viewing family engaged in relational loafing.

The one "skill" still required of family members is the hardest one of all—the emotional work of forging, deepening or repairing family relationships. It takes time to develop this skill, and even then things can go awry. Family ties are complicated. People get hurt. Yet as broken homes become more common—and as the sense of belonging to a geographical community grows less and less secure in an age of mobility—the corporate world has created a sense of "neighborhood," of "feminine culture," of family at work. Life at work can be insecure; the company can fire workers. But workers aren't so secure at home, either. Many employees have been working for Amerco for 20 years but are on their second or third marriages or relationships. The shifting balance between these two "divorce rates" may be the most powerful reason why tired parents flee a world of unresolved quarrels and unwashed laundry for the orderliness, harmony and managed cheer of work. People are getting their "pink slips" at home.

Amerco workers have not only turned their offices into "home" and their homes into workplaces; many have also begun to "Taylorize" time at home, where families are succumbing to a cult of efficiency previously associated mainly with the office and factory. Meanwhile, work time, with its ever longer hours, has become more hospitable to sociability—periods of talking with friends on E-mail, patching up quarrels, gossiping. Within the long workday of many Amerco employees are great hidden pockets of inefficiency while, in the far smaller number of waking weekday hours at home, they are, despite themselves, forced to act increasingly time-conscious and efficient.

The Averys respond to their time bind at home by trying to value and protect "quality time." A concept unknown to their parents and grandparents, "quality time" has become a powerful symbol of the struggle against the growing pressures at home. . . .

ESSAY

Quality time holds out the hope that scheduling intense periods of togetherness can compensate for an overall loss of time in such a way that a relationship will suffer no loss of quality. But this is just another way of transferring the cult of efficiency from office to home. We must now get our relationships in good repair in less time. Instead of nine hours a day with a child, we declare ourselves capable of getting "the same result" with one intensely focused hour. . . . .

Part of modern parenthood seems to include coping with the resistance of real children who are not so eager to get their cereal so fast. Some parents try desperately not to appease their children with special gifts or smooth-talking promises about the future. But when time is scarce, even the best parents find themselves passing a system-wide familial speed-up along to the most vulnerable workers on the line. Parents are then obliged to try to control the damage done by a reversal of worlds. They monitor mealtime, homework time, bedtime, trying to cut out "wasted" time.

In response, children often protest the pace, the deadlines, the grand irrationality of "efficient" family life. Children dawdle. They refuse to leave places when it's time to leave. They insist on leaving places when it's not time to leave. Surely, this is part of the usual stop-and-go of childhood itself, but perhaps, too, it is the plea of children for more family time, and more control over what time there is. This only adds to the feeling that life at home has become hard work.

Instead of trying to arrange shorter or more flexible work schedules, Amerco parents often avoid confronting the reality of the time bind. Some minimize their ideas about how much care a child, a partner or they themselves "really need." They make do with less time, less attention, less understanding and less support at home than they once imagined possible. They *emotionally downsize* life. In essence, they deny the needs of family members, and they themselves become emotional ascetics. If they once "needed" time with each other, they are now increasingly "fine" without it. . . .

Obviously, not everyone, not even a majority of Americans, is making a home out of work and a workplace out of home. But in the working world, it is a growing reality, and one we need to face. Increasing numbers of women are discovering a great male secret—that work can be an escape from the pressures of home, pressures that the changing nature of work itself are only intensifying. Neither men nor women are going to take up "family friendly" policies, whether corporate or governmental, as long as the current realities of work and home remain as they are. For a substantial number of time-bound parents, the stripped-down home and the neighborhood devoid of community are simply losing out to the pull of the workplace.

# Leo Tolstoy, *The Death of Ivan Ilyich*

Ivan Ilyich's life had been most simple and commonplace—and most horrifying.

He died at the age of forty-five, a member of the Court of Justice. He was the son of an official who, in various Petersburg ministries and departments, had established the sort of career whereby men reach a stage at which, owing to their rank and years of service, they cannot be dismissed, even though they are clearly unfit for any responsible work; and therefore they receive fictitious appointments, especially designed for them, and by no means fictitious salaries of from six to ten thousand on which they live to a ripe old age.

Such was the Privy Councillor Ilya Efimovich Golovin, superfluous member of various superfluous institutions.

He had three sons, of whom Ivan Ilyich was the second. The eldest had established the same type of career as his father, except in a different ministry, and was rapidly approaching the stage where men obtain sinecures. The third son was a failure. He had ruined his prospects in a number of positions and was now serving in the Railway Division. His father and brothers, and especially their wives, not only hated meeting him but, unless compelled to do otherwise, managed to forget his existence. The sister had married Baron Greff, the same sort of Petersburg official as his father-in-law. Ivan Ilyich, as they said, was *le phenix de la famille.* He was neither as cold and punctilious as his elder brother nor as reckless as his younger. He was a happy mean between the two— a clever, lively, pleasant, and respectable man. He and his younger brother had both attended the school of jurisprudence. The younger brother never graduated, for he was expelled when he reached the fifth course. On the other hand, Ivan Ilyich completed the program creditably. As a law student he had become exactly what he was to remain the rest of his life: a capable, cheerful, good-natured, and sociable man but one strict to carry out whatever he considered his duty, and he considered his duty all things that were so designated by people in authority. Neither as a boy nor as an adult had he been a toady, but from his earliest youth he had been drawn to people of high standing in society as a moth is to light; he had adopted their manners and their views on life and had established friendly relations with them. All the enthusiasms of childhood and youth passed, leaving no appreciable impact on him; he had succumbed to sensuality and vanity and, in his last years at school, to liberalism, but strictly within the limits his instinct unerringly prescribed.

As a student he had done things which at the time, seemed to him extremely vile and made him feel disgusted with himself; but later, seeing that people of high standing had no qualms about doing these things, he was not

quite able to consider them good but managed to dismiss them and not feel
the least perturbed when he recalled them.

When he graduated from law school with a degree qualifying him for the
tenth rank of civil service, and had obtained money from his father for his
outfit, he ordered some suits at Sharmer's, the fashionable tailor, hung a me-
dallion inscribed *respice finem* on his watch chain, took leave of his mentor
and prince, who was patron of the school, dined in state with his friends at
Donon's, and then, with fashionable new luggage, linen, clothes, shaving and
other toilet articles, and a traveling rug (all ordered and purchased at the finest
shops), he set off for one of the provinces to assume a post his father had secured for him there as assistant on special commissions to the governor.

Ivan Ilyich immediately made his life in the provinces as easy and pleasant
as it had been at law school. He worked, saw to his career, and at the same time,
engaged in proper and pleasant forms of diversion. When from time to time
he traveled to country districts on official business, he maintained his dignity
with both his superiors and inferiors and fulfilled the duties entrusted to him
(primarily cases involving a group of religious sectarians) with an exactitude
and incorruptibility in which he could only take pride.

In his official duties, despite his youth and love of light forms of amusement, he was exceedingly reserved, punctilious, and even severe; but in society
he was often playful and witty, always good-humored and polite—a *bon enfant*
as the governor and his wife, with whom he was like one of the family, used
to say of him.

In the provinces he had an affair with one of the ladies who threw themselves at the chic young lawyer; there was also a milliner; there were drinking
bouts with visiting aides-de-camp and after-supper trips to a certain street on
the outskirts of town; there were also attempts to curry favor with his chief
and even with his chief's wife. But all this had such a heightened air of respectability that nothing bad could be said about it. It could all be summed
up by the French saying, "*Il faut que jeunesse se passe.*" It was all done with
clean hands, in clean shirts, and with French phrases, and, most importantly,
among people of the best society—consequently, with the approval of those in
high rank.

Ivan Ilyich spent five years of his service career in this manner, and at the
end of that time there was a change in his official life. New judicial institutions
had been formed and new men were needed.

Ivan Ilyich became such a new man.

He was offered a post as examining magistrate and he accepted it, even
though it meant moving to another province, giving up the connections he had
formed, and establishing new ones. His friends met to bid him farewell: they

had a group photograph taken and presented him with a silver cigarette case, and he set off to assume his new position.

As an examining magistrate, Ivan Ilyich was just as *comme il faut* and respectable, just as capable of separating his official duties from his private life and of inspiring general respect as he had been while acting as assistant on special commissions. He found the work of a magistrate far more interesting and appealing than his former duties. In his previous position he had enjoyed the opportunity to stride freely and easily in his Sharmer uniform past the crowd of anxious, envious petitioners and officials waiting to be heard by the governor, to go straight into his chief's office and sit with him over a cup of tea and a cigarette. But few people had been directly under his control then—only the district police officers and religious sectarians he encountered when sent out on special commissions. And he loved to treat these people courteously, almost as comrades, loved to make them feel that he who had the power to crush them was dealing with them in such a friendly, unpretentious manner. But there had been few such people. Now, as an examining magistrate, Ivan Ilyich felt that all, without exception—including the most important and self-satisfied people—all were in his power, and that he had only to write certain words on a sheet of paper with an official heading and this or that important, self-satisfied person would be brought to him as a defendant or a witness, and if Ivan Ilyich did not choose to have him sit, he would be forced to stand to answer his questions. Ivan Ilyich never abused his power; on the contrary, he tried to exercise it leniently; but the awareness of that power and the opportunity to be lenient constituted the chief interest and appeal of his new post. In the work itself—that is, in conducting investigations—Ivan Ilyich soon mastered the technique of dispensing with all considerations that did not pertain to his job as examining magistrate, and of writing up even the most complicated cases in a style that reduced them to their externals, bore no trace of his personal opinion, and, most importantly, adhered to all the prescribed formalities. This type of work was new, and he was one of the first men to give practical application to the judicial reforms instituted by the Code of 1864.

On taking up the post of examining magistrate in the new town, Ivan Ilyich made new acquaintances and connections, adopted a new stance, and assumed a somewhat different tone. He put a suitable amount of distance between himself and the provincial authorities, chose his friends from among the best circle of lawyers and wealthy gentry in the town, and assumed an air of mild dissatisfaction with the government, of moderate liberalism, of enlightened civic responsibility. And though he remained as fastidious as ever about his attire, he stopped shaving his chin and allowed his beard to grow freely.

In the new town, too, life turned out to be very pleasant for Ivan Ilyich. The people opposed to the governor were friendly and congenial, his salary was higher, and he began to play whist, which added considerably to the pleasure of his life, for he had an ability to maintain his good spirits while playing and to reason quickly and subtly, so that he usually came out ahead.

After he had been working in the town for two years, Ivan Ilyich met his future wife. Praskovya Fyodorovna Mikhel was the most attractive, intelligent, and outstanding young lady of the set in which Ivan Ilyich moved. In addition to the other amusements and relaxations that provided relief from his work as an examining magistrate, Ivan Ilyich began a light flirtation with Praskovya Fyodorovna.

As an assistant on special commissions Ivan Ilyich had, as a rule, danced; as an examining magistrate he danced as an exception. He danced to show that although he was a representative of the reformed legal institutions and an official of the fifth rank, when it came to dancing, he could also excel at that. So he occasionally danced with Praskovya Fyodorovna at the end of an evening, and it was mainly during the time they danced together that he conquered her. She fell in love with him. Ivan Ilyich had no clear and definite intention of marrying, but when the girl fell in love with him, he asked himself: "Really, why shouldn't I get married?"

Praskovya Fyodorovna came from a good family and was quite attractive; she also had a little money. Ivan Ilyich could have counted on a more illustrious match, but even this one was quite good. He had his salary, and her income, he hoped, would bring in an equal amount. It would be a good alliance: she was a sweet, pretty, and extremely well-bred young woman. To say that Ivan Ilyich married because he fell in love with his fiancee and found her sympathetic to his views on life would be as mistaken as to say that he married because the people in his circle approved of the match. Ivan Ilyich married for both reasons: in acquiring such a wife he did something that gave him pleasure and, at the same time, did what people of the highest standard considered correct.

And so Ivan Ilyich got married.

The preparations for marriage and the first period of married life, with its conjugal caresses, new furniture, new dishes, new linen—the period up to his wife's pregnancy—went very well, so that Ivan Ilyich began to think that marriage would not disrupt the easy, pleasant, cheerful, and respectable life approved of by society (a pattern he believed to be universal); that it would even enhance such a life. But during the first months of his wife's pregnancy, something new, unexpected, and disagreeable manifested itself, something painful and unseemly, which he had no way of anticipating and could do nothing to avoid.

For no reason at all, so it seemed to Ivan Ilyich—*de gaite de coeur,* as he told himself—his wife began to undermine the pleasure and propriety of their life: she became jealous without cause, demanded he be more attentive to her, found fault with everything, and created distasteful and ill-mannered scenes.

At first Ivan Ilyich hoped to escape from this unpleasant state of affairs by preserving the same carefree and proper approach to life that had served him in the past. He tried to ignore his wife's bad moods, went on living in a pleasant and easygoing fashion, invited friends over for cards, and made an effort to get away to his club or his friends' homes. But on one occasion his wife lashed out at him with such fury and such foul language, and persisted in attacking him every time he failed to satisfy her demands (apparently having resolved not to let up until he submitted—that is, until he stayed home and moped as she did) that Ivan Ilyich was horrified. He realized that married life—at least with his wife—was not always conducive to the pleasures and proprieties of life but, on the contrary, frequently disrupted them, and for that reason he must guard against disruptions. Ivan Ilyich tried to find some means of doing this. His work was the one thing that made any impression on Praskovya Fyodorovna, and so he began to use his work and the obligations it entailed as a way of combating his wife and safeguarding his independence.

With the birth of the baby, the attempts to feed it and the various difficulties, the real and imaginary illnesses of mother and child, which Ivan Ilyich was supposed to sympathize with but failed to understand, his need to fence off a world for himself outside the family became even more imperative.

To the degree that his wife became more irritable and demanding, Ivan Ilyich increasingly made work the center of gravity in his life. He grew more attached to his job and more ambitious than before.

Very soon, within a year after his wedding, Ivan Ilyich realized that married life, though it offered certain conveniences, was in fact a very complex and difficult business, and that to do one's duty to it—that is, to lead a proper, socially acceptable life—one had to develop a clearly defined attitude to it, just as one did with respect to work.

And Ivan Ilyich developed such an attitude. Of married life he demanded only the conveniences it could provide—dinners at home, a well-run household, a partner in bed, and, above all, a veneer of respectability which public opinion required. As for the rest, he tried to find enjoyment in family life, and, if he succeeded, was very grateful; but if he met with resistance and querulousness, he immediately withdrew into his separate, entrenched world of work and found pleasure there.

Ivan Ilyich was esteemed for his diligent service, and after three years he was made assistant public prosecutor. His new duties, the importance of them, the possibility of indicting and imprisoning anyone he chose, the publicity his speeches received and the success they brought him—all this further enhanced the appeal of his work.

Other children were born. His wife became more and more petulant and irascible, but the attitude Ivan Ilyich had adopted toward domestic life made him almost impervious to her carping. After serving for seven years in this town, Ivan Ilyich was transferred to another province as public prosecutor. They moved, they were short of money, and his wife disliked the new town. Although his salary was higher, the cost of living was greater; moreover, two of their children had died, and so family life became even more unpleasant for Ivan Ilyich.

Praskovya Fyodorovna blamed her husband for every setback they experienced in the new town. Most of the topics of conversation between husband and wife, especially the children's education, brought up issues on which they remembered having quarreled, and these quarrels were apt to flare up again at any moment. All they had left were the rare periods of amorousness that came over them, but these did not last long. They were merely little islands at which the couple anchored for a while before setting out again on a sea of veiled hostility, which took the form of estrangement from one another. This estrangement might have distressed Ivan Ilyich had he felt it should not exist, but by now he not only regarded it as a normal state of affairs, but as a goal he sought to achieve in family life. That goal was to free himself more and more from these disturbances, to make them appear innocuous and respectable. He managed to do this by spending less and less time with his family and, when obliged to be at home, tried to safeguard his position through the presence of outsiders. But what mattered most was that Ivan Ilyich had his work. His entire interest in life was centered in the world of official duties and that interest totally absorbed him. The awareness of his power, the chance to run whomever he chose, the importance attached even to his entry into the courtroom and manner of conferring with his subordinates, the success he enjoyed both with them and his superiors, and, above all, his own recognition of the skill with which he handled cases—all this gave him cause for rejoicing and, together with chats with his colleagues, dinner invitations, and whist, made his life full. So that on the whole Ivan Ilyich's life proceeded as he felt it should—pleasantly and properly.

# Judith Martin, *Common Courtesy*

## Banned from trade, American ladies go abroad to acquire suitable dresses and gentlemen

In Europe, there was always that clear-cut division between those who made the money and those who enjoyed it. One was either in trade or one was in society, but it was impossible to be in both. (The item of men's clothing known in America as the "business suit" is, in England, called a "lounge suite.") The essence of being in trade is working to get ever ahead, while the essence of being in society is knowing how to enjoy the leisure afforded by having arrived.

Bridging this dichotomy diachronically, with earlier generations in trade and subsequent ones in society, is obviously not suitable in the land of the self-made man, where everyone is created equal. In nineteenth-century America, a synchronic solution was found, a sexually dimorphic division of the tasks of making and spending within concurrent generations of the same family. Until fairly recently, the pattern was that the father and sons worked, and, to whatever extent their earnings allowed, the mother and daughters were supposed to display culture, religion, luxury, and other assorted fine feelings of society (in addition to seeing that the housework got done).

This system of working men and supposedly leisured women is not as old as those who are trying to revive it, or to root out the remains of it, seem to imagine. Before the rise of the middle class during the industrial revolution, gender had little to do with whether one worked. All the poor, men, women, and children, worked, and all the rich didn't work. The nonworking of the rich was known as "looking after the property," a unisex form of housewifery, except that the man looked after the estate manager who looked after the outdoor property, and the woman looked after the household staff who looked after the indoor property. In America, rich men would satisfy our belief in the virtue of labor by venturing "downtown" to look after the cash property, but that was not supposed to interfere with leisure duties. Edith Wharton lamented the misfortune of serious male employment invading the upper classes at the turn of the century, and the demise of the long delightful drunken society luncheon. If only she had lived to see the coeducational expense-account lunch.

The American-style family division, by gender, of earning and spending made trouble from the beginning. When money made the women socially mobile, Mamma would take the daughters to Europe to find them noble husbands unsullied by work, and the last thing they needed to have around was old money-grubbing papa. Now even aristocratic societies are abandoning the idea of full-time leisure. There isn't a countess left in Europe who doesn't run a boutique, or aspire to, and every idiot son of an old family identifies himself as a photographer. We have also finally noticed that dividing the tasks of work and leisure by gender leaves a lot of dissatisfied people—overburdened men and bored women.

This system has now come to an end. We have tried to improve upon it by adding or subtracting, and ended up with twice-as-overworked women, and dropouts of both sexes from the professional structure, who couldn't figure out what to do with themselves and got zonked. College women are typically given to declaring for one or the other (in my day, for marriage; now, generally, for careers), and only later finding to their surprise that they must cope with both—while their men may be trying to figure out how to get out of doing both. The simple idea that everyone needs a reasonable amount of challenging work in his or her life, and also a personal life, complete with noncompetitive leisure has never really taken hold.


### Admitted to trade, the ladies leave the private realm unstaffed

A new social problem has replaced the old one. Now that virtually everyone works, including middle-class women and upper-class men, the private realm, which included not only extensive family life and society, but keeping neighborhood, civic, philanthropic, cultural, and religious institutions viable, has all but disappeared. There is no one left to run it.

Everything is business. What is referred to as society in the newspapers consists of parties celebrating merchants or new merchandise, or of charity luncheons or balls to which tickets are sold. More exclusive, so called private, social life is routinely used unabashedly as opportunities to further the guests' careers. The successful host is one who can command "movers and shakers," although it is not clear why one would want to have one's dinner table moving and shaking.

Such mongrel practices as expense-account entertaining, the tax-deductible home party, the private letter on office letterhead, the opening question at parties of "What do you do?" (still considered in Europe to be as rude as "How much money do you make?") are ubiquitous. In return for professional sponsorship of their entertainment, people have surrendered the very concept of leisure. I never thought I would see the return of cards nowadays to hand out at parties. Does anyone besides me still have social cards? Does anyone have a social identity?

Private houses are treated by their guests as public accommodations, or worse. A restaurant may be entitled to demand reservations, but a private invitation is not only not thought worth the bother of a reply, but considered an entitlement to bring along one's own guests. If the Second Coming were scheduled for next week, my mail would be full of letters asking, "Can I bring a date?" Even the White House has yielded to this, and issues "and guest" invitations. Mrs. Guest is the most popular person in the country—she goes simply everywhere.

Just about every etiquette question I receive concerning weddings provides financial information as the presumptive basis for my ruling on social matters. "We're paying for it ourselves, so why do we have to invite my mother's cousins whom I can't stand?" "If my step-father is paying for the liquor, shouldn't he give me away, rather than my father, who's only paying for the flowers?" "How can we tell people that we already have all the household things we want but we like cash?" There seems to be a general belief that social, and even family, honors are for sale, and that there is an acknowledged admission charge to wedding guests.

Private standards, such as reticence and loyalty, have given way to commercial ones of advertising and competition. The best place to discuss your intimate problems is on television. If it is discovered that you are so successful that you don't seem to have any problems, it will be assumed that "dealing with success" is a problem, a chief manifestation of which must be the jealous resentment (politely called feelings of "inadequacy") of your family and friends. The friends you left behind professionally are as embarrassing in your new life as the relatives locked in the attic once were.

Business techniques are applied to the most personal situations. If you're ready to fall in love, you run a classified advertisement announcing a vacancy and including a job description with the most detailed skill requirements. It is permissible to fire lovers, but only with cause. "I don't love you any more" is not considered acceptable; "You don't meet my present needs" is more suitably businesslike. In what used to be known as free love, contractual obligation after obligation is being established until, ultimately, the free lovers will have reinvented marriage.

Friends are only friends if they fit exactly with one's stage of life and momentary interests. They should not only be able to advance one's career, but also to solve, or at least share, one's immediate social problems. That person whose agenda is to find romance doesn't bother with married people, and married couples only bother with people who are childless, if they are, or have children of the same age group they do, so that competitions can be held over which child first talks, gets into college, or marries. Acquiring or losing a spouse or a job means that one also loses one's friends.

I suppose one couldn't argue with applying M.B.A. techniques to running personal life if they worked. But loneliness has never been more widespread a societal phenomenon. There was no singles problem until singles got so single-minded that they stopped wasting time with anyone ineligible. Before that, it was understood that one of society's main tasks was matchmaking. People with lifelong friendships and ties to local nonprofessional organizations did not have to fear that isolation would accompany retirement, old age, or losing a spouse. Overburdened householders could count on the assistance not only of their own extended families, but of the American tradition of neighborliness.

### Now that society is abandoned, one's only friend is one's bank

Meanwhile, the empty forms of social behavior survive inappropriately in business situations. We all know that when a business sends its customers "friendly reminders," it really means business.

There is a pretense, by using the social model in commerce, that professional inequalities do not exist. "Hi, I'm Kimberly, and I'm going to be bringing you your dinner. How ya doing?" "We're not just your bank, we're your friend." Never trust your luggage to an airline that has promised to be your friend, because the other side of that means that the business will not be held accountable any more than a friend would. Kimberly never does bring you the dinner you ordered when you wanted it, but is hurt if you complain. If a friend does his or her best, or has an excuse, or just botches something, or doesn't feel like it, it is rude to berate him for not doing a favor.

American businesses now seem to specialize in explaining to the customer why things were not done, rather than in doing them. "I wasn't here then," "We're short-staffed today," "That's not my responsibility" are the routine answers to complaints. Individual responses of nonaccountability are given, each employee refusing to accept the symbolic representation of the company. They are just there as "themselves," so the customer would have to be familiar with everyone's employment conditions and records if he is to find who is to blame for what has gone wrong, much less someone who feels interested in correcting it.

Using the social model, it seems rude to say, "I don't care how many people were out sick or whose fault it was—I want what I paid for." Of course the presumption that the customer is always right, or even that the business should be run for his convenience rather than the employees', is considered inappropriate among friends.

Privacy, or the ability to select one's friends on the mere grounds of personal preference, also comes to be considered rude. If everyone is a friend, one of them can't be excluded from the conversation just because he happens to be driving the taxi that the others have hired.

Nobody knows anymore what true social obligations are. A mockery has been made of traditional American openness, so that everyone is considered open, all the time, to all social advances. Where "the roof" was considered to constitute an introduction, the sky now serves the same purpose. In this age where people do not feel obliged to be polite to their spouses, I get dozens of letters from young ladies who want to know how to discourage the lewd advances of strangers without seeming rude. Sometimes they kindly specify that the method of fending off these men should not result in making them feel rejected.

This confusion of friendship and business not only blinds people to their own interests, but leads them to unrealistic expectations from others. I always have to start the New Year reading pitiful letters from those who, thinking the office Christmas party a social occasion where everyone is equal, used it to have a frank talk with the boss. I remember how handicapped my union, the Newspaper Guild, always was by the fact that reporters who called their editors by their first names and drank with them misunderstood their relationship at contract time. Much of the membership would act personally hurt and aggreived by betrayed friendship—or else they would refuse to believe that their friends were acting in opposition to them.

One spring, I attended the Orioles' opening game of the baseball season in Baltimore—where the football team had just decamped to Indianapolis—in the company of Washingtonians who were still angry over the Senators' betrayal by moving away so many years ago. The perfidy of professional teams was bemoaned the whole bus ride to and from Baltimore. Fans are led to act on the personal model, which includes geographical loyalty, and so they are astonished and outraged when the teams, which are clearly in business, act, as they must, on financial considerations. It was like listening to a man who had married a prostitute complain about her infidelity.

### In which it is lamented that ladies are not taught the difference between a drawing room and a board room

A major handicap of women in the business world is that while men were taught the difference between social and professional manners—the phrases "an officer and a gentleman," and "a gentleman and a scholar" suggest that different behavior is appropriate in the drawing room than on the battlefield or even in the library—women were brought up to have only one set of manners. A woman was either a lady or she wasn't, and we all know what the latter meant. Not even momentary lapses were allowed; there is no female equivalent of the boys-will-be-boys concept.

A lady (or a gentleman in the drawing room, for that matter) never discusses money, never brags, and never pushes or makes herself conspicuous. It is amazing, in this time of forgotten manners, how many women are reluctant to ask for raises or take credit for work done, attributing any career progress to luck. This does not make for great professional success.

Women are quite right to suspect that when social standards are applied to them at business—when the wrong person picks up the check at a business lunch, or a woman is accused of being "rude," rather than unprofessional, on the job; or supposedly insurmountable etiquette problems are cited as a reason for not giving a woman a good job—somebody is up to no good. At various times, the United States Government declared it impossible to find the form of address for the husband of an ambassador or for a female Supreme Court justice; and the etiquette problems involved if a women were to become Vice President of the United States became a major topic of the 1984 campaign.

In the professional world, precedence is correctly based strictly on rank, not gender. If you are going to stand up for anyone, or get down on your knees, it is going to be for the president of the company, male or female; and the president always has precedence over the vice-president. It is as simple as that. The female equivalent of "Mr.," as in "Mr. President" or "Mr. Justice," is "Madam," as respectable a word as "mistress" used to be. (One wonders why professionally useful female titles always seem to pick dirty connotations.) Spouses of officials have no official rank, but are accorded, by courtesy, those of their husbands or wives.

I don't in the least mean to suggest that I do not approve of an unashamed recognition of the importance of trade in American life, and of the dignity of all honest labor. But how can the equality of all citizens be represented symbolically in the decidedly unequal world of business, where some people are bosses and others are their employees? It cannot. Only in the private realm, where each citizen can exercise autonomy and choice, is full equality possible.

When there is no private realm, rank derives only from jobs, and a person without a job, no matter how charming, amusing, educated, beautiful, or rich, is a person without social identification or standing. This is why women who were once proud of single-handedly maintaining private, domestic, community, social, and cultural life for men who could manage only one job apiece, are now ashamed or defensive about being housewives. Many try to justify themselves by inventing pseudo-business titles for themselves, such as "domestic engineer," or reciting how much their skills would cost if they hired themselves out to their families. They are only conceding that it is more respectable for a lady to sell her services to her husband, than to give them away.

# William F. May, *The Physician's Covenant*

The bureaucratic emphasis on the office, rather than the person, creates difficulties for physicians and administrators in three directions: it produces conflicts with duties to patients, to oneself, and to colleagues.

Patients sense acutely the deprivations that result from official, officious, and impersonal treatment. Tolstoy's Ivan Ilych put it most trenchantly:

> There was the usual waiting and the important air assumed by the doctor with which he was so familiar (resembling that which he himself assumed in court). . . . To Ivan Ilych only one question was important: was his case serious or not? But the doctor ignored that inappropriate question. From his point of view it was not the one under consideration, the real question was to decide between a floating kidney, chronic catarrh or appendicitis. It was not a question of life or death, but one between a floating kidney and appendicitis.

Dealing in huge numbers and attempting to deal fairly combine to force the large organization to deal impersonally. Patients, clients, and consumers complain of impersonal treatment, and the existentialists developed this complaint into a broadside against modern mass society. They bemoaned a culture that reduces subjects to objects, persons to things. The manager symbolizes this reduction, for the very term "manager," like "manipulation," derives from the Latin word for hands; the manager "handles" others, a mode of relationship that has less to do with the personal predilections and sensitivity of the manager than with the very structure and scale of the institution.

This criticism has an important element of truth. The ideal physician should not simply treat the disease but reckon with the patient. The failure to do so in the large-scale organization has led to the exploration of significant alternatives and supplements to the prevailing health care system: the self-care movement, the hospice movement, and the holistic health care movement.

Within limits, sensitive administrators and professionals working in a bureaucracy can lean against some of its tendencies toward institutional callousness. Some reforms, particularly in the allocation of time to patients and in the training of residents, will help considerably to give the hospital a "human face." But some superficial efforts at "personalizing" relationships only remind the inmate of the highly impersonal environment that engulfs a person there. "Personalizing" relationships smacks too much of Sanforizing pants. The very process industrializes intimacy. Physicians, managers, and administrators must also accept without false dismay the incompleteness of their contacts with those over whom they exercise control. In doing their limited jobs, they often serve persons well whose fellowship, in personal terms, they will never enjoy.

The organizational emphasis upon the impersonal rather than the personal runs a second danger of impoverishing the self that fills the office; it conflicts with one's duties to oneself. The careerist totally subordinates himself or herself to the office and becomes, in the course of time, a cipher, a spectral being, deferring satisfactions and evading pain by referring it from its deeper psychic levels to petty frustrations. Such a person becomes guilty of what Nietzsche called the "work neurosis." The "now" generation criticized such careerism for its tunnel vision; Jungians took it to task for its one-sidedness. Careerism prefers the *animus* to the *anima*, the rational to the affective, the manipulative to the sensitive, and thereby diminishes the self. Resentful spouses, broken marriages, alienated children, drug addiction, early health problems, and career burnout reflect this psychic disarray. Wrongly interpreted, a covenantal ethic would appear to contribute to a self-consuming, eventually destructive commitment. As stated earlier, the notion of covenant cuts deeper into personal identity than either a limited contractual or a technical interpretation of professional duty. But I also noted earlier that the biblical notion of covenant produces an inner freedom and nonchalance that makes a deeper commitment to others tolerable. The religious tradition imparts a sense of the final extraterritoriality of the person that makes it possible to function in a "hardship post," as it were, without being annihilated thereby. One can take a job seriously precisely because one does not take it too seriously. It has not become the sole arena of self-realization. One can also accept the lesser distinctions between the office and the person without finding them disconcertingly schizophrenic. Meanwhile, official roles and social masks do not necessarily impoverish or stifle the agent who must play and wear them. On the contrary, they provide the self with a social fig leaf; they permit some measure of personal life to thrive behind them.

Finally, the bureaucratic emphasis on the impersonal at the expense of the personal presents difficulties, especially for Americans, in dealings with colleagues. American professionals find themselves caught between the pressure of a social structure that is highly formal, bureaucratic, and competitive—energized throughout by the rewards of promotion—and a social style predicated on friendliness, informality, and intimacy as its ideal. The impersonal strains against the personal; the hierarchical against the egalitarian; and the competitive against the impulse to help others. The resultant moral conflicts between loyalty to the institution and loyalty to friends can be immense.

Some societies protect their members from such conflicts by separating the public order of work from the private order of friendship. But Americans peculiarly combine these orders at the risk of corrupting them both. Caught between the demands of an impersonal social system and a social style in which friendliness counts for so much, Americans carry a heavy burden of guilt over betrayal of the friend or compromise of the institution. They make friends at work, but then find themselves making professional judgments and decisions about those befriended. The confidences of friendship inspire some measure of personal loyalty, but they also render two people more vulnerable to each other in their weaknesses. The course of friendship reveals secrets and confidences. But then it can happen that a man finds himself suddenly called upon to judge impersonally those in whom he has confided and who have confided in him. Uncomfortably, he helps turn them over to the machinery of the system—not entirely certain that the system itself hands out justice as it reviews the individual case. Friendship, moreover, in the bureaucratic setting has its darker side. Irrespective of the formal table of organization, staff members polarize into shifting patterns of friendship and enmity. It becomes even more difficult to make unclouded professional judgments about colleagues adversarially defined.

The social mobility of Americans increases the competitive tension throughout the system. The social system lacks a ceiling above and a floor below. Thus, the rewards for backbiting can tempt; the threat of the betrayal by others can chill. Under these circumstances, the prevailing social style remains outwardly friendly and direct; but inwardly a wariness takes possession of the soul and corrodes the workplace with distrust.

It must be frankly conceded that covenantal obligations to friends and institutions can conflict. But the earlier discussion of professional self-regulation makes it clear why the heavier accent must fall on obligations to the institution—as defined by professional purpose. The immense powers professionals wield, in and out of the institutional setting, and the fateful consequences of their actions for patients, forbid the professional to warp judgment for reasons of friendship. This does not mean that a covenantal ethic depresses altogether the claims of friendship or obligations to one's colleagues. The chief obstacle to friendship comes not from conflicting institutional obligations but from a careerist preoccupation with one's self. The word "career" perhaps not accidentally derives from the same root as "car," in our culture a self-driven vehicle. Today a vocation deteriorates only too often into a career that is a kind of self-driven vehicle through life, that deals expediently with both institutions and friends in the nervous effort to get ahead. Rightly understood, a covenantal ethic should help strengthen both institutional and collegial ties.

# Sidney Callahan, *Parents Forever*

They should put "an ability to do career counseling" in the parental job description packet! One mother reported that her son's nine-month job search after coming home from graduate school was worse than any pregnancy she had undergone. She and her husband made efforts to support their son before job interviews and after disappointing rejections but it was not clear that anything was of any help. In a depressed economic scene it is no easy feat for a young person to get a good job, or for parents to maintain cheerful confidence and benign detachment from the process.

As the weeks of unemployment mounted these parents had to stave off mounting doubts. Had they raised a son who could not compete in the marketplace? James was making money as a skilled painter of houses but his efforts to find work in his professional field were meeting with no success. Was it really a problem of bad times or did their son have some problem with competition and self-presentation? It does not always help to know that jobs in general are scarce, because if anyone is getting work out there, parents can reason that their son should be able to do so as well. Anxieties over jobs are a new and strange problem for a generation of parents who started their own careers in boom times. In an earlier day all you needed to get a good job was proof of your educational preparation and a demonstration of good will. If you did your part and went to a decent school, many opportunities awaited you. In these more competitive times of recession and depression getting started in a career and keeping a job can be a struggle. The outlook is particularly tough for what is known as "the trailing edge" of baby boomers, those born from 1955 to 1964.

James's parents were hard pressed to try to think up helpful strategies and advice, and to remain encouraging. They did not have any contacts or connections in their son's chosen field so they could not help him get an interview. This mother felt particularly worried in this crisis because the siblings of this hardworking eldest son, who had toiled through the established path of graduate school, were watching his job search with some skepticism. If James couldn't get a job after doing everything right, why should they buckle down to more years of education?

James finally got a good job in his field after months of trying, but the stress accompanying this all too typical job search provides several lessons. The obvious one might be that everyone today needs a backup subsistence skill, like painting or typing, to support periods of unemployment in his or her profession. Another moral that is penetrating the middle class for the first time is how important it can be for young people to be able to look forward to work opportunities. Suddenly the high unemployment statistics of the ghetto, the barrio, or northern Ireland, become more of a reality. It can happen here.

Joblessness is a social plague that induces a crippling sense of helplessness and dependency. It is frightening to read that, at age twenty-nine, nearly 40 percent of American men have failed to find a stable, long-term job. Young men and women are taking longer to get established, and tend to return home when unemployed or in the throes of career changes or after being laid off, or "excessed." Parents who are secure enough not to have to worry about their own employment find themselves footing the bills for the returnees' room and board, as well as contributing to tuition for adult children entering graduate school as they change careers.

Parents may have tried very hard to keep their children from graduating college without a crushing load of student debt. Some affluent parents succeed, but for others it may be impossible. But when an expensive graduate school tuition is added on, young adult debt becomes a hidden social reality. It is a shadow deficit weighing down the initial stages of a young person's working life. The pressure to payback expensive student loans gets added on to other strains surrounding work and careers. Getting a job becomes urgent.

Few parents can guarantee a job or successfully stage-manage a career for a son or daughter. Gone are the days when parents could help provide for their children's livelihood by arranging apprenticeships or entry jobs at the parental place of work or at a friend of the family's business. Nepotism is frowned upon except in the building and plumbing trades or in the remaining family businesses. And who has a farm to pass on to children anymore? Parents can help pay for schooling and if they are very fortunate they can provide contacts and family connections to gain an entry interview, or more rarely an entry level job, but little else. . . .

Most Americans have been prepared to pay the price involved in having one's child get more education than they did and move up in the class system. A father who has been a factory worker cannot have firsthand experiences of what his son, the college professor, meets in his working conditions. If there has been an education gap the father and mother may find it impossible to advise a child who faces entirely new decisions in a more technical field. But an immigrant and internally migrating people is prepared for this kind of distancing between the generations, however painful it may be. The parents are proud that their children have problems they can't understand. It is part of the American dream to see one's children fly up, up, and away.

Yet dreams are smashed quite regularly. Individual children may not succeed in work because of their own incapacities, but hard times can ensure that even the most talented and hardworking young adults won't get a fair chance to succeed in a career. Parents can have fears and anxieties over the future as they see more and more good workers fired or laid off during a recession or depression. The thought that your offspring will do worse than you did in the world of work is painful. Downward mobility for offspring means that the quantity and quality of work available to them, and the money they can earn doing it, will be less than that of their parents. . . .

Success, partly symbolized by money earned, is still the jealous bitch goddess of America. Parents of young workaholics can wonder if they helped induct their children into this consuming cult of success and achievement. Parents in mid-life may reflect upon their own past and wonder whether they too were driven in their earlier work patterns. Certainly many older men of high achievement regret that they did not pay as much attention to their children as they should have when the children were growing up. Career women also worry whether their determination to be Wonderwoman may have been costly to their children. Such regrets over earlier career choices can engender worries over a grown child's work obsession.

If, however, parents were always thwarted in their work, they may sense that they have subtly pressed their children to make up for their own deficiencies. Those who failed at work and careers may invest heavily in their offspring's success. Women who never had the opportunities for careers may push their daughter's career achievements. The temptation is always there for parents to push adult children into fulfilling their own hidden or not so hidden agendas.

When daughters and sons are too consumed by work to find a mate, or too involved in their work to have children, parents may worry. But isn't this worry just another hidden parental agenda coming to the fore? Yes, the selfish thought does arise that the biological clock is ticking away one's chances for in-laws and grandchildren, but more altruistic concerns can also be on a parent's mind. Will my child who is so caught up today in a career, miss out in the long run on having a family of his or her own? Parents who are renewed by their relationships with their grown children are saddened by the possibility that their children may miss this rich experience for themselves. Social analysts have noted that many people now turn their work situations into substitute families with daddy and mommy bosses and sibling coworkers. These observations do not give parents in a young adult's real family much comfort.

The prevalence of our obsession with work and achievement in America creates what has been called a harried leisure class. No other elite in history has ever worked such long hours. Have we really progressed all that much from a society in which perpetual drudgery was a curse and unceasing toil took its toll in health and happiness? Today fancier forms of competition and overwork are doing damage to our leisure, family life, and communities. The mediating institutions of life, from family to churches, to neighborhood associations, to service clubs and political parties, are based upon volunteers expending energy and time that is not job related. The public sphere and the common good suffer when the best and the brightest are too busy to help build the good society.

Parents who have had time to reflect on the balance between work, leisure, and family life can help their adult children truly value work and the work ethic and yet keep it in its place. Like little bear's porridge, the commitment to work should not be either too hot or too cold, but just right. Getting the right mix of work and the rest of life can be an ongoing project. Family discussions, family exemplars and family support can help adult children fight against the mindless pressures of the times. . . .

Many of today's well-educated parents were taught to admire a leisured life devoted to creative art and literature. Yet in reality a life devoted to creating art demands years of highly focused, disciplined effort. The life of an artist is hard, and quite different from the undisciplined life of the dabbling dilettante. Without supreme dedication, along with good fortune, an artist can never have a successful career, much less hope to come near financial independence. Many great artists lived in near poverty and only survived because of generous patronage.

And who will be the modern equivalent of a patron? A young adult's parent? Parents who have adult children pursuing the arts are faced with interesting judgment calls. Is my child really talented and is his or her pursuit of an artistic career a truly disciplined dedicated effort or is it a way of evading work and responsibility? It is hard to tell. In the meantime young adults leading Bohemian, alternate life-styles do not have job security, long-term benefits, or even immediate protection against hospitalization or illness. As one parent said ruefully, "I never thought I would become so fixated on health insurance and job benefits."

Parents can find themselves paying for their struggling adult children's health insurance. Should they? Is this really their problem? Alas, yes—it can be. Affluent parents know that if their son or daughter faced a medical emergency they would not be able to stand by and see their child denied adequate treatment; they would end up footing the bill. So in a way, it is a parental problem, and parents end up paying for health insurance in self-defense. But it can be depressing to confront an adult child's inability to earn money, and/or their lack of foresight or insight into economic realities.

The old parable of the ant and the grasshopper becomes relevant. Middle-class young adults who choose an alternative life-style with shaky economic security often can aspire to such paths because of their parents' conformity and success in the system. The prudent toiling ant has made the life of the grasshopper possible; but mindful of what happens to grasshoppers in the winter, should the ant continue to pay? How long should well-to-do, hard-working parents subsidize their young adult child's aspirations for creative work?

Much depends upon how hard the young adult works at his or her craft, and how probable are the chances for success. Outside assessment by persons in the field may be one way to know whether a young adult has talent or a real chance. In some fields like acting and music, the odds are stacked against anyone's being able to make it. Waiting for the big break may become futile. The more prudent life course is to find a backup way to make a living, in alternate scenarios such as teaching.

Many parents have found it necessary to cut the purse strings and end their role as patrons of unsuccessful artistic careers or other idealistic ventures. They make the justifiable demand that their adult child find work that may not be as artistically fulfilling, but can provide an adequate living in the long run. Honest work serves the good purpose of provisioning one's self and others, even if it is boring. The dignity of work, which is not illegal or destructive, comes from the human person who works to meet human needs.

At some point parental economic support given in the cause of finding the perfect career can become a handicapping prop for prolonging behavior that is immature and maladaptive. It is an old and painful pattern to see self-made parents who labored and struggled for their success, weaken their children by overprotecting and overindulging them. The fair-haired and thoroughly cosseted young prince or princess can become a failed adult who cannot move from entitlement to giving to others. If there are dependents or children involved, the duty to work is increased. To choose to make an artistic statement and sacrifice material goods for one's self is one thing, to deprive one's family of necessities is reprehensible.

# Barbara Dafoe Whitehead, "Lost in Work"

It's little wonder that *E.R.* has become America's favorite television show. An emergency room is the perfect metaphor for today's culture of work: a 24-hour work day; a workplace loaded with dazzling technology; a buzz induced by adrenaline and fueled by caffeine; and an overwhelming sense of urgency and importance. For the medical team in the E.R., no other domain offers comparable attractions.

For a growing number of Americans, work is gobbling up not only our time but also our loyalties. Especially for the most well-educated and successfully employed Americans, work identities are overtaking other identities. Work itself is crowding out other life pursuits. Partly because of the personal and portable technologies, partly because of our acquiescence to its claims, work has become an imperial presence—setting up outposts everywhere.

*Take family life:* The technology that makes it possible for parents to work ⓵ at home also turns home into a 24-hour workplace. Just when it's time to put the kids to bed, the fax spurts an urgent communication, the pager beeps, the e-mail dings. Along with home as workplace, we are getting workplace as home. Businesses now offer emergency childcare so their employees can work overtime or on weekends; others provide temporary childcare for children who are sick or on school vacations. I know a mother whose boss so valued her services that when she threatened to quit to spend more time with her children, he offered to provide a chauffeured limousine to take her kids to Little League and music lessons. Most employees, as well as advocates for family-friendly workplaces, find these efforts praiseworthy, and they do accomplish the goal of making parents more reliable employees. But we should not be fooled about what is going on here. The workplace is bidding for and acquiring ⓶ time once pledged to children, and children have no way to make a reasonable counteroffer.

*Take neighborhood and community life:* Membership in community organi- ⓷ zations is declining. Some people attribute this trend to increases in women's workforce participation and this is a factor. However, there has also been a 25 percent drop in men's participation in community groups over roughly the past decade. One reason to suspect that work plays a role in the disengagement from civic life is that membership in professional associations has not suffered a similar decline but in fact has been rising. (I suspect the same might be said for memberships in private health clubs.)

*Take vacations:* The "getting-away-from-it-all" vacation is disappearing as more Americans tote lap-tops, cellular phones, and portable faxes to the

cottage and the beach. Not only is this practice spreading from senior execu-
tives to mid- and lower-level managers, but it is establishing a new work norm:
never leave the office.

*Take Sundays:* Sunday has become another work day. Once dedicated to
churchgoing and late sleeping, Sunday mornings are increasingly devoted to
work or work disguised as leisure. According to a recent biography, Senator
Robert Dole watches political talk shows on Sunday morning while he rides an
exercycle. He goes to church only when his wife drags him there. In Massachusetts, businesses are challenging the blue laws on the grounds that opening
stores on Sunday mornings is friendly to families, providing jobs and expanded
hours for grocery shopping. Similarly, work is taking over Sunday evenings.
According to one unscientific study, home technologies begin to hum on Sundays around four P.M. People start calling on Sunday night to set up the next
day's meetings, assignments, appointments.

*Take marriage:* According to divorce researcher Judith Wallerstein, the institution of marriage and the institution of work may be on a collision course.
In particular, the marriages of two-career couples who have children are
"frighteningly fragile." The demands and pressures of building a career, often
coinciding with the peak childrearing years, can introduce tension and conflict
between spouses, particularly when the strain of holding it all together seems
to fall on one parent more than the other.

*Take last but certainly not least, love and sex:* Our intimate lives are increasingly described not in the language of love and romance, but in the language
of work. We are encouraged to "work" on our relationships, to develop new
"skills" in our love lives, to use computerized technologies to locate potential
partners, even to engage in sex as a form of aerobic exercise. (Moderate inten-
sity sex, says one woman's magazine, can burn off 40 calories an hour.) Too,
there is the exhaustion factor. One working mother confesses: I don't crave sex.
I crave sleep.

If pursuit of our work lives has crowded out pursuit of our lives as husbands and wives, mothers and fathers, neighbors, friends, and citizens, does it
matter? It may matter a lot. To begin, it makes for a more atomized and disconnected society, where workers jostle and contend in the marketplace, leaving empty chairs at the PTA meetings and volunteer fire departments and
church suppers. The result is a weakened and impoverished civil society, a reduced sense of social trust and responsibility, and a decline in the nation's social capital.

The incursions of work into family and community life may prove especially detrimental to children. Children are the last American provincials,
bound to a particular family and local geography, dependent on the richness
and resources of a social world created by adults. That social world is growing

more meager and fragile as the work world claims the loyalties and investments of the grownups.

From time to time, I read an obituary that describes the recently deceased not as an executive for a pharmaceutical firm or a successful lobbyist, but as a church member or a Red Cross volunteer. Yet it is increasingly difficult to imagine a successful life in these terms—because we cannot imagine ourselves defined by anything but our work.

# IID. Historical Transformations

1. Michael Novak, pp. 119–25 of *Business as a Calling: Work and the Examined Life* (New York: Free Press, 1996). Michael Novak (1933–) is a contemporary American intellectual who writes on religious, political, and economic topics.

2. Peter F. Drucker, selections from pp. 53–72 of "The Age of Social Transformation," *Atlantic Monthly* (November 1994). Peter Drucker (1909–) is well known as the leading modern theorist of both the theory and technique of management.

3. Michael Novak, pp. 177–82 of *Business as a Calling: Work and the Examined Life* (New York: Free Press, 1996).

4. Richard Sennett, selections from pp. 15–27 of *The Corrosion of Character: The Personal Consequences of Work in the New Capitalism* (New York: W. W. Norton, 1998). Richard Sennett (1943–), a sociologist and social critic, explores changes in the meaning of work over the last quarter century.

5. Alasdair MacIntyre, selections from pp. 84–102 of *After Virtue: A Study in Moral Theory* (Notre Dame, Ind.: University of Notre Dame Press, 1981). *After Virtue* by MacIntyre (1929–) has been one of the most influential works of philosophy written in the last decades of the twentieth century.

6. John P. Robinson and Geoffrey Godbey, "Are Average Americans Really Overworked?" *American Enterprise* 6 (September/October 1995), p. 43.

# Michael Novak, *Business as a Calling*

## The Virtue of Creativity

> The ultimate resource in economic development is people. It is people,
> not capital or raw materials, that develop an economy. The greatest need
> in the underdeveloped countries is people who can do the new orga-
> nizing job, the job of building an effective organization of skilled and
> trained people exercising judgment and making responsible decisions.
> ———Peter F. Drucker

Most of us first learned to think about the ethic of capitalism from Max
Weber's *The Protestant Ethic and the Spirit of Capitalism* (1904). It was Weber's
great achievement to bring to consciousness the fact that cultural forces are
essential to the definition of capitalism; capitalism is not a system solely about
things but about the human spirit. Nonetheless, there is some question whether
Max Weber actually caught the spirit of capitalism in his sights. I think he
scored a near-miss. He thought the essence of capitalism is calculation, a
strictly cost-conscious analysis of means in relation to ends. He saw in it the
growth of bureaucracy, like a rushing locomotive that would confine human
spontaneity to "iron rails." He seemed to have in mind the huge industrial en-
terprises of the turn of the century, and he expressed some dread of the ad-
vancing locomotive.

In all this, he missed something much closer to the heart of the matter:
discovery, invention, serendipity, surprise—what my colleague Rocco But-
tiglione of the International Academy of Philosophy in Lichtenstein (and now
chairman of Italy's new party, Christian Democrats United) calls the "Don
Quixote" factor.

At the very heart of capitalism, as Friedrich Hayek, Joseph Schumpeter,
and the American Israel Kirzner have shown, is the creative habit of enterprise.
Enterprise is, in its first moment, the inclination to notice, the habit of discern-
ing, the tendency to discover what other people don't yet see. It is also the capacity to act on insight, so as to bring into reality things not before seen. It is
the ability to foresee both the needs of others and the combinations of productive factors most adapted to satisfying those needs. This habit of intellect
constitutes an important source of wealth in modern society. Organizing such
a productive effort, planning its duration in time, making sure that it corresponds in a positive way to the demands it must satisfy, and taking the necessary risks: all this has been a source of new wealth in the past 200 years. In

this way, the role of initiative and entrepreneurial ability have become increasingly decisive.

Many critics seem never to have imagined the sheer fun and creative pleasure involved in bringing a new business to birth. Such creativity has the stamp of a distinctive personality all over it. In the pleasure it affords its creator, it rivals, in its way, artistic creativity.

To verify this, visit a business in the presence of its builder. It is quite possible that no actress was ever so pleased with her standing-ovation performance as an entrepreneur is with what she has built. Note, too, that a rapidly increasing proportion of entrepreneurs worldwide is female; enterprise is a vocation made to order for newcomers into markets.

In precapitalist centuries, the chief form of wealth was land. For thousands of years, the natural fruitfulness of the earth was the primary factor of wealth; work and invention were bent to the increase of this fruitfulness. Under capitalism, the newcomer among economic systems, enterprise turned work in new directions. Enterprise itself—invention and discovery and new ideas—became the most dynamic source of wealth the world had ever known.

In brief, the new system linked work more and more with knowledge. *And this is the crucial switch.* This is the point missed by some (like Marx) who hold to the labor theory of value. It is not so much labor, in the sense of physical labor, that adds value, but working *smart*—adding enterprise and invention to everything one does. Work becomes ever more fruitful and productive to the extent that people become more knowledgeable of the productive potentialities of the earth and more profoundly cognizant of the needs of those for whom their work is done. The cause of wealth is knowledge. This cause lies in the human mind.

"What is the cause of the wealth of nations?" This is the question that Adam Smith was the first to raise in 1776; Pope Leo XIII alluded to it in *Rerum Novarum* in 1891. Pope John Paul II, a hundred years later, had his own crisp reply:

> In our time, in particular there exists another form of ownership which is becoming no less important than land: *the possession of know-how, technology and skill.* The wealth of the industrialized nations is based much more on this kind of ownership than on natural resources.

The chief cause of wealth is intellectual capital. Since the wealth of nations is based much more on intellectual property and know-how than on natural resources, some nations that are very wealthy in natural resources (such as Brazil) may remain poor, while other nations that have virtually no natural resources (like Japan) can become among the richest in the world.

Whereas at one time the decisive factor of production was the land and later capital—understood (in Marx's sense) as ownership of the means of production—today the decisive factor is increasingly human knowledge, especially scientific knowledge. Yet enterprise depends also on a capacity for interrelated and compact organization, and on an ability to perceive the needs of others and to satisfy them. These are exactly the factors in which Japan is preeminent: scientific knowledge, a capacity for organization, and ability to perceive the needs of others and to satisfy them. Through these factors, the Japanese, whose country is extremely poor in natural resources, have made themselves economically preeminent among the nations.

Of course, natural resources are still important. But if human beings do not see their value and figure out ways to bring them into universal use, natural resources may lie fallow, forever undiscovered and unused. Oil lay beneath the sands of Arabia for thousands of years, unused, regarded as a nuisance, until human beings developed the piston engine and learned how to convert crude oil into gasoline. It is human beings who made useless crude into a "natural resource."

For this reason, inanimate things are not the deepest, best, or most inexhaustible resources. The human mind is, as Julian Simon puts it, the "ultimate resource." It is not the things of earth that set limits to the wealth of the world. On this question over twenty years ago the Club of Rome, drastically exaggerating the scarcity of material resources, made an elementary mistake. Many of the things of this earth are useful at some times and not at other times—whale oil is a good example—depending on the value the human mind sees in them. In this sense, the mind of human beings is the primary source of wealth. And no wonder: it participates from afar in the source of all knowledge, the Creator. Sharing in God's creativity, so to speak, the principal resource of humans is their own inventiveness. Their intelligence enables them to discover the earth's productive potential, but also the many different ways in which human needs can be satisfied.

Pope John Paul II sees three ways in which human knowledge is a source of wealth. First is the *ability to foresee* both the needs of others and the combinations of productive factors most adapted to satisfying those needs. Second, many goods cannot be adequately produced through the work of an isolated individual; they require the cooperation of many people working toward a common goal. Thus, a second kind of knowledge entails *knowing how to organize the large-scale community* necessary to produce even so simple an object as a pencil.

It does not ordinarily occur to theologians, but it is a matter of everyday experience to businesspeople, that even so simple an object as a pencil is made up of elements of graphite, wood, metal, rubber, and lacquer (to mention only the most visible, and to leave aside others that only specialists know about), which come from vastly separated parts of this earth. The knowledge and skills needed to prepare each one of these separate elements for the precise role they will play in the pencil represent a huge body of scientific and practical knowledge, which is almost certainly not present in the mind of any one individual. On the contrary, it is widely dispersed among researchers, managers, and workers in factories and workplaces in different parts of the world. All of these factors of production—materials, knowledge, and skilled workers—must be brought together before anyone holds a pencil.

So far, we have seen two kinds of knowledge at work in human economic creativity: accurate insight into the needs of others and practical knowledge concerning how to organize a worldwide productive effort. But there is also a third kind: the *painstaking effort to discover the earth's productive potential.* Consider briefly several discoveries whose diffusion has done so much to change the world since 1980: the invention of fiber optics, which in so many places are replacing copper (and thus contributing to the difficulties of Chile's copper industry); the invention of the word processor and electronic processes in general (which are doing so much to shift the basis of industry from mechanical to electronic technologies); the use of satellites and electronic impulses to link the entire world in a single, instantaneous communications network; and many medical breakthroughs, including genetic medicine. Such breathtaking discoveries are the fruit of the principal human resource: creative intelligence.

It is no accident that a capitalist economy grew up first in the part of the world deeply influenced by Judaism and Christianity. Millions of people over many centuries learned from Judaism and Christianity not to regard the earth as a realm merely to accept, never to investigate or experiment with; but, rather, as a place in which to exercise human powers of inquiry, creativity, and invention.

The philosopher Alfred North Whitehead once remarked that the rise of modern science was inconceivable apart from the habits human beings learned during long centuries of tutelage under Judaism and Christianity. Judaism and Christianity taught humans that the whole world and everything in it are intelligible, because all things—even contingent and seemingly accidental events—spring from the mind of an all-knowing Creator. This teaching had great consequences in the practical order.

Man the discoverer is made in the image of God. To be creative, to cooperate in bringing creation itself to its perfection is an important element of the human vocation. This belief that each human being is *imago Dei*—made in the image of God—was bound to lead, in an evolutionary and experimental way, to the development of an economic system whose first premise is that the principal cause of wealth is human creativity.

# Peter F. Drucker, "The Age of Social Transformation"

No century in recorded history has experienced so many social transformations and such radical ones as the twentieth century. They, I submit, may turn out to be the most significant events of this, our century, and its lasting legacy. In the developed free-market countries—which contain less than a fifth of the earth's population but are a model for the rest—work and work force, society and polity, are all, in the last decade of this century, *qualitatively* and *quantitatively* different not only from what they were in the first years of this century but also from what has existed at any other time in history: in their configurations, in their processes, in their problems, and in their structures. . . .

## The Social Structure Transformed

Before the First World War, farmers composed the largest single group in every country. They no longer made up the population everywhere, as they had from the dawn of history to the end of the Napoleonic Wars, a hundred years earlier. But farmers still made up a near-majority in every developed country except England and Belgium—in Germany, France, Japan, the United States—and, of course, in all underdeveloped countries, too. On the eve of the First World War it was considered a self-evident axiom that developed countries—the United States and Canada being the only exceptions—would increasingly have to rely on food imports from nonindustrial, nondeveloped areas.

Today only Japan among major developed free-market countries is a heavy importer of food. (It is one unnecessarily, for its weakness as a food producer is largely the result of an obsolete rice-subsidy policy that prevents the country from developing a modern, productive agriculture.) And in all developed free-market countries, including Japan, farmers today are at most five percent of the population and work force—that is, one tenth of the proportion of eighty years ago. Actually productive farmers make up less than half of the total farm population, or no more than two percent of the work force. And these agricultural producers are not "farmers" in most senses of the word: they are "agribusiness," which is arguably the most capital-intensive, most technology-intensive, and most information-intensive industry around. Traditional farmers are close to extinction even in Japan. And those that remain have become a protected species kept alive only by enormous subsidies.

The second-largest group in the population and work force of every developed country around 1900 was composed of live-in servants. They were considered as much a law of nature as farmers were. Census categories of the time defined a "lower middle class" household as one that employed fewer than three servants, and as a percentage of the work force domestics grew steadily up to the First World War. Eighty years later live-in domestic servants scarcely exist in developed countries. Few people born since the Second World War— that is, few people under fifty—have even seen any except on the stage or in old movies.

In the developed society of 2000 farmers are little but objects of nostalgia, and domestic servants are not even that.

Yet these enormous transformations in all developed free market countries were accomplished without civil war and, in fact, in almost total silence. Only now that their farm population has shrunk to near zero do the totally urban French loudly assert that theirs should be a "rural country" with a "rural civilization."

### The Rise and Fall of the Blue-Collar Worker

One reason why the transformations caused so little stir (indeed, the main reason) was that by 1900 a new class, the blue-collar worker in manufacturing industry—Marx's "proletarian"—had become socially dominant. Farmers were loudly adjured to "raise less corn and more hell," but they paid little attention. Domestic servants were clearly the most exploited class around. But when people before the First World War talked or wrote about the "social question," they meant blue-collar industrial workers. Blue-collar industrial workers were still a fairly small minority of the population and work force—right up to 1914 they made up an eighth or a sixth of the total at most—and were still vastly outnumbered by the traditional lower classes of farmers and domestic servants. But early-twentieth-century society was obsessed with blue-collar workers, fixated on them, bewitched by them. . . .

No class in history has ever risen faster than the blue-collar worker. And no class in history has ever fallen faster.

In 1883, the year of Marx's death, "proletarians" were still a minority not just of the population but also of industrial workers. The majority in industry were then skilled workers employed in small craft shops, each containing twenty or thirty workers at most. Of the anti-heroes of the nineteenth century's best "proletarian" novel, *The Princess Casamassima,* by Henry James— published in 1886 (and surely only Henry James could have given such a title to a story of working-class terrorists!)—one is a highly skilled bookbinder, the other an equally skilled pharmacist. By 1900 "industrial worker" had become synonymous with "machine operator" and implied employment in a factory along with hundreds if not thousands of people. These factory workers were indeed Marx's proletarians—without social position, without political power, without economic or purchasing power.

The workers of 1900—and even of 1913—received no pensions, no paid vacation, no overtime pay, no extra pay for Sunday or night work, no health or old-age insurance (except in Germany), no unemployment compensation (except, after 1911, in Britain); they had no job security whatever. Fifty years later, in the 1950s, industrial workers had become the largest single group in every developed country, and unionized industrial workers in mass-production industry (which was then dominant everywhere) had attained upper-middle-class income levels. They had extensive job security, pensions, long paid vacations, and comprehensive unemployment insurance or "lifetime employment." Above all, they had achieved political power. In Britain the labor unions were considered to be the "real government," with greater power than the Prime Minister and Parliament, and much the same was true elsewhere. In the United States, too—as in Germany, France, and Italy—the labor unions had emerged as the country's most powerful and best organized *political* force. And in Japan they had come close, in the Toyota and Nissan strikes of the late forties and early fifties, to overturning the system and taking power themselves.

Thirty-five years later, in 1990, industrial workers and their unions were in retreat. They had become marginal in numbers. Whereas industrial workers who make or move things had accounted for two fifths of the American work force in the 1950s, they accounted for less than one fifth in the early 1990s—that is, for no more than they had accounted for in 1900, when their meteoric rise began. In the other developed free-market countries the decline was slower at first, but after 1980 it began to accelerate everywhere. By the year 2000 or 2010, in every developed free-market country, industrial workers will account for no more than an eighth of the work force. Union power has been declining just as fast.

Unlike domestic servants, industrial workers will not disappear—any more than agricultural producers have disappeared or will disappear. But just as the traditional small farmer has become a recipient of subsidies rather than a producer, so will the traditional industrial worker become an auxiliary employee. His place is already being taken by the "technologist"—someone who works both with hands and with theoretical knowledge. (Examples are computer technicians, x-ray technicians, physical therapists, medical-lab technicians, pulmonary technicians, and so on, who together have made up the fastest-growing group in the U.S. labor force since 1980.) And instead of a class—a coherent, recognizable, defined, and self-conscious group—industrial workers may soon be just another "pressure group." . . .

Contrary to Marxist and syndicalist predictions, the rise of the industrial worker did not destabilize society. Instead it has emerged as the century's most stabilizing social development. It explains why the disappearance of the farmer and the domestic servant produced no social crises. Both the flight from the land and the flight from domestic service were voluntary. Farmers and maids were not "pushed off" or "displaced." They went into industrial employment as fast as they could. Industrial jobs required no skills they did not already possess, and no additional knowledge. In fact, farmers on the whole had a good deal more skill than was required to be a machine operator in a mass-production plant—and so did many domestic servants. To be sure, industrial work paid poorly until the First World War. But it paid better than farming or household work. Industrial workers in the United States until 1913—and in some countries, including Japan until the Second World War—worked long hours. But they worked shorter hours than farmers and domestic servants. What's more, they worked *specified* hours: the rest of the day was their own, which was true neither of work on the farm nor of domestic work.

The history books record the squalor of early industry, the poverty of the industrial workers, and their exploitation. Workers did indeed live in squalor and poverty, and they were exploited. But they lived better than those on a farm or in a household and were generally treated better. . . .

For farmers and domestic servants, industrial work was an opportunity. It was, in fact, the first opportunity that social history had given them to better themselves substantially without having to emigrate. In the developed free-market countries over the past 100 or 150 years every generation has been able to expect to do substantially better than the generation preceding it. The main reason has been that farmers and domestic servants could and did become industrial workers. . . .

### The Rise of the Knowledge Worker

The rise of the class succeeding industrial workers is not an opportunity for industrial workers. It is a challenge. The newly emerging dominant group is "knowledge workers." . . . By the end of this century knowledge workers will make up a third or more of the work force in the United States—as large a proportion as manufacturing workers ever made up, except in wartime. The majority of them will be paid at least as well as, or better than, manufacturing workers ever were. And the new jobs offer much greater opportunities.

But—and this is a big but—the great majority of the new jobs require qualifications the industrial worker does not possess and is poorly equipped to acquire. They require a good deal of formal education and the ability to acquire and to apply theoretical and analytical knowledge. They require a different approach to work and a different mind-set. Above all, they require a habit of continuous learning. Displaced industrial workers thus cannot simply move into knowledge work or services the way displaced farmers and domestic workers moved into industrial work. At the very least they have to change their basic attitudes, values, and beliefs. . . .

In the United States the shift had by 1990 or so largely been accomplished. But so far it has occurred only in the United States. In the other developed free-market countries, in western and northern Europe and in Japan, it is just beginning in the 1990s. It is, however, certain to proceed rapidly in these countries from now on, perhaps faster than it originally did in the United States. The fall of the industrial worker in the developed free-market countries will also have a major impact outside the developed world. Developing countries can no longer expect to base their development on their comparative labor advantage—that is, on cheap industrial labor. . . .

But for the developed countries, too, the shift to knowledge-based work poses enormous social challenges. Despite the factory, industrial society was still essentially a traditional society in its basic social relationships of production. But the emerging society, the one based on knowledge and knowledge workers, is not. It is the first society in which ordinary people—and that means most people—do not earn their daily bread by the sweat of their brow. It is the first society in which "honest work," does not mean a callused hand. It is also the first society in which not everybody does the same work, as was the case when the huge majority were farmers or, as seemed likely only forty or thirty years ago, were going to be machine operators.

This is far more than a social change. It is a change in the human condition. What it means—what are the values, the commitments, the problems, of the new society—we do not know. But we do know that much will be different.

### The Emerging Knowledge Society

Knowledge workers will not be the majority in the knowledge society, but in many if not most developed societies they will be the largest single population and work-force group. And even where outnumbered by other groups, knowledge workers will give the emerging knowledge society its character, its leadership, its social profile. They may not be the ruling class of the knowledge society, but they are already its leading class. And in their characteristics, social position, values, and expectations, they differ fundamentally from any group in history that has ever occupied the leading position.

In the first place, knowledge workers gain access to jobs and social position through formal education. A great deal of knowledge work requires highly developed manual skill and involves substantial work with one's hands. An extreme example is neurosurgery. The neurosurgeon's performance capacity rests on formal education and theoretical knowledge. An absence of manual skill disqualifies one for work as a neurosurgeon. But manual skill alone, no matter how advanced, will never enable anyone to be a neurosurgeon. The education that is required for neurosurgery and other kinds of knowledge work can be acquired only through formal schooling. It cannot be acquired through apprenticeship.

Knowledge work varies tremendously in the amount and kind of formal knowledge required. Some jobs have fairly low requirements, and others require the kind of knowledge the neurosurgeon possesses. But even if the knowledge itself is quite primitive, only formal education can provide it.

Education will become the center of the knowledge society, and the school its key institution. What knowledge must everybody have? What is "quality" in learning and teaching? These will of necessity become central concerns of the knowledge society, and central political issues. In fact, the acquisition and distribution of formal knowledge may come to occupy the place in the politics of the knowledge society which the acquisition and distribution of property and income have occupied in our politics over the two or three centuries that we have come to call the Age of Capitalism.

In the knowledge society, clearly, more and more knowledge, and especially advanced knowledge, will be acquired well past the age of formal schooling and increasingly, perhaps, through educational processes that do not center on the traditional school. But at the same time, the performance of the schools and the basic values of the schools will be of increasing concern to society as a whole, rather than being considered professional matters that can safely be left to "educators."

We can also predict with confidence that we will redefine what it means to be an educated person. Traditionally, and especially during the past 300 years (perhaps since 1700 or so, at least in the West, and since about that time in Japan as well), an educated person was somebody who had a prescribed stock of formal knowledge. The Germans called this knowledge *allgemeine Bildung,* and the English (and, following them, the nineteenth-century Americans) called it the liberal arts. Increasingly, an educated person will be somebody who has learned how to learn, and who continues learning, especially by formal education, throughout his or her lifetime. . . .

A society in which knowledge workers dominate is under threat from a new class conflict: between the large minority of knowledge workers and the majority of people, who will make their living traditionally, either by manual work, whether skilled or unskilled, or by work in services, whether skilled or unskilled. The productivity of knowledge work—still abysmally low—will become the economic challenge of the knowledge society. On it will depend the competitive position of every single country, every single industry, every single institution within society. The productivity of the non-knowledge, services worker will become the social challenge of the knowledge society. On it will depend the ability of the knowledge society to give decent incomes. and with them dignity and status, to non-knowledge workers.

No society in history has faced these challenges. But equally new are the opportunities of the knowledge society. In the knowledge society, for the first time in history, the possibility of leadership will be open to all. Also, the possibility of acquiring knowledge will no longer depend on obtaining a prescribed education at a given age. Learning will become the tool of the individual—available to him or her at any age—if only because so much skill and knowledge can be acquired by means of the new learning technologies.

Another implication is that how well an individual, an organization, an industry, a country, does in acquiring and applying knowledge will become the key competitive factor. The knowledge society will inevitably become far more competitive than any society we have yet known—for the simple reason that with knowledge being universally accessible, there will be no excuses for non-performance. There will be no "poor" countries. There will only be ignorant countries. And the same will be true for companies, industries, and organizations of all kinds. It will be true for individuals, too. In fact, developed societies have already become infinitely more competitive for individuals than were the societies of the beginning of this century, let alone earlier ones.

I have been speaking of knowledge. But a more accurate term is "knowledges," because the knowledge of the knowledge society will be fundamentally different from what was considered knowledge in earlier societies—and, in fact, from what is still widely considered knowledge. The knowledge of the German *allgemeine Bildung* or of the Anglo-American liberal arts had little to do with one's life's work. It focused on the person and the person's development, rather than on any application—if, indeed, it did not, like the nineteenth-century liberal arts, pride itself on having no utility whatever. In the knowledge society knowledge for the most part exists only in application. Nothing the x-ray technician needs to know can be applied to market research, for instance, or to teaching medieval history. The central work force in the knowledge society will therefore consist of highly specialized people. In fact, it is a mistake to speak of "generalists." What we will increasingly mean by that term is people who have learned how to acquire additional specialties rapidly in order to move from one kind of job to another—for example, from market research into management, or from nursing into hospital administration. But "generalists" in the sense in which we used to talk of them are coming to be seen as dilettantes rather than educated people. . . .

## How Knowledge Works

18      That knowledge in the knowledge society has to be highly specialized to be productive implies two new requirements: that knowledge workers work in teams, and that if knowledge workers are not employees, they must at least be affiliated with an organization.

19      There is a great deal of talk these days about "teams" and "teamwork." Most of it starts out with the wrong assumption—namely, that we have never before worked in teams. Actually people have always worked in teams; very few people ever could work effectively by themselves. The farmer had to have a wife, and the farm wife had to have a husband. The two worked as a team. And both worked as a team with their employees, the hired hands. The craftsman also had to have a wife, with whom he worked as a team—he took care of the craft work, and she took care of the customers, the apprentices, and the business altogether. And both worked as a team with journeymen and apprentices. Much discussion today assumes that there is only one kind of team. Actually there are quite a few. But until now the emphasis has been on the individual worker and not on the team. With knowledge work growing increasingly effective as it is increasingly specialized, teams become the work unit rather than the individual himself.

20

The team that is being touted now—I call it the "jazz combo" team—is only one kind of team. It is actually the most difficult kind of team both to assemble and to make work effectively, and the kind that requires the longest time to gain performance capacity. We will have to learn to use different kinds of teams for different purposes. We will have to learn to understand teams—and this is something to which, so far, very little attention has been paid. The understanding of teams, the performance capacities of different kinds of teams, their strengths and limitations, and the tradeoffs between various kinds of teams will thus become central concerns in the management of people.

21      Equally important is the second implication of the fact that knowledge workers are of necessity specialists: the need for them to work as members of an organization. Only the organization can provide the basic continuity that knowledge workers need in order to be effective. Only the organization can convert the specialized knowledge of the knowledge worker into performance.

By itself, specialized knowledge does not yield performance. The surgeon is not effective unless there is a diagnosis—which, by and large, is not the surgeon's task and not even within the surgeon's competence. As a loner in his or her research and writing, the historian can be very effective. But to educate students, a great many other specialists have to contribute—people whose specialty may be literature, or mathematics, or other areas of history. And this requires that the specialist have access to an organization.

This access may be as a consultant, or it may be as a provider of specialized services. But for the majority of knowledge workers it will be as employees, full-time or part-time, of an organization, such as a government agency, a hospital, a university, a business, or a labor union. In the knowledge society it is not the individual who performs. The individual is a cost center rather than a performance center. It is the organization that performs.

### What Is an Employee?

Most knowledge workers will spend most if not all of their working lives as "employees." But the meaning of the term will be different from what it has been traditionally—and not only in English but in German, Spanish, and Japanese as well.

Individually, knowledge workers are dependent on the job. They receive a wage or salary. They have been hired and can be fired. Legally each is an employee. But collectively they are the capitalists; increasingly, through their pension funds and other savings, the employees own the means of production. In traditional economics—and by no means only in Marxist economics—there is a sharp distinction between the "wage fund," all of which goes into consumption, and the "capital fund," or that part of the total income stream that is available for investment. And most social theory of industrial society is based, one way or another, on the relationship between the two, whether in conflict or in necessary and beneficial cooperation and balance. In the knowledge society the two merge. The pension fund is "deferred wages," and as such is a wage fund. But it is also increasingly the main source of capital for the knowledge society.

22    Perhaps more important, in the knowledge society the employees—that is, knowledge workers—own the tools of production. Marx's great insight was that the factory worker does not and cannot own the tools of production, and therefore is "alienated." There was no way, Marx pointed out, for the worker to own the steam engine and to be able to take it with him when moving from one job to another. The capitalist had to own the steam engine and to control it. Increasingly, the true investment in the knowledge society is not in machines and tools but in the knowledge of the knowledge worker. Without that knowledge the machines, no matter how advanced and sophisticated, are unproductive.

*Link this w/ Job hopping*

The market researcher needs a computer. But increasingly this is the researcher's own personal computer, and it goes along wherever he or she goes. The true "capital equipment" of market research is the knowledge of markets, of statistics, and of the application of market research to business strategy, which is lodged between the researcher's ears and is his or her exclusive and inalienable property. The surgeon needs the operating room of the hospital and all its expensive capital equipment. But the surgeon's true capital invest-ment is twelve or fifteen years of training and the resulting knowledge, which the surgeon takes from one hospital to the next. Without that knowledge the hospital's expensive operating rooms are so much waste and scrap. . . .

### Management in the Knowledge Society

One additional conclusion: Because the knowledge society perforce has to be a society of organizations, its central and distinctive organ is management.

When our society began to talk of management, the term meant "business management"—because large-scale business was the first of the new organiza-tions to become visible. But we have learned in this past half century that man-agement is the distinctive organ of all organizations. All of them require man-agement, whether they use the term or not. All managers do the same things, whatever the purpose of their organization. All of them have to bring people— each possessing different knowledge—together for joint performance. All of them have to make human strengths productive in performance and human weaknesses irrelevant. All of them have to think through what results are wanted in the organization—and have then to define objectives. All of them are responsible for thinking through what I call the theory of the business— that is, the assumptions on which the organization bases its performance and actions, and the assumptions that the organization has made in deciding what not to do. All of them must think through strategies—that is, the means through which the goals of the organization become performance. All of them have to define the values of the organization, its system of rewards and pun-ishments, its spirit and its culture. In all organizations managers need both the knowledge of management as work and discipline and the knowledge and understanding of the organization itself—its purposes, its values, its environ-ment and markets, its core competencies.

Management as a practice is very old. The most successful executive in all history was surely that Egyptian who, 4,500 years or more ago, first conceived the pyramid, without any precedent, designed it, and built it, and did so in an astonishingly short time. That first pyramid still stands. But as a discipline management is barely fifty years old. It was first dimly perceived around the time of the First World War. It did not emerge until the Second World War, and then did so primarily in the United States. Since then it has been the fastest-growing new function, and the study of it the fastest-growing new dis-cipline. No function in history has emerged as quickly as has management in the past fifty or sixty years, and surely none has had such worldwide sweep in such a short period.

Management is still taught in most business schools as a bundle of techniques, such as budgeting and personnel relations. To be sure, management, like any other work, has its own tools and its own techniques. But just as the essence of medicine is not urinalysis (important though that is), the essence of management is not techniques and procedures. The essence of management is to make knowledges productive. Management, in other words, is a social function. And in its practice management is truly a liberal art.

25

# Michael Novak, *Business as a Calling*

### The Bad Side of Downsizing

In the early chapters of this book we encountered at least two examples of the anguish caused to managers by the necessity of letting good people go in order to save the firm.

In communist societies, dissidents and other "misfits" were often punished by being removed from their jobs. Sometimes they were sent to prison, sometimes placed in menial employment. My good friend Pavel Bratinka of the Czech Republic, now deputy foreign minister, was a distinguished young physicist until he joined the dissident movement Charter 77. He was summarily deprived of his opportunities for research and teaching and sentenced to working as a stoker in the coal-burning heating units of a large building. The current cardinal archbishop of Prague was sentenced to working as a window washer.

Nonetheless, practically everybody in communist societies was put to work. Even if much of this work was senseless—simply to meet production quotas piling up steel beams that nobody wanted to buy outside the plant in Nowa Huta, Poland, where they rusted away; bringing in fish from the cold Bering Sea to rot in broken refrigeration units—today some remember those days with nostalgia: "We were all equal and everybody had a job."

In a far more intelligent way, based on the dynamism of markets and invention, the German social market economy goes to extraordinary lengths to protect workers, once hired, from being laid off. It also provides very high benefits and expensive social plans for any who are let go. In protecting the security of the workforce, the German system (imitated in other European nations) has given democracy a stable popular base. Having experienced devastating periods of insecurity during World War I, the skyrocketing inflation of the 1920s, the Great Depression, and then World War II and its at first bleak aftermath, Germans tend to value security higher than most other social goods. They also tend to favor equality over opportunity. They prefer a stable society in which the incomes of all are more or less equal to a society in which there are more risks but chances for greater rewards. Even when assured that the incomes of all would be higher in the opportunity society but more unequal, they prefer equality at lower levels.

One disadvantage from which the German system suffers is that employers fear hiring new workers because of the high and lasting costs to which each employment contract commits them. Those currently employed are privileged;

entry for others is difficult. Another disadvantage is that the German system sets many legal and financial hurdles before new entrepreneurs. The result is low rates of new business formation and high rates of unemployment.

A third disadvantage is that in the new international competition, German firms are more straitjacketed than their U.S. and Japanese counterparts. It is far harder for them to restructure themselves and redeploy their energies.

Fourth, as German women continue to have fewer children, the aging of the working population and the swelling ranks of the retired elderly are straining the finances of the welfare state. A similar situation in the United States is somewhat eased by the great influx of immigrants, most of whom become citizens. Since 1970, America has welcomed nearly 20 million legal immigrants (as well as many illegals). This immigration has increased the younger U.S. workforce by a number larger than the workforce of several medium-sized European nations put together.

Nonetheless, if it makes little sense for the United States to imitate German ways, we still need to improve the way in which assistance is offered to those laid off as a result of downsizing and restructuring. The situation of middle-aged and older workers is particularly affecting.

One important reform would be to vest health care plans in each worker, so that each plan will go wherever the individual goes. There is no reason, only historical accident, that companies should be the carriers of health care plans. In fact, much of the increase in workers' compensation packages in recent decades comes from increases in health care coverage—both to cover higher costs and to include new medical technologies. This is a major reason that the wages of many have grown only slowly; they are taking an ever larger proportion of their compensation in benefit packages, including enriched health care benefits. For example, the health care costs for all workers at General Motors in 1970 were $359 million, but by 1992 $3.7 billion. (In constant 1970 dollars, the jump was from $359 million to $1.03 billion.)

One reason for raising compensation by way of benefits rather than wages goes back to the wage and price controls introduced by the Nixon administration. Another is that benefits come to the worker tax free, and this fact appeals to workers. Receiving such benefits through the company, however, has had negative side effects: because workers are tied to the company as never before, to depart from the company means losing benefits. Lack of portability makes workers dependent.

High labor costs resulting from generous benefit packages also give companies an incentive to alter their approach to labor in unfortunate ways—by shedding many long-term jobs, for example. Large corporations began contracting out many services (security, maintenance and clean-up, food services, accounting, etc.) that were formerly supplied through the organization itself. Lack of stability in the labor force has badly affected morale, among white-collar workers as well as blue collar, and not least in middle management.

The tragedy of recent decades is that many senior workers, in higher as well as lower ranks, suffered a double disadvantage. First, their very jobs became vulnerable to cost-cutting and restructuring. Second, those whose jobs were terminated abruptly found themselves without basic benefits on which they and their families had come to rely, most notably health care protection and in many cases pension benefits.

To remedy this situation, another structural reform that has won considerable political support among both Democrats and Republicans is to make not only health care but also pensions portable. Instead of belonging to the company, such benefits would be owned by individual workers. Through programs such as TIAA-CREF, for example, most universities, colleges, and nonprofit organizations (such as museums, research institutes, and foundations) provide pension plans that insure a multitude of institutions while granting ownership in the benefits to each individual worker, and allowing each to choose (up to certain limits) certain options for themselves: how much additional money to save tax-free in their personal accounts; in which investment vehicle to invest it; and how they wish to receive the benefits when they become eligible for them. Such workers carry these benefits with them from job to job.

In general, individual retirement accounts (IRAs) heighten a sense of individual responsibility, independence, and mobility. Since such savings are tax-free, they also provide powerful incentives for lifetime investment.

Analogously, well short of the ill-fated "comprehensive" health care plan proposed by the Clinton administration, considerable consensus exists on *incremental* health care reforms, medical IRAs, for example.

*Forbes* magazine has pioneered an intermediate arrangement. While offering its employees a form of catastrophic medical insurance, insuring them against unexpectedly high medical costs, the company also offers a package covering ordinary medical claims but with a twist. The entire package of ordinary health care is worth $1,500 per year, but individuals are offered an incentive to keep actual costs lower. For every dollar in their personal medical account that they choose *not* to spend in that year, up to $500, *Forbes* will double that amount in a cash payment to that individual. In other words, for every dollar that individuals save (up to $500) of their own medical bills or simply do not withdraw from their individual annual account, they will be paid an equal amount in cash. This plan gives employees a financial incentive to keep a close watch on their out-of-pocket health expenses, to make their own medical decisions, and to keep group costs low. Each year since the plan was instituted in 1992, employees have received greater cash benefits, and medical costs to *Forbes* have fallen. Individual responsibility—and satisfaction—have been enhanced.

One of the disadvantages of the "creative destruction" inherent in a system based on invention, creativity, and new methods, in short, is the insecurity of employees. Creative thinking about how to diminish this insecurity is very much in order. The personal ownership of benefit packages, particularly for pension and health care benefits, and their portability from job to job, are two powerful steps in the right direction.

# Richard Sennett, *The Corrosion of Character*

Recently I met someone in an airport whom I hadn't seen for fifteen years. I had interviewed the father of Rico (as I shall call him) a quarter century ago when I wrote a book about blue-collar workers in America, *The Hidden Injuries of Class*. Enrico, his father, then worked as a janitor, and had high hopes for this boy, who was just entering adolescence, a bright kid good at sports. When I lost touch with his father a decade later, Rico had just finished college. In the airline lounge, Rico looked as if he had fulfilled his father's dreams. He carried a computer in a smart leather case, dressed in a suit I couldn't afford, and sported a signet ring with a crest.

Enrico had spent twenty years by the time we first met cleaning toilets and mopping floors in a downtown office building. He did so without complaining, but also without any hype about living out the American Dream. His work had one single and durable purpose, the service of his family. It had taken him fifteen years to save the money for a house, which he purchased in a suburb near Boston, cutting ties with his old Italian neighborhood because a house in the suburbs was better for the kids. Then his wife, Flavia, had gone to work, as a presser in a dry-cleaning plant; by the time I met Enrico in 1970, both parents were saving for the college education of their two sons.

What had most struck me about Enrico and his generation was how linear time was in their lives: year after year of working in jobs which seldom varied from day to day. And along that line of time, achievement was cumulative: Enrico and Flavia checked the increase in their savings every week, measured their domesticity by the various improvements and additions they had made to their ranch house. Finally, the time they lived was predictable. The upheavals of the Great Depression and World War II had faded, unions protected their jobs; though he was only forty when I first met him, Enrico knew precisely when he would retire and how much money he would have. . . .

He carved out a clear story for himself in which his experience accumulated materially and psychically; his life thus made sense to him as a linear narrative. Though a snob might dismiss Enrico as boring, he experienced the years as a dramatic story moving forward repair by repair, interest payment by interest payment. The janitor felt he became the author of his life, and though he was a man low on the social scale, this narrative provided him a sense of self-respect. . . .

Though Enrico felt he had achieved a measure of social honor, he hardly wanted his son Rico to repeat his own life. The American dream of upward mobility for the children powerfully drove my friend. "I don't understand a word he says," Enrico boasted to me several times when Rico had come home from school and was at work on math. I heard many other parents of sons and daughters like Rico say something like "I don't understand him" in harder tones, as though the kids had abandoned them. We all violate in some way the place assigned us in the family myth, but upward mobility gives that passage a peculiar twist. Rico and other youngsters headed up the social ladder sometimes betrayed shame about their parents' working-class accents and rough manners, but more often felt suffocated by the endless strategizing over pennies and the reckoning of time in tiny steps. These favored children wanted to embark on a less constrained journey.

Now, many years later, thanks to the encounter at the airport, I had the chance to see how it had turned out for Enrico's son. In the airport lounge, I must confess, I didn't much like what I saw. Rico's expensive suit could have been just business plumage, but the crested signet ring—a mark of elite family background—seemed both a lie and a betrayal of the father. However, circumstances threw Rico and me together on a long flight. He and I did not have one of those American journeys in which a stranger spills out his or her emotional guts to you, gathers more tangible baggage when the plane lands, and disappears forever. I took the seat next to Rico without being asked, and for the first hour of a long flight from New York to Vienna had to pry information out of him.

Rico, I learned, has fulfilled his father's desire for upward mobility, but has indeed rejected the way of his father. Rico scorns "time-servers" and others wrapped in the armor of bureaucracy; instead he believes in being open to change and in taking risks. And he has prospered; whereas Enrico had an income in the bottom quarter of the wage scale, Rico's has shot up to the top 5 percent. Yet this is not an entirely happy story for Rico.

After graduating from a local university in electrical engineering, Rico went to a business school in New York. There he married a fellow student, a young Protestant woman from a better family. School prepared the young couple to move and change jobs frequently, and they've done so. Since graduation, in fourteen years at work Rico has moved four times.

Rico began as a technology adviser to a venture capital firm on the West Coast, in the early, heady days of the developing computer industry in Silicon Valley; he then moved to Chicago, where he also did well. But the next move was for the sake of his wife's career. If Rico were an ambition-driven character out of the pages of Balzac, he would never have done it, for he gained no larger salary, and he left hotbeds of high-tech activity for a more retired, if leafy, office park in Missouri. Enrico felt somewhat ashamed when Flavia went to work; Rico sees Jeannette, his wife, as an equal working partner, and has adapted to her. It was at this point, when Jeannette's career took off, that their children began arriving.

In the Missouri office park, the uncertainties of the new economy caught up with the young man. While Jeannette was promoted, Rico was downsized—his firm was absorbed by another, larger firm that had its own analysts. So the couple made a fourth move, back East to a suburb outside New York. Jeannette now manages a big team of accountants, and he has started a small consulting firm.

Prosperous as they are, the very acme of an adaptable, mutually supportive couple, both husband and wife often fear they are on the edge of losing control over their lives. This fear is built into their work histories.

In Rico's case, the fear of lacking control is straightforward: it concerns managing time. When Rico told his peers he was going to start his own consulting firm, most approved; consulting seems the road to independence. But in getting started he found himself plunged into many menial tasks, like doing his own photocopying, which before he'd taken for granted. He found himself plunged into the sheer flux of networking; every call had to be answered, the slightest acquaintance pursued. To find work, he has fallen subservient to the schedules of people who are in no way obliged to respond to him. Like other consultants, he wants to work in accordance with contracts setting out just what the consultant will do. But these contracts, he says, are largely fictions. A consultant usually has to tack one way and another in response to the changing whims or thoughts of those who pay; Rico has no fixed role that allows him to say to others, "This is what I do, this is what I am responsible for." . . .

Rico told me that he and Jeannette have made friends mostly with the people they see at work, and have lost many of these friendships during the moves of the last twelve years, "though we stay 'netted.'" Rico looks to electronic communications for the sense of community which Enrico most enjoyed when he attended meetings of the janitors' union, but the son finds communications on-line short and hurried. "It's like with your kids—when you're not there, all you get is news later."

In each of his four moves, Rico's new neighbors have treated his advent as an arrival which closes past chapters of his life; they ask him about Silicon Valley or the Missouri office park, but, Rico says, "they don't *see* other places"; their imaginations are not engaged. This is a very American fear. The classic American suburb was a bedroom community; in the last generation a different kind of suburb has arisen, more economically independent of the urban core, but not really town or village either; a place springs into life with the wave of a developer's wand, flourishes, and begins to decay all within a generation. Such communities are not empty of sociability or neighborliness, but no one in them becomes a long-term witness to another person's life.

The fugitive quality of friendship and local community form the background to the most important of Rico's inner worries, his family. Like Enrico,

Rico views work as his service to the family; unlike Enrico, Rico finds that the demands of the job interfere with achieving the end. At first I thought he was talking about the all too familiar conflict between work time and time for family. "We get home at seven, do dinner, try to find an hour for the kids' homework, and then deal with our own paperwork." When things get tough for months at a time in his consulting firm, "it's like I don't know who my kids are." He worries about the frequent anarchy into which his family plunges, and about neglecting his children, whose needs can't be programmed to fit into the demands of his job. . . .

He therefore wants to set for his son and daughters an example of resolution and purpose, "but you can't just tell kids to be like that"; he has to set an example. The objective example he could set, his upward mobility, is something they take for granted, a history that belongs to a past not their own, a story which is over. But his deepest worry is that he cannot offer the substance of his work life as an example to his children of how they should conduct themselves ethically. The qualities of good work are not the qualities of good character.

As I came later to understand, the gravity of this fear comes from a gap separating Enrico and Rico's generations. Business leaders and journalists emphasize the global marketplace and the use of new technologies as the hallmarks of the capitalism of our time. This is true enough, but misses another dimension of change: new ways of organizing time, particularly working time.

The most tangible sign of that change might be the motto "No long term." In work, the traditional career progressing step by step through the corridors of one or two institutions is withering: so is the deployment of a single set of skills through the course of a working life. Today, a young American with at least two years of college can expect to change jobs at least eleven times in the course of working, and change his or her skill base at least three times during those forty years of labor.

An executive for ATT points out that the motto "No long term" is altering the very meaning of work:

> In ATT we have to promote the whole concept of the work force being contingent, though most of the contingent workers are inside our walls. "Jobs" are being replaced by "projects" and "fields of work."

Corporations have also farmed out many of the tasks they once did permanently in-house to small firms and to individuals employed on short-term contracts. The fastest-growing sector of the American labor force, for instance, is people who work for temporary job agencies. . . .

A change in modern institutional structure has accompanied short-term, contract, or episodic labor. Corporations have sought to remove layers of bureaucracy, to become flatter and more flexible organizations. In place of organizations as pyramids, management wants now to think of organizations as networks. "Networklike arrangements are lighter on their feet" than pyramidal hierarchies, the sociologist Walter Powell declares; "they are more readily decomposable or redefinable than the fixed assets of hierarchies." This means that promotions and dismissals tend not to be based on clear, fixed rules, nor are tasks crisply defined; the network is constantly redefining its structure. . . .

For all these reasons, Enrico's experience of long-term, narrative time in fixed channels has become dysfunctional. What Rico sought to explain to me—and perhaps to himself—is that the material changes embodied in the motto, "No long term" have become dysfunctional for him too, but as guides to personal character, particularly in relation to his family life.

Take the matter of commitment and loyalty. "No long term" is a principle which corrodes trust, loyalty, and mutual commitment. Trust can, of course, be a purely formal matter, as when people agree to a business deal or rely on another to observe the rules in a game. But usually deeper experiences of trust are more informal, as when people learn on whom they can rely when given a difficult or impossible task. Such social bonds take time to develop, slowly rooting into the cracks and crevices of institutions. . . .

It is the time dimension of the new capitalism, rather than high-tech data transmission, global stock markets, or free trade, which most directly affects people's emotional lives outside the workplace. Transposed to the family realm, "No long term" means keep moving, don't commit yourself, and don't sacrifice. Rico suddenly erupted on the plane, "You can't imagine how stupid I feel when I talk to my kids about commitment. It's an abstract virtue to them; they don't see it anywhere." Over dinner I simply didn't understand the outburst, which seemed apropos of nothing. But his meaning is now clearer to me as a reflection upon himself. He means the children don't see the commitment practiced in the lives of their parents or their parents' generation.

Similarly, Rico hates the emphasis on teamwork and open discussion which marks an enlightened, flexible workplace once those values are transposed to the intimate realm. Practiced at home, teamwork is destructive, marking an absence of authority and of firm guidance in raising children. He and Jeannette, he says, have seen too many parents who have talked every family issue to death for fear of saying "No!," parents who listen too well, who understand beautifully rather than lay down the law; they have seen as a result too many disoriented kids. . . .

Behavior which earns success or even just survival at work thus gives Rico little to offer in the way of a parental role model. In fact, for this modern couple, the problem is just the reverse: how can they protect family relations from succumbing to the short-term behavior, the meeting mind-set, and above all the weaknesses of loyalty and commitment which mark the modern work-place? In place of the chameleon values of the new economy, the family—as Rico sees it—should emphasize instead formal obligation, trustworthiness, commitment, and purpose. These are all long-term virtues.

This conflict between family and work poses some questions about adult experience itself. How can long-term purposes be pursued in a short-term so-ciety? How can durable social relations be sustained? How can a human being develop a narrative of identity and life history in a society composed of epi-sodes and fragments? The conditions of the new economy feed instead on experience which drifts in time, from place to place, from job to job. If I could state Rico's dilemma more largely, short-term capitalism threatens to cor-rode his character, particularly those qualities of character which bind human beings to one another and furnishes each with a sense of sustainable self.

# Alasdair MacIntyre, *After Virtue*

## Chapter 8: The Character of Generalizations in Social Science and their Lack of Predictive Power

What managerial expertise requires for its vindication is a justified conception of social science as providing a stock of law-like generalizations with strong predictive power. It might therefore seem at first sight that the claims of managerial expertise can be easily sustained. For just this conception of social science has dominated the philosophy of social science for two hundred years. According to this conventional account—from the Enlightenment through Comte and Mill to Hempel—the aim of the social sciences is to explain specifically social phenomena by supplying law-like generalizations to which the managerial expert would have to appeal. This account however seems to entail—what is certainly not the case—that the social sciences are almost or perhaps completely devoid of achievement. For the salient fact about those sciences is the absence of the discovery of any law-like generalizations whatsoever. . . .

Given then that conventional philosophy of social science has asserted that the task of the social scientist is the production of law-like generalizations, and given further that social science does not produce generalizations of this kind, one might have expected a hostile and dismissive attitude on the part of many social scientists to the conventional philosophy of social science. Yet this has certainly not occurred, and I have already identified one good reason for not being too surprised at this.

It is of course that if social science does not present its findings in the form of law-like generalizations, the grounds for employing social scientists as expert advisors to government or to private corporations become unclear and the very notion of managerial expertise is imperiled. For the central function of the social scientist as expert advisor or manager is to depict the outcomes of alternative policies, and if his predictions do not derive from a knowledge of law-like generalizations, the status of the social scientist as predictor becomes endangered—as, so it turns out, it ought to be; for the record of social scientists as predictors is very bad indeed, insofar as the record can be pieced together. No economist predicted 'stagflation' before it occurred, the writings of monetary theorists have signally failed to predict the rates of inflation correctly (Levy 1975) and D. J. C. Smyth and J. C. K. Ash have shown that the forecasts produced on the basis of the most sophisticated economic theory for OECD since 1967 have produced less successful predictions than would have been arrived at by using the commonsense, or as they say, naive methods of forecasting rates of growth by taking the average rate of growth for the last ten years as a guide or rates of inflation by assuming that the next six months will resemble the last six months (Smyth and Ash 1975). . . .

That the social sciences are predictively weak *and* that they do not discover law-like generalizations may clearly turn out to be two symptoms of the same condition. But what is that condition? Ought we simply to conclude that predictive weakness reinforces the conclusion implied by the conjunction of the conventional philosophy of social sciences and the facts about what social scientists do and do not achieve; namely, that the social sciences have substantially failed at their task? Or ought we perhaps instead to question both the conventional philosophy of social science *and* the claim to expertise by social scientists who seek to hire themselves out to government and corporations? What I am suggesting is that the true achievements of the social sciences are being concealed from us—and from many social scientists themselves—by systematic misinterpretation. Consider for example four highly interesting generalizations that have been advanced by modern social scientists.

The first is James C. Davies's famous thesis (1962) which generalizes—to revolutions as a class—Tocqueville's observation that the French revolution occurred when a period of rising and to some degree gratified expectations was followed by a period of set-back when expectations continued to rise and were sharply disappointed. The second is Oscar Newman's generalization that the crime rate rises in high-rise buildings with the height of the building up to a height of thirteen floors, but at more than thirteen floors levels off (Newman 1973, p. 25). The third is Egon Bittner's discovery of the differences between the understanding of the import of law embodied in police work and the understanding of that same import embodied in the practice of courts and of lawyers (Bittner 1970). The fourth is the contention advanced by Rosalind and Ivo Feierabend (1966) that the most and least modernized societies are the most stable and least violent, whereas those at midpoint in the approach to modernity are most liable to instability and political violence.

All four of these generalizations rest on distinguished research; all are buttressed by an impressive set of confirming instances. But they share three notable characteristics. First of all, they all coexist in their disciplines with recognized counter-examples, and the recognition of these counter-examples—if not by the authors of the generalizations themselves, at least by colleagues at work in the same areas—does not seem to affect the standing of the generalizations in anything like the way in which it would affect the standing of generalizations in physics or chemistry. Some critics from outside the social scientific disciplines—the historian Walter Laqueur, for example (1972)—have treated these counter-examples as affording new reasons for dismissing both such generalizations and the disciplines that are so lax as to allow generalizations and counter-examples to coexist. So Laqueur has cited the Russian revolution of 1917 and the Chinese of 1949 as examples *refuting* Davies's generalization and the patterns of political violence in Latin America as *refuting* the Feierabends' claim. For the moment all I want to note is that social scientists themselves characteristically and for the most part do in fact adopt just such a tolerant attitude to counter-examples, an attitude very different from that of either natural scientists themselves or of Popperian philosophers of sciences and to leave open the question of whether their attitudes might not after all be justified.

A second characteristic, closely linked to the first, of all four generalizations is that they lack not only universal quantifiers but also scope modifiers. That is, they are not only not genuinely of the form 'For all $x$ and some $y$ if $x$ has property $\phi$, then $y$ has property $\psi$', but we cannot say of them in any precise way under what conditions they hold. Of the gas law equations relating pressure, temperature and volume we know not only that they hold of all gases; but the original formulation whereby they were held to hold under all conditions has since been revised to modify their scope. We now know that they hold for all gases under all conditions except those *of very low temperature and very high pressure* (where we can say exactly what we mean by 'very high' and 'very low'). None of our four social scientific generalizations is presented with such clauses attached.

Thirdly, these generalizations do not entail any well-defined set of counterfactual conditionals in the way that the law-like generalizations of physics and chemistry do. We do not know how to apply them systematically beyond the limits of observation to unobserved or hypothetical instances. Thus they are not laws, whatever else they may be. What then *is* their status? To respond to this question is not going to be easy, because we do not possess any philosophical account of them which respects them for what they are, rather than treating them as failed attempts at the formulations of laws. Some social scientists, it is true, have seen no problem here. Confronted with the kind of consideration which I have adduced they have thought it appropriate to reply: 'What the social sciences discover are probabilistic generalizations; and where a generalization is only probabilistic of course there can be cases which would be counter-examples if the generalization was non-probabilistic and universal.' But this reply misses the point completely. For if the type of generalization which I have cited is to be a generalization at all, it must be something more than a mere list of instances. The probabilistic generalizations of natural science—those, say, of statistical mechanics—are indeed more than this precisely because they are as law-like as any non-probabilistic generalizations. They possess universal quantifiers—quantification is over sets, not over individuals—they entail well-defined sets of counter-factual conditionals and they are refuted by counter-examples in precisely the same way and to the same degree that other law-like generalizations are. Hence we throw no light on the status of the characteristic generalizations of the social sciences by calling them probabilistic; for they are as different from the generalizations of statistical mechanics as they are from the generalizations of Newtonian mechanics or the gas law equations.

We therefore have to start out afresh and in so doing to consider whether the social sciences may not have looked in the wrong place for their philosophical ancestry as well as for their logical structure. It is because modern social scientists have seen themselves as the successors of Comte and Mill and Buckle, of Helvétius and Diderot and Condorcet, that they have presented their writings as attempted answers to the questions of their eighteenth- and nineteenth-century masters. But let us suppose once again that the eighteenth and nineteenth centuries, brilliant and creative as they were, were in fact centuries not as we and they take them to be of Enlightenment, but of a peculiar kind of darkness in which men so dazzled themselves that they could no longer see and ask whether the social sciences might not have an alternative ancestry.

The name I wish to invoke is that of Machiavelli, for Machiavelli takes a very different view of the relationship between explanation and prediction from that taken by the Enlightenment. The thinkers of the Enlightenment were infant Hempelians. To explain is on their view to invoke a law-like generalization retrospectively; to predict is to invoke a similar generalization prospectively. For this tradition the diminution of predictive failure is the mark of progress in science; and those social scientists who have espoused it must face the fact that if they are right at some point an unpredicted war or revolution will become as disgraceful for a political scientist, an unpredicted change in the rate of inflation as disgraceful for an economist, as would an unpredicted eclipse for an astronomer. That this has not occurred yet has itself to be explained within this tradition and explanations have not been lacking: the human sciences are still young sciences, it is said—but clearly falsely. They are in fact as old as the natural sciences. Or it is said that the natural sciences attract the most able individuals in modern culture and the social sciences only those not able enough to do natural science—this was the claim of H. T. Buckle in the nineteenth century and there is some evidence that it is still partly true. A 1960 study of the I.Q.s of those completing Ph.D. requirements in various disciplines showed that natural scientists *are* significantly more intelligent than social scientists (although chemists drag down the natural science averages and economists raise the social science average). But the same reasons that make me reluctant to judge deprived minority children by their I.Q. scores make me equally reluctant to judge my colleagues by them—or myself. Yet perhaps explanations are not needed, for perhaps the failure that the dominant tradition tries to explain is like King Charles II's dead fish. Charles II once invited the members of the Royal Society to explain to him why a dead fish weighs more than the same fish alive; a number of subtle explanations were offered to him. He then pointed out that it does not.

Wherein does Machiavelli differ from the Enlightenment tradition? Above all in his concept of *Fortuna*. Machiavelli certainly believed as passionately as any thinker of the Enlightenment that our investigations should issue in generalizations which may furnish maxims for enlightened practice. But he also believed that no matter how good a stock of generalizations one amassed and no matter how well one reformulated them, the factor of *Fortuna* was ineliminable from human life. Machiavelli also believed that we might be able to contrive a quantitative measure of *Fortuna*'s influence in human affairs; but this belief for the moment I shall set on one side. What I want to emphasize is Machiavelli's belief that, given the best possible stock of generalizations, we may on the day be defeated by an unpredicted and unpredictable counterexample—and yet still see no way to improve upon our generalizations and still have no reason to abandon them or even to reformulate them. We can by improvements in our knowledge limit the sovereignty of *Fortuna*, bitch-goddess of unpredictability; we cannot dethrone her. If Machiavelli was right, the logical condition of the four generalizations which we inspected would be that which we could expect to hold for the most successful generalizations of the social sciences; it would in no way be a mark of failure. But was he right?

I want to argue that there are four sources of systematic unpredictability in human affairs. The first derives from the nature of radical conceptual innovation. Sir Karl Popper suggested the following example. Some time in the Old Stone Age you and I are discussing the future and I predict that within the next ten years someone will invent the wheel. 'Wheel?' you ask. 'What is that?' I then describe the wheel to you, finding words, doubtless with difficulty, for the very first time to say what a rim, spokes, a hub and perhaps an axle will be. Then I pause, aghast. 'But no one can be *going to* invent the wheel, for I have just invented it.' In other words, the invention of the wheel cannot be predicted. For a necessary part of predicting an invention is to say what a wheel is; and to say what a wheel is just *is* to invent it. It is easy to see how this example can be generalized. Any invention, any discovery, which consists essentially in the elaboration of a radically new concept cannot be predicted, for a necessary part of the prediction is the present elaboration of the very concept whose discovery or invention was to take place only in the future. The notion of the prediction of radical conceptual innovation is itself conceptually incoherent. . . .

The second type of systematic unpredictability to which I now turn is that which derives from the way in which the unpredictability of certain of his own future actions by each agent individually generates another element of unpredictability as such in the social world. It is at first sight a trivial truth that when I have not yet made up my mind which of two or more alternative and mutually exclusive courses of action to take I cannot predict which I shall take. Decisions contemplated but not yet made by me entail unpredictability of me by me in the relevant areas. But this truth seems trivial precisely because what I cannot predict of myself others may well be able to predict about me. My own future from my point of view may be representable only as a set of ramifying alternatives with each node in the branching system representing a point of as yet unmade decision-making. But from the point of view of an adequately informed observer provided both with the relevant data about me and the relevant stock of generalizations concerning people of my type, my future, so it seems, may be representable as an entirely determinable set of stages. Yet a difficulty at once arises. For this observer who is able to predict what I cannot is of course unable to predict his own future in just the way that I am unable to predict mine; and one of the features which he will be unable to predict, since it depends in substantial part upon decisions as yet unmade by him, is how far his actions will impact upon and change the decisions made by others—both what alternatives they will choose and what sets of alternatives will be offered to them for choice. Now among those others is me. It follows that insofar as the observer cannot predict the impact of his future actions on my future decision-making, he cannot predict my future actions any more than he can his own; and this clearly holds for all agents and observers. The unpre- dictability of my future by me does indeed generate an important degree of unpredictability as such. . . .

Another way of putting the same point would be to note that omniscience excludes the making of decisions. If God knows everything that will occur, he confronts no as yet unmade decision. He has a single will (*Summa Contra Gentiles,* cap. LXXIX, *Quod Deus Vult Etiam Ea Quae Nondum Sunt*). It is precisely insofar as we differ from God that unpredictability invades our lives. This way of putting the point has one particular merit: it suggests precisely what project those who seek to eliminate unpredictability from the social world or to deny it may in fact be engaging in.

A third source of systematic unpredictability arises from the game-theoretic character of social life. To some theorists in political science the formal structures of game theory have served to provide a possible basis for explanatory and predictive theory incorporating law-like generalizations. Take the formal structure of an *n*-person game, identify the relevant interests of the players in some empirical situation and we shall at the very least be able to predict what alliances and coalitions a fully rational player will enter into and, at a perhaps Utopian most, the pressures upon and the subsequent behavior of not fully

rational players. This recipe and its criticism have inspired some notable work
(especially that of William H. Riker). But the large hope that it embodied in
its original optimistic form seems to be illusory. Consider three types of obstacle to the transfer of the formal structures of game theory to the interpretation of actual social and political situations.

The first concerns the indefinite reflexivity of game-theoretic situations. I
am trying to predict what move you will make; in order to predict this I must
predict what you will predict as to what move I will make; and in order to
predict this I must predict what you will predict about what I will predict about
what you will predict . . . and so on. At each stage each of us will simultaneously be trying to render himself or herself unpredictable by the other; and
each of us will also be relying on the knowledge that the other will be trying
to make himself or herself unpredictable in forming his or her own predictions. Here the formal structures of the situation can never be an adequate
guide. A knowledge of them may be necessary, but even a knowledge of them
backed by a knowledge of each player's interest cannot tell us what the simul-
taneous attempt to render others predictable and oneself unpredictable will
produce.

This first type of obstacle may not by itself be insuperable. The chances
that it will be are however heightened by the existence of a second type of
obstacle. Game-theoretic situations are characteristically situations of imper-
fect knowledge, and this is no accident. For it is a major interest of each actor
to maximize the imperfection of the information of certain other actors at
the same time as he improves his own. Moreover a condition of success at mis-
informing other actors is likely to be the successful production of false im-
pressions in external observers too. This leads to an interesting inversion of
Collingwood's odd thesis that we can only hope to understand the actions of
the victorious and the successful, while those of the defeated must remain
opaque to us. But if I am right the conditions of success include the ability to
deceive successfully and hence it is the defeated whom we are more likely to be
able to understand and it is those who are going to be defeated whose behavior
we are more likely to be able to predict.

Once again this second type of obstacle need not be insuperable, even in
conjunction with the first. But there is yet a third type of obstacle to prediction
in game-theoretic situations. Consider the following familiar type of situation.
The management of a major industry are negotiating the terms of the next
long-term contract with the labor union leadership. Representatives of the government are present, not only in an arbitrating and mediating role, but because
the government has a particular interest in the industry—its products are crucial for defence, say, or it is an industry which powerfully affects the rest of the
economy. At first sight it ought to be easy to map this situation in game-

theoretic terms: three collective players each with a distinctive interest. But now let us introduce some of those features that so often make social reality so messy and untidy in contrast with the neat examples in the textbooks.

Some of the union leadership are approaching the time when they are going to retire from their posts in the union. If they cannot obtain relatively highly paid jobs with either the employers or the government, they may have to return to the shop floor. The employers are not only concerned with government in its present public interest capacity; they have a longer-term concern with obtaining a different type of government contract. One of the representatives of government is considering running for elected office in a district where the labor vote is crucial. That is to say, in any given social situation it is frequently the case that many different transactions are taking place at one and the same time between members of the same group. Not one game is being played, but several, and if the game metaphor may be stretched further, the problem about real life is that moving one's knight to QB3 may always be replied to with a lob across the net.

Even when we can identify with some certainty what game is being played, there is another problem. In real life situations, unlike both games and the examples in books about game-theory, we often do not start with a determinate set of players and pieces or a determinate area in which the game is to take place. There is—or perhaps used to be—on the market a cardboard and plastic version of the battle of Gettysburg which reproduces with great accuracy the terrain, the chronology and the units involved in that battle. It had this peculiarity, that a moderately good player taking the Confederate side can win. Yet clearly no player of war games is likely to be as intelligent at generalship as Lee was, and he lost. Why? The answer of course is that the player knows from the outset what Lee did not—what the time scale of the preliminary stages of the battle must be, precisely what units are going to get involved, what the limits to the terrain are on which the battle is to be fought. And all this entails that the game does *not* reproduce Lee's situation. For Lee did not and could not know that it was the *Battle of Gettysburg*—an episode on which a determinate shape was conferred only retrospectively by its outcome—which was about to be fought. Failure to realize this affects the predictive power of many computer simulations which seek to transfer analyses of past determinate situations to the prediction of future indeterminate ones. . . .

I turn now to the fourth such source: pure contingency. J. B. Bury once followed Pascal in suggesting that the cause of the foundation of the Roman Empire was the length of Cleopatra's nose: had her features not been perfectly proportioned, Mark Antony would not have been entranced; had he not been entranced he would not have allied himself with Egypt against Octavian; had he not made that alliance, the battle of Actium would not have been fought—

13  and so on. One does not need to accept Bury's argument to see that trivial
contingencies can powerfully influence the outcome of great events: the molehill which killed William III or Napoleon's cold at Waterloo which led him to
delegate command to Ney, who in turn had four horses shot from under him
that day, which led to faults in judgment, most notably in sending in the *Garde
Imperiale* two hours too late. There is no way in which all such contingencies
as moles and bacteria provide can be allowed for in battle plans. . . .

14a  Given then that there are these unpredictable elements in social life, it is
crucial to notice their intimate relationship to the predictable elements. What
are the predictable elements? They are of at least four kinds. The first arises
from the necessity of scheduling and coordinating our social actions. In every
culture most people most of the time structure their activities in terms of some
notion of a normal day. They get up at roughly the same time each day, dress
and wash or fail to wash, eat meals at set times, go to work and return from
work at set times and so on. Those who prepare the food have to be able to
expect those who eat to appear in particular times and particular places; the
secretary who picks up the telephone in one office has to be able to expect the
secretary in another office to answer it; the bus and train must meet the trav-
ellers at prearranged points. We all have a great deal of tacit, unspelled-out
knowledge of the predictable expectations of others as well as a large stock of
explicitly-stored information. Thomas Schelling in a famous experiment told
a group of a hundred subjects that they had the task of meeting an unknown
person in Manhattan on a given date. The only other fact they knew about the
unknown person was that he knew everything that they knew. What they had
to supply was the time and place for the encounter. More than eighty of them
selected the spot under the large clock in the Concourse of Grand Central Station at twelve noon; and precisely because over eighty per cent gave this answer
it is the right answer. What Schelling's experiment suggests is that we all know
more about what other people's expectations about our expectations are—and
vice versa—than we usually recognize.

14b  A second source of systematic predictability in human behavior arises
from statistical regularities. We know that we all tend to catch more colds in
winter, that the suicide rate rises sharply around Christmas, that multiplying
the number of qualified scientists at work on a well-defined problem increases
the probability that it will be solved sooner rather than later, that Irishmen are
more likely than Danes to be mentally ill, that the best indicator of how a man
will vote in Britain is how his best friend votes, that your wife or husband is
more likely to murder you than a criminal stranger, and that everything in
Texas tends to be bigger including the homicide rates. What is interesting about
this knowledge is its relative independence of causal knowledge.

No one knows the causes of some of these phenomena and about others many of us actually have false causal beliefs. Just as unpredictability does not entail inexplicability, so predictability does not entail explicability. Knowledge of statistical regularities plays as important a part in our elaboration and carrying out of plans and projects as does knowledge of scheduling and coordinated expectations. Lacking either we would not be able to make rational choices between alternative plans in terms of their chances of success and failure. This is also true of the two other sources of predictability in social life. 14 c The first of these is the knowledge of the causal regularities of nature: snowstorms, earthquakes, plague bacilli, height, malnutrition and the properties of protein all place constraints on human possibility. The second is the knowledge 14 d of causal regularities in social life. Although the status of the generalizations which express such knowledge is in fact the object of my enquiry, that there are such generalizations and that they do have some predictive power is after all quite clear. An example to add to the fourth that I gave earlier would be the generalization that in societies such as Britain and Germany in the nineteenth and twentieth centuries by and large one's place in the class structure determined one's educational opportunities. Here I am talking about genuine causal knowledge and not mere knowledge of statistical regularity.

We now at last are in a position to approach the question of the relation- 15 ship of predictability to unpredictability in social life with a view to casting some positive light on the status of the generalizations of the social sciences. It is at once clear that many of the central features of human life derive from the particular and peculiar ways in which predictability and unpredictability interlock. It is the degree of predictability which our social structures possess which enables us to plan and engage in long-term projects; and the ability to plan and to engage in long-term projects is a necessary condition of being able to find life meaningful. A life lived from moment to moment, from episode to episode, unconnected by threads of large-scale intention, would lack the basis for many characteristically human institutions: marriage, war, the remembrance of the lives of the dead, the carrying on of families, cities and services through generations and so on. But the pervasive unpredictability in human life also renders all our plans and projects permanently vulnerable and fragile. . . .

Each of us, individually and as a member of particular social groups, seeks to embody his own plans and projects in the natural and social world. A condition of achieving this is to render as much of our natural and social environment as possible predictable and the importance of both natural and social science in our lives derives at least in part—although only in part—from their contribution to this project. At the same time each of us, individually and as a member of particular social groups, aspires to preserve his independence, his freedom, his creativity, and that inner reflection which plays so great a part in freedom and creativity, from invasion by others. We wish to disclose of ourselves no more than we think right and nobody wishes to disclose all of himself—except perhaps under the influence of some psycho-analytic illusion. We need to remain to some degree *opaque and unpredictable*, particularly when threatened by the predictive practices of others. The satisfaction of this need to at least some degree supplies another necessary condition for human life being meaningful in the ways that it is and can be. It is necessary, if life is to be meaningful, for us to be able to engage in long-term projects, and this requires predictability; it is necessary, if life is to be meaningful, for us to be in possession of ourselves and not merely to be the creations of other people's projects, intentions, and desires, and this requires unpredictability. We are thus involved in a work in which we are simultaneously trying to render the rest of society predictable and ourselves unpredictable, to devise generalizations which will capture the behavior of others and to cast our own behavior into forms which will elude the generalizations which others frame. If these are general features of social life, what will be the characteristics of the best possible available stock of generalizations about social life?

It seems probable that they will have three important characteristics. They will be based on a good deal of research, but their inductively-founded character will appear in their failure to approach law-likeness. No matter how well-framed they are the best of them may have to coexist with counter-examples, since the constant creation of counter-examples is a feature of human life. And we shall never be able to say of the best of them precisely what their scope is. It follows of course that they will not entail well-defined sets of counterfactual conditionals. They will be prefaced not by universal quantifiers but by some such phrase as "Characteristically and for the most part . . . "

But just these, as I pointed out earlier, turned out to be the characteristics of the generalizations which actual empirical social scientists claim with good reason to have discovered. In other words the logical form of these generalizations—or the lack of it—turns out to be rooted in the form—or lack of it—of human life. We should not be surprised or disappointed that the generalizations and maxims of the best social science share certain characteristics of their predecessors—the proverbs of folk societies, the generalizations of jurists, the maxims of Machiavelli. And it is indeed to Machiavelli that we can now return.

What the argument shows is that *Fortuna* is ineliminable. But this does not mean that we cannot say some more about her in at least two respects. The first concerns the possibility of a measure of *Fortuna*. One of the problems created by the conventional philosophy of science is that it suggests to scientists in general and social scientists in particular that they should treat predictive error merely as a form of failure, except when some crucial question of falsification arises. If instead we kept careful records of error, and made of error itself a topic for research, my guess is that we should discover that predictive error is not randomly distributed. To learn whether this is so or not would be a first step to doing more than I have done in this chapter; that is, to talking about the specific parts played by *Fortuna* in different areas of human life rather than merely about the general role of *Fortuna* in all human life.

The second aspect of *Fortuna* which requires comment concerns its permanence. I earlier disclaimed the status of proof for my arguments; how then can I have grounds for believing in the permanence of *Fortuna*? My reasons are partly empirical. For suppose that someone were to accept the argument so far and to agree in the identification of the four systematic sources of unpredictability, but was then to propose that we try to eliminate or at least to limit as far as possible the part that these sources of unpredictability play in social life. He proposes to prevent as far as possible the occurrence of situations in which conceptual innovation, or the unforeseen consequences of unmade decisions, or the game-theoretic character of human life or pure contingency can disrupt the predictions already made, the regularities already identified. Could such a man achieve his goal? Could he render a now-unpredictable social world wholly or largely predictable?

Clearly his first step would have to be the creation of an organization to provide an instrument for his project and equally clearly his first task would have to be to render the activity of his own organization wholly or largely predictable. For if he were unable to achieve this, he could scarcely achieve his larger goal. But he would also have to render his organization efficient and effective, capable of dealing with its highly original task and of surviving in the very environment which it is committed to changing. Unfortunately these two characteristics, total or near total predictability on the one hand and organizational effectiveness on the other, turn out on the basis of the best empirical studies we have to be incompatible. Defining the conditions of effectiveness in an environment that requires innovative adaptation Tom Burns has listed such characteristics as 'continual redefinition of individual task', 'communication which consists of information and advice rather than instructions and decisions', 'knowledge may be located anywhere in the network' and so on (Burns 1963 and Burns and Stalker 1968). One can safely generalize what Burns and Stalker say about the need to allow for individual initiative, a flexible response to changes in knowledge, the multiplication of centres of problem-solving and decision-making as adding up to the thesis that an effective organization has to be able to tolerate a high degree of unpredictability within itself. Other studies confirm this. Attempts to monitor what every subordinate is doing all the time tend to be counter-productive; attempts to make the activity of others predictable necessarily routinize, suppress intelligence and flexibility and turn the energies of subordinates to frustrating the projects of at least some of their superiors (Kaufman 1973, and see also Burns & Stalker on the effects of attempts to subvert and circumvent managerial hierarchies).

Since organizational success and organizational predictability exclude one another, the project of creating a wholly or largely predictable society is doomed and doomed by the facts about social life. Totalitarianism of a certain kind, as imagined by Aldous Huxley or George Orwell, is therefore impossible. What the totalitarian project will always produce will be a kind of rigidity and inefficiency which may contribute in the long run to its defeat. We need to remember however the voices from Auschwitz and Gulag Archipelago which tell us just how long that long run is.

There is then nothing paradoxical in offering a prediction, vulnerable in the way that all social predictions are, about the permanent unpredictability of human life. Underlying that prediction is a vindication of the practice and of the findings of empirical social science and a rebuttal of what has been the dominant ideology of much social science as well as of the conventional philosophy of social science.

But that rebuttal entails also a large rejection of the claims of what I called bureaucratic managerial expertise. And with this rejection one part of my argument at least has been completed. The expert's claim to status and reward is fatally undermined when we recognize that he possesses no sound stock of law-like generalizations and when we realize how weak the predictive power available to him is. The concept of managerial effectiveness is after all one more contemporary moral fiction and perhaps the most important of them all. The dominance of the manipulative mode in our culture is not and cannot be accompanied by very much actual success in manipulation. I do not of course mean that the activities of purported experts do not have effects and that we do not suffer from those effects and suffer gravely. But the notion of social control embodied in the notion of expertise is indeed a masquerade. Our social order is in a very literal sense out of our, and indeed anyone's, control. No one is or could be in charge.

Belief in managerial expertise *is* then, on the view that I have taken, very like what belief in God was thought to be by Carnap and Ayer. It is one more illusion and a peculiarly modern one, the illusion of a power not ourselves that claims to make for righteousness. Hence the manager as *character* is other than he at first sight seems to be: the social world of everyday hard-headed practical pragmatic no-nonsense realism which is the environment of management is one which depends for its sustained existence on the systematic perpetuation of misunderstanding and of belief in fictions. The fetishism of commodities has been supplemented by another just as important fetishism, that of bureaucratic skills. For it follows from my whole argument that the realm of managerial expertise is one in which what purport to be objectively-grounded claims function in fact as expressions of arbitrary, but disguised, will and preference. . . .

To this many managers and many bureaucrats will reply: you are attacking a straw man of your own construction. We make no large claims, Weberian or otherwise. We are as keenly aware of the limitations of social scientific generalizations as you are. We perform a modest function with a modest and unpretentious competence. But we do have specialized knowledge, we are entitled in our own limited fields to be called experts.

Nothing in my argument impugns these modest claims; but it is not claims of this kind which achieve power and authority either within or for bureaucratic corporations, whether public or private. For claims of this modest kind could never legitimate the possession or the uses of power either within or by bureaucratic corporations in anything like the way or on anything like the scale on which that power is wielded. So the modest and unpretentious claims embodied in this reply to my argument may themselves be highly misleading, as much to those who utter them as anyone else. For they seem to function not as a rebuttal of my argument that a metaphysical belief in managerial expertise has been institutionalized in our corporations, but as an excuse for continuing to participate in the charades which are consequently enacted. The histrionic talents of the player with small walking-on parts are as necessary to the bureaucratic drama as the contributions of the great managerial character actors.

# John P. Robinson and Geoffrey Godbey, "Are Average Americans Really Overworked?"

In her best-selling book *The Overworked American,* Harvard economist Juliet Schor claimed that Americans were running endless circles in the "squirrel cage of capitalism" and consequently had few moments left to themselves. "According to my estimates," she wrote, "the average employed person is now on the job an additional 163 hours, or the equivalent of an extra month, a year." This argument hit a resounding chord in the American psyche.

In numerous surveys, Americans have indicated that the amount of free time they have is limited, less than they want, and less than they used to have. In one 1991 study, they estimated they had an average of only about 17 hours of free time per week, after taking care of their work and household obligations. Free time, an earlier Harris survey indicated, had declined by as much as one-third from the 1970s.

The idea that we have lost control of our time fits well with the psychology of victimization that flourishes today. There *must* be something keeping us from achieving all we're entitled to. It couldn't be just that our expectations are too vast and open-ended, or that we have used an increasing amount of free time poorly (such as 17 hours per week of television, on average). We *must* be working longer, because we feel so rushed now. As the McDonald's jingle says, "You deserve a break today."

Unfortunately, little attention has been given to the frailty of the numbers on which Schor's case is built. She relied heavily on people's ability to estimate, in response to a snap survey question, where their time goes during the week. Yet there is strong evidence that that technique does not produce reliable figures.

For this reason, we have carefully formulated an alternative method of determining what people do with their day—a complete time diary. Since 1965, we have been asking scientific samples of respondents to report, in written diaries, exactly what they did yesterday during specific time blocks. We ask them to report that single day's activity in their own words, not ours. We build in cross-checks to be sure that all their daily activities are accounted for.

These diary accounts give a much more accurate and detailed picture of a day in the life of Americans. When one compares the entries of people in time diaries with their survey estimates of working time, an escalating pattern of overestimation appears. For instance, workers whose diaries show 40 hours per week of paid work estimate they worked 43 hours. Workers who actually worked 55 hours estimate 80 hours on the job. Perhaps it feels that way to the toiler. But it's not true.

Moreover, comparisons of diary and survey data show that overestimation of total work hours has increased over the years—from about one hour in 1965 to an average of 7 hours a week too much in 1985. And overestimation is not peculiar to Americans. Virtually the same pattern is found in eight other Western countries where we have compared estimated and diary data.

So the snap survey judgments Americans make about how long they work should not be believed. When one looks instead at time-diary data, they do not show any mass overwork syndrome at all. Quite the opposite: *they show that free time is on the rise. . . .* Incidentally, government statistics on work hours collected from *employers* back up our diary data; they too show that work hours declined over the last few decades.

Thus, no reliable evidence supports claims of an increase in the workweek. Among women, of course, there has been a significant increase in the number of individuals at work. This leads to more employed workhours for women in total—but not to increases per average worker. And the greater likelihood of employment among women has been offset by the shorter hours of employment among women and men both, as well as by the declining levels of work among people ages 55 and older.

A variety of factors may account for Americans' false impression of overwork. Perhaps first and foremost, Americans do feel more rushed. Our 1992 research shows that 38 percent of the adult public now says they "always" feel rushed, an increase from 22 percent in 1971. People who feel more rushed and more stressed, we suggest, are more likely to overestimate how long they work. The myriad reasons for feeling rushed include the racing rate of change in the contemporary world, accelerating consumption of goods and experiences, more small and single-person households (which eliminates economies of housework), and increases in commuting time associated with sharp increases in suburban living. Additionally, uncertainty about jobs, the increasing need to meet deadlines, more reliance on instant communication, and other factors can make the pace of life more harried.

But however stressed we feel, we should maintain a true perspective: our parents and grandparents had less free time than we do.

# III. REST

1. Genesis 2:1–3. Translation is the Revised Standard Version.

2. Exodus 16:1–30. Translation is the Revised Standard Version.

3. Exodus 20:8–11. Translation is the Revised Standard Version.

4. Psalm 95:8–11. Translation is the Revised Standard Version.

5. Luke 10:25–42. Translation is the Revised Standard Version.

6. George Herbert, "The Parson in Circuit," pp. 75–77 of "The Country Parson," in John N. Wall, Jr., ed., *George Herbert: The Country Parson, The Temple* (New York: Paulist Press, 1981). George Herbert (1593–1633) is known chiefly as a great religious poet. But he was also a priest in the Church of England, and "The Country Parson" depicts the proper manner of life of a priest.

7. Josef Pieper, pp. 141–42 of "Leisure and Its Threefold Opposition," in Josef Pieper, *An Anthology* (San Francisco: Ignatius Press, 1989). Josef Pieper (1904–1997) was a German philosopher and a Roman Catholic. His book *Leisure: The Basis of Culture* is a classic discussion of its subject.

8. Kenneth Kirk, pp. 179–86 of *The Vision of God*, abridged ed. (Greenwood, S.C.: Attic Press, 1934). Kenneth Kirk (1886–1954) was the foremost Anglican moral theologian of the twentieth century. *The Vision of God* was first delivered as the Bampton Lectures in 1928.

9. Michael Walzer, selections from pp. 185–88, 190–95 of *Spheres of Justice* (New York: Basic Books, 1983). In this selection, Walzer, a political theorist, considers what a just distribution of "free time" would be, a subject that leads him to discuss the sabbath as one form of free time.

10. Joseph Epstein, selections from "Observing the Sabbath," pp. 194–204 in *Familiar Territory: Observations on American Life* (New York: Oxford University Press, 1979). Joseph Epstein (1937–) is one of the great essayists of twentieth-century America and was for many years editor of the *American Scholar.*

11. Abraham Joshua Heschel, pp. 3–10, 27–29 of *The Sabbath: Its Meaning for Modern Man* (New York: Farrar, Straus & Giroux, 1951). Heschel (1907–1972) was born in Warsaw, Poland. From 1945 until his death he was Professor of Jewish Ethics and Mysticism at the Jewish Theological Seminary in New York.

12. This evening prayer is taken from the Office of Compline ("Prayer at the Close of Day") in the *Lutheran Book of Worship* (Minneapolis: Augsburg, 1978).

# Genesis 2:1–3

Thus the heavens and the earth were finished, and all the host of them. And on the seventh day God finished his work which he had done, and he rested on the seventh day from all his work which he had done. So God blessed the seventh day and hallowed it, because on it God rested from all his work which he had done in creation.

# Exodus 16:1–30

They set out from Elim, and all the congregation of the people of Israel came to the wilderness of Sin, which is between Elim and Sinai, on the fifteenth day of the second month after they had departed from the land of Egypt. And the whole congregation of the people of Israel murmured against Moses and Aaron in the wilderness, and said to them, "Would that we had died by the hand of the LORD in the land of Egypt, when we sat by the fleshpots and ate bread to the full; for you have brought us out into this wilderness to kill this whole assembly with hunger."

Then the LORD said to Moses, "Behold, I will rain bread from heaven for you; and the people shall go out and gather a day's portion every day, that I may prove them, whether they will walk in my law or not. On the sixth day, when they prepare what they bring in, it will be twice as much as they gather daily." So Moses and Aaron said to all the people of Israel, "At evening you shall know that it was the LORD who brought you out of the land of Egypt, and in the morning you shall see the glory of the LORD, because he has heard your murmurings against the LORD. For what are we, that you murmur against us?" And Moses said, "When the LORD gives you in the evening flesh to eat and in the morning bread to the full, because the LORD has heard your murmurings which you murmur against him—what are we? Your murmurings are not against us but against the LORD."

And Moses said to Aaron, "Say to the whole congregation of the people of Israel, 'Come near before the LORD, for he has heard your murmurings.'" And as Aaron spoke to the whole congregation of the people of Israel, they looked toward the wilderness, and behold, the glory of the LORD appeared in the cloud. And the LORD said to Moses, "I have heard the murmurings of the people of Israel; say to them, 'At twilight you shall eat flesh, and in the morning you shall be filled with bread; then you shall know that I am the LORD your God.'"

In the evening quails came up and covered the camp; and in the morning dew lay round about the camp. And when the dew had gone up, there was on the face of the wilderness, a fine flakelike thing, fine as hoarfrost on the ground. When the people of Israel saw it, they said to one another, "What is it?" For they did not know what it was. And Moses said to them, "It is the bread which the LORD has given you to eat. This is what the LORD has commanded: 'Gather of it, every man of you, as much as he can eat; you shall take an omer apiece, according to the number of the persons whom each of you has in his tent.'" And the people of Israel did so; they gathered, some more, some less. But when they measured it with an omer, he that gathered much had nothing over, and he that gathered little had no lack; each gathered according to what he could eat. And Moses said to them, "Let no man leave any of it till the morning." But they did not listen to Moses; some left part of it till the morning, and it bred worms and became foul; and Moses was angry with them. Morning by morning they gathered it, each as much as he could eat; but when the sun grew hot, it melted.

On the sixth day they gathered twice as much bread, two omers apiece; and when all the leaders of the congregation came and told Moses, he said to them, "This is what the LORD has commanded: 'Tomorrow is a day of solemn rest, a holy sabbath to the LORD; bake what you will bake and boil what you will boil, and all that is left over lay by to be kept till the morning.'" So they laid it by till the morning, as Moses bade them; and it did not become foul, and there were no worms in it. Moses said, "Eat it today, for today is a sabbath to the LORD; today you will not find it in the field. Six days you shall gather it; but on the seventh day, which is a sabbath, there will be none." On the seventh day some of the people went out to gather, and they found none. And the LORD said to Moses, "How long do you refuse to keep my commandments and my laws? See! The LORD has given you the sabbath, therefore the sixth day he gives you bread for two days; remain every man of you in his place, let no man go out of his place on the seventh day." So the people rested on the seventh day.

# Exodus 20:8–11

Remember the sabbath day, to keep it holy. Six days you shall labor, and do all your work; but the seventh day is a sabbath to the LORD your God; in it you shall not do any work, you, or your son, or your daughter, your manservant, or your maidservant, or your cattle, or the sojourner who is within your gates; for in six days the LORD made heaven and earth, the sea, and all that is in them, and rested the seventh day; therefore the LORD blessed the sabbath day and hallowed it.

# Psalm 95:8–11

O that today you would hearken to his voice!
  Harden not your hearts, as at Meribah,
  as on the day at Massah in the wilderness,
when your fathers tested me,
  and put me to the proof, though they had seen my work.
For forty years I loathed that generation
  and said, "They are a people who err in heart,
  and they do not regard my ways."
Therefore I swore in my anger
  that they should not enter my rest.

# Luke 10:25–42

And behold, a lawyer stood up to put him to the test, saying, "Teacher, what shall I do to inherit eternal life?" He said to him, "What is written in the law? How do you read?" And he answered, "You shall love the Lord your God with all your heart, and with all your soul, and with all your strength, and with all your mind; and your neighbor as yourself." And he said to him, "You have answered right; do this, and you will live."

But he, desiring to justify himself, said to Jesus, "And who is my neighbor?" Jesus replied, "A man was going down from Jerusalem to Jericho, and he fell among robbers, who stripped him and beat him, and departed, leaving him half dead. Now by chance a priest was going down that road; and when he saw him he passed by on the other side. So likewise a Levite, when he came to the place and saw him, passed by on the other side. But a Samaritan, as he journeyed, came to where he was; and when he saw him, he had compassion, and went to him and bound up his wounds, pouring on oil and wine; then he set him on his own beast and brought him to an inn, and took care of him. And the next day he took out two denarii and gave them to the innkeeper, saying, 'Take care of him; and whatever more you spend, I will repay you when I come back.' Which of these three, do you think, proved neighbor to the man who fell among the robbers?" He said, "The one who showed mercy on him." And Jesus said to him, "Go and do likewise."

Now as they went on their way, he entered a village; and a woman named Martha received him into her house. And she had a sister called Mary, who sat at the Lord's feet and listened to his teaching. But Martha was distracted with much serving; and she went to him and said, "Lord, do you not care that my sister has left me to serve alone? Tell her then to help me." But the Lord answered her, "Martha, Martha, you are anxious and troubled about many things; one thing is needful. Mary has chosen the good portion, which shall not be taken away from her."

# George Herbert, "The Parson in Circuit"

The Country Parson upon the afternoons in the weekdays, takes occasion sometimes to visit in person, now one quarter of his Parish, now another. For there he shall find his flock most naturally as they are, wallowing in the midst of their affairs: whereas on Sundays it is easy for them to compose themselves to order, which they put on as their holy-day clothes, and come to Church in frame, but commonly the next day put off both. When he comes to any house, first he blesseth it, and then as he finds the persons of the house employed, so he forms his discourse. Those that he finds religiously employed, he both commends them much, and furthers them when he is gone, in their employment; as if he finds them reading, he furnisheth them with good books; if curing poor people, he supplies them with Receipts, and instructs them further in that skill, showing them how acceptable such works are to God, and wishing them ever to do the Cures with their own hands, and not to put them over to servants. Those that he finds busy in the works of their calling, he commendeth them also: for it is a good and just thing for everyone to do their own business. But then he admonisheth them of two things; first, that they dive not too deep into worldly affairs, plunging themselves over head and ears into carking [anxious thoughts], and caring; but that they so labor, as neither to labor anxiously, nor distrustfully, nor profanely. Then they labor anxiously, when they overdo it, to the loss of their quiet, and health: then distrustfully, when they doubt God's providence, thinking that their own labor is the cause of their thriving, as if it were in their own hands to thrive, or not to thrive. *Then they labor profanely, when they set themselves to work like brute beasts, never raising their thoughts to God, nor sanctifying their labor with daily prayer; when on the Lord's day they do unnecessary servile work, or in time of divine service on other holy days, except in the cases of extreme poverty, and in the seasons of Seed-time, and Harvest.* Secondly, he adviseth them so to labor for wealth and maintenance, as that they make not that the end of their labor, but that they may have wherewithal to serve God the better, and to do good deeds. After these discourses, if they be poor and needy, whom he thus finds laboring, he gives them somewhat; and opens not only his mouth, but his purse to their relief, that so they go on more cheerfully in their vocation, and himself be ever the more welcome to them. Those that the Parson finds idle, or ill-employed, he chides not at first, for that were neither civil, nor profitable; but always in the close, before he departs from them: yet in this he distinguisheth; for if he be a plain countryman, he reproves him plainly; for they are not sensible of fineness: if they be of higher quality, they commonly are quick, and sensible, and very tender of reproof: and therefore he lays his discourse so, that he comes to the point very leisurely, and oftentimes as *Nathan* did, in the person of another, asking them to reprove themselves. However, one way or other, he ever reproves them, that he may keep himself pure, and not be entangled in others' sins. Neither in this doth he forbear, though there be company by: for as when the offense is particular, and against me, I am to follow our Savior's rule, and to take my brother aside, and reprove him; so when the offense is public and against God, I am then to follow the Apostle's rule (I *Tim.* 5:20), and to *rebuke openly* that which is done openly. Besides these occasional discourses, the Parson questions what order is kept in the house, as about prayers morning, and evening on their knees, reading of Scripture, catechizing, singing of Psalms at their work, and on holy days; who can read, who not; and sometimes he hears the children read himself, and blesseth, encouraging also the servants to learn to read, and offering to have them taught on holy days by his servants. If the Parson were ashamed of particularizing in these things, he were not fit to be a Parson: but he holds the Rule, that Nothing is little in God's service: If it once have the honor of that Name, it grows great instantly. Wherefore neither disdaineth he to enter into the poorest Cottage, though he even creep into it, and though it smell never so loathsomely. For both God is there also, and those for whom God died: and so much the rather doth he so, as his access to the poor is more comfortable [i.e., providing comfort], than to the rich; and in regard of himself, it is more humiliation. These are the Parson's general aims in his Circuit; but with these he mingles other discourses for conversation sake, and to make his higher purposes slip the more easily.

# Josef Pieper, "Leisure and
Its Threefold Opposition"

It is well known that physicians for some time now have reminded us how important it is for our health to have leisure—and they are certainly correct. But: it is impossible to "achieve leisure" in order to stay or to become healthy, not even in order to "save our culture!" Some things can be approached only if they are seen as meaningful in and by themselves. They cannot be accomplished "in order to" effect something else. (Thus it is impossible, for example, to love someone "in order to . . . " and "for the purpose of . . . ".) The order of certain realities cannot be reversed; to try it anyway is not only inappropriate but simply doomed to failure.

Related to our question, this means: if leisure is not conceived as meaningful in and by itself, then it is plainly impossible to achieve. Here we should once again mention the celebration of a feast. Such a celebration combines all three elements that also constitute leisure: first, nonactivity and repose; second, ease and absence of exertion; third, leave from the everyday functions and work. Everybody knows how difficult an endeavor it is for us moderns really to celebrate. Indeed, this difficulty is identical with our inability to achieve leisure. The reason that our celebrations fail is the same reason that we fail to achieve leisure.

At this point there appears an inevitable consideration that to most people, as I have frequently experienced, seems quite uncomfortable. Put in a nutshell, it is this: to celebrate means to proclaim, in a setting different from the ordinary everyday, our approval of the world as such. Those who do not consider reality as fundamentally "good" and "in the right order" are not able to truly celebrate, no more than they are able to "achieve leisure". In other words: leisure depends on the precondition that we find the world and our own selves agreeable. And here follows the offensive but inevitable consequence: the highest conceivable form of approving of the world as such is found in the worship of God, in the praise of the Creator, in the liturgy. With this we have finally identified the deepest root of leisure.

We should expect, I believe that humanity will make strenuous efforts to escape the consequences of this insight. It may try, for example, to establish "artificial" feast days in order to avoid the ultimate and true approval of reality—while producing a resemblance of genuine celebration through the immense display of outward arrangements supported by the political authorities. In reality, the "organized" recreation of such pseudocelebrations is merely a more hectic form of work.

It would be a misconception to assume that this proposition regarding the cultic essence of all celebration and the cultic roots of leisure and culture would be a specifically Christian thesis. What in our days is called "secularism" represents perhaps not so much the loss of a Christian outlook as rather the loss of some more fundamental insights that have traditionally constituted humanity's patrimony of natural wisdom. I believe that our thesis on leisure and culture is part of this patrimony. It was the Greek Plato, long before Christi- *6* anity, who in his old age formulated this thesis by employing the imagery of a magnificent myth. Plato asks whether there would be no respite for the human race, destined as it seems for labor and suffering. And he replies, Yes indeed, there is a respite: "The gods, out of compassion for us humans who are born into hardship, provided respite by granting periodic cultic celebrations, and by giving us, to join in our feasts, the Muses with their leaders Apollo and Dionysus, so that we may be sustained by joyfully conversing with the gods, and be lifted up and given a sense of direction."

# Kenneth Kirk, *The Vision of God*

## "Worship" and "Service"

Post-Reformation developments of thought, both in Protestant and in Catholic circles, combined, therefore, to challenge the traditional primacy of the doctrine of the vision of God. By evacuating prayer of all but its 'practical' aspect, by denying (in effect) that communion with God through worship can be an end in itself for human life, they voiced in the most pointed manner a criticism—or, rather, two alternative criticisms—of which many Christians catch an echo in the secrecy of their own reflections. (i) Against that traditional development of thought which, from New Testament or even from pre-Christian times, has taught that the goal of human life is to see God, it is urged, in the first place, that such an ideal is essentially and pre-eminently selfish, in that it proposes a course of life devoted solely to the attainment of personal satisfaction. But (ii) even if it could be shown that the ideal of the vision of God is no more selfish than one of explicit altruism, it might yet be said that on utilitarian grounds alone the latter is the higher of the two. The doctrine of the vision of God makes worship the primary human activity; and as compared with the ideal of service worship has all the appearance of a barren, limited and anti-social aspiration. If then, we are to estimate the value of that vast concentration of Christian thought upon worship to which the preceding chapters bear witness, we must be prepared to explore these criticisms, each in its turn, and to ask how far they can be met satisfactorily.

### (a) Is the quest for the Vision of God a Selfish Ideal?

It would be foolish to deny that the desire to see God in pre-Christian religious thought appealed often enough to motives rightly deserving the adjectives 'selfish' or 'interested.' In the main it seems to have been animated by a passion for a personal experience—for the attaining of a particular state of consciousness, or indeed, in some cases, of unconsciousness. The special characteristics of this state, as conceived or experienced by different persons or groups, do not affect the question of principle—whether God was 'seen' in ecstasy, or in dreams, or in a calm untroubled communion with nature, matters nothing. At heart, in all these aspirations, the believer was in pursuit of something *for himself*—regardless, it may almost be said, of the interests of any other, whether God or his neighbour.

Large parts of Christendom, again, in every generation have adopted this same ideal, and can without hesitation be accused of selfishness for that reason.

But here the accusation holds at best only within certain limits. The Christian *3*
seeker after God was rarely content with solitary enjoyment of the vision. To
S. Paul and S. John it could have no other context than that of the Church— *4*
now militant, but in eternity triumphant. Clement's gnostic—a person at first
sight wholly self-contained—longs for a city like Plato's 'set up as a pattern in
heaven'—an 'ordered multitude' of the blessed; to Augustine the vision of God
in the city of God was an ideal from which the one member could no more be
subtracted than the other.

Christian poetry tells the same tale. No account of the vision of God and
its influence upon the history of Christian ideals could be complete without
some allusion to the 'Divina Commedia.' But the reference is specially appropriate at this point. In the final cantos of the 'Purgatorio' the animated crowds
which hitherto have marked the poet's journey have gradually been with-
drawn, and on the threshold of the 'Paradiso' he stands alone with Beatrice in
the terrestrial Paradise. As they rise towards the empyrean, heaven grows ra-
diant around them with the spirits of the blest—the 'myriad splendours, living
and victorious'; the 'jewels dear and fair' of the celestial court. The final vision
portrays the great Rose of God and His innumerable saints, word-painted as
no other poet has ever found it possible to depict them:—

> 'Thus in the form of a white rose revealed itself to me that saintly host, which
> Christ espoused in His own blood. Therewith that other host—the angels—which
> as it soars, contemplates and chants the glory of Him Who fills it with love, and
> the goodness which made it so great—like as a swarm of bees, which one while
> settles within the flowers and anon returns to the hive where its work is stored in
> sweetness—now lighted down upon the great flower with its coronal of many
> petals; now again soared aloft to the place where its love doth for ever dwell.
> And all their faces were of living flame, and of gold their wings; and for the rest
> they were all white beyond the whiteness of snow. . . . This realm of security and
> joy, peopled by folk alike of old time and of new, centred its looks and its love
> upon one mark alone. O threefold light, whose bright radiance, shed in a single
> beam upon their eyes, doth so content them, look hither down upon our storm-
> tossed lives.'

The vision then is to be a corporate one; and this makes the quest for it, in *5*
any case, something less than wholly selfish. But this is only half the truth. The
greatest saints have always recognized that to make enjoyment even though it
be a communal enjoyment, the goal of life, is to import a motive less than the
purest into ethics. The emphatic protests against 'panhedonism' in any one
of its different forms, which we have noticed at different stages, are evidence
that Christianity was alive to the danger; and that however much lesser minds

succumbed to it, the greatest figures in the history of the Church knew that it represented something in essence at once immoral and un-Christian.

The doctrine that the 'end of man is the vision of God,' as a practical maxim for life, implies that the Christian should set himself first of all to focus his thought upon God in the spirit of worship. It implies this of necessity, and of necessity it implies nothing more—nothing whatever as to the achieving of pleasures, rapture, exaltation in the act of worship. The only achievement man has the right to hope for is that of greater Christian saintliness—greater zeal for service—coming from this direction of the heart and mind to God. It can hardly be denied that in so far as unselfishness is possible in this life at all (to anticipate for a moment another question), this is an unselfish ideal. To look towards God, and from that 'look' to acquire insight both into the follies of one's own heart and the needs of one's neighbours, with power to correct the one no less than to serve the other—this is something very remote from any quest for 'religious experience' for its own sake. Yet this, and nothing else, is what the vision of God has meant in the fully developed thought of historic Christianity.

### (b) Is 'Worship' a Higher Ideal than 'Service'?

The second question prompted by this review of Christian thought has many aspects. Granted that 'worship' is unselfish, it may be said, surely 'service' may be unselfish too? And further, a comparison of worship and service, viewed in relation to the world's deepest needs, both spiritual and temporal, suggests that service—the unremitting service of God and man—is the more urgently needed of the two. The most, then, that can be allowed to worship is that it is a means, and only a means, to better service. It has no independent value. The true Christian must set before himself as the goal of his efforts the realization of the kingdom of God or the brotherhood of man; must form his thought and centre his activity upon these ideals. Prayer and meditation, if they are to have a place in life at all, must make no such claim as will seriously detract from the time available for action. Every hour they monopolize must show fruit in enhanced efficiency if it is to be accounted anything but wasted. This is the plea of the champion of 'service.' Virile, philanthropic, restless in his zeal to do good, he is jealous of every moment given to prayer; he tolerates it simply as a tonic or stimulant to fit him for new ventures of heroic activity. That in its own nature worship is a service no less heroic than any other, is a sentiment from which his whole being recoils.

If this conclusion of the apostles of energy is accepted, the whole development of Christian thought about the vision of God must be adjudged a wasteful, if not a tragic, mistake. Selfish the ideal of seeing God may not be;

erroneous it is. It mistakes the means for the end, and in so doing veils the true end from men's eyes. It diverts them from the king's highway of loving energy into a maze of contemplative prayer wholly at fault, that is how robust common sense, even among Christians, has always regarded, and to-day more than ever regards, those who insist that worship or contemplation has the primary place in the ideal life. Its test is wholly pragmatic. If it uplifts, then, but only then, is worship commendable; if it strengthens and purifies, so far, but only so far, has it a place. But it has no value for its own sake, or apart from these possible influences which it may exert. And in any case, a little of it goes a long way; it must never be allowed to oust positive benevolence from its position as the Christian's first, final, and only genuine duty.

This is a serious criticism: but even so the Christian tradition of the vision of God seems to have a message for the restless energizers of the modern world, with their problems, programmes, and calls to discipleship. The concept of service embraces two very different ideas. Only one of these is Christian— indeed, only one of them realizes the ideal of service at all; for service of the other kind is self-destructive and nugatory. For the purposes of the present discussion, they may be called the *service of humility,* and the *service of patronage.* It should not be difficult to see that only the former of these two has real worth. Once this is recognized, it becomes not unreasonable to suggest that worship alone guarantees to service that quality of humility without which it is no service at all; and therefore that worship may claim and must be allowed a substantive position in the Christian ideal once more. So far from being a selfish goal, worship is the only way to unselfishness which the Christian has at his command.

To serve humanity in the spirit of patronage—as a genius condescending to stupidity, as an expert coming to the help of the inefficient, as a millionaire lavishing gifts upon the destitute—is there anything in the world which breeds more dissension, discontent, just resentment and open revolt than this? The question has only to be asked to be answered; every generation has writhed under the well-meant patronage of Ladies Bountiful. Yet apart from an atmosphere of worship, every act of service avails only to inflate the agent's sense of patronage. He is the doctor, humanity is his patient: he is the Samaritan, his neighbour the crippled wayfarer: he is the instructor, others are merely his pupils. Gratitude (if they show gratitude) only confirms his conviction of his own importance; resentment (if they resent his services) only ministers to the glow of self-esteem with which he comforts himself in secret. The phenomenon has been the commonplace of satirists since the world began. Not only so—we recognize in it as well a principal cause of the divisions of Christendom, of the stultifying effort, of the disillusionment of enthusiasts. The experts quarrel over rival panaceas; the hierophants jostle each other at the altar; and the more there is of such 'service,' the less the cause of humanity is in truth served at all.

A man must be blind not to recognize something of himself in this picture; he must be no less callous if he fails to long for the spirit of humility. But humility cannot be acquired by taking thought for oneself; that way, as S. Paul's condemnation of the law has once for all made clear, lie only the alternatives of pride and despair. The way of worship is the only way left open. Even worship is not altogether exempt from the dangers of pride and despair. But in so far as contemplation, or worship, is to be distinguished from service—and the distinction is one which the world has agreed to make—it is surely true to say that contemplation ministers to humility just as service ministers to patronage. The man who 'serves'—who plans, and organizes, and issues instructions, advice or exhortations—is doing so from the vantage ground of independence. He thinks of himself as a free agent, dowered with talents to be employed for the benefit of others. In worship, on the contrary, the worshipper puts himself in an attitude of dependence. In looking towards God, who is All in All, he sees himself to be nothing; in worshipping his Redeemer, he knows himself incapable of redeeming even the least of God's creatures. The most he can hope for is that God will deign to use him for the forwarding of His high designs. Worship tells us much good of God, but little good of ourselves, except that we are the work of God's hands. For that we may praise Him, but it leaves us nothing upon which to pride ourselves.

Thus the danger of 'service,' as an ideal, is that it fosters the spirit of patronage: the glory of worship is to elicit the grace of humility. Without humility there can be no service worth the name; patronizing service is self-destructive—it may be the greatest of all disservices. Hence to serve his fellows *at all*—to avoid doing them harm greater even than the good he proposed to confer on them—a man must find a place for worship in his life. The truth is not that worship (as the advocate of action allowed us to assert) will help him to serve *better*. The alternative lies not between service of a better kind and a worse kind; it lies between service and no service at all. If we would attempt to do good with any sure hope that it will prove good and not evil, we must act in the spirit of humility; and worship alone can make us humble. There is no other cause.

This is no more than to carry to its conclusion what we have noticed already on more than one occasion, that a system of thought which is primarily moralistic, in so far as it sets before men a rule of conduct by which it is their first duty to measure themselves, is in essence egocentric. It is only one of the many forms which selfishness can take, even though its rule appear superficially altruistic. The ultimate purpose which its devotee has in view is not the well-being of others, but the vindication of his own personal worth. This gives us material for a conclusion. 'Your ideal of service,'—so we may imagine traditional Christianity answering robust common sense—'necessarily leads up to the ideal of worship as its consummation. Without the latter you cannot achieve the former; and, if worship languishes, service will once more degenerate into mere self-assertion. The two are, at least, co-ordinate parts of the same ideal whole.'

Disinterested service, then, is the only service that is serviceable; and disinterestedness comes by the life of worship alone.

# Michael Walzer, *Spheres of Justice*

## The Meaning of Leisure

For most people, leisure is simply the opposite of work; idleness, its essence. The etymological root of the Greek *schole,* as of the Hebrew *shabbat,* is the verb "to cease" or "to stop." Presumably, it is work that is stopped, and the result is quiet, peace, rest (also enjoyment, play, celebration). But there is an alternative understanding of leisure that requires at least a brief description here. Free time is not only "vacant" time; it is also time at one's command. That lovely phrase "one's own sweet time" doesn't always mean that one has nothing to do, but rather that there is nothing that one has to do. We might say, then, that the opposite of leisure isn't work simply but necessary work, work under the constraint of nature or the market or, most important, the foreman or the boss. So there is a leisurely way of working (at one's own pace), and there are forms of work compatible with a life of leisure. "For leisure does not mean idleness," wrote T. H. Marshall in an essay on professionalism. "It means the freedom to choose your activities according to your own preferences and your own standards of what is best." Professionals once eagerly claimed this freedom; it made them gentlemen, for though they earned their living working, they worked in a leisurely way. It's not difficult to imagine a setting in which this same freedom would make, not for gentility, but for citizenship. Consider, for example, the Greek artisan, whose aim in life, it has been said, was "to preserve his full personal liberty and freedom of action, to work when he felt inclined and when his duties as a citizen permitted him, to harmonize his work with all the other occupations that filled [his days], to participate in the government, to take his seat in the courts, to join in the games and festivals." The picture is certainly idealized, but it is important to note that the ideal is that of a working man all of whose time is free time, who does not need a "vacation with pay" in order to enjoy a moment of leisure.

Aristotle argued that only the philosopher could rightly be said to live a leisured life, for philosophy was the only human activity pursued without the constraint of some further end. Every other occupation, including politics, was tied to a purpose and was ultimately unfree, but philosophy was an end in itself. The artisan was a slave not only to the market where he sold his products, but to the products themselves. I suppose that the books we currently attribute to Aristotle were, by contrast, not products at all but mere by-products of philosophical contemplation. They were not written to make money or to win tenure or even eternal fame. Ideally, philosophy has no issue; at least, it is not pursued for the sake of its issue. One can see here the source (or perhaps it is already a reflection) of the aristocratic disdain for productive work. But it is both an unnecessary and a self-serving restriction on the meaning of leisure to make nonproductivity its central feature. That the philosopher's thoughts do not taint the idea of leisure, but the artisan's table or vase or statue do, is a thought likely to appeal only to philosophers. From a moral standpoint, it seems more important that human activity be directed from within than that it have no outside end or material outcome. And if we focus on self-direction, a wide variety of purposive activities can be brought within the compass of a life of leisure. Intellectual work is certainly one of these, not because it is useless—one can never be certain about that—but because intellectuals are commonly able to design, to their own specifications, the work they do. But other sorts of work can also be designed (planned, scheduled, organized) by the workers themselves, either individually or collectively; and then it isn't implausible to describe the work as "free activity" and the time as "free time."

Human beings also need a "cessation from rest," Marx once wrote, criticizing Adam Smith's description of rest as the ideal human condition, identical with freedom and happiness. "Certainly the measure of work seems externally given by the goal to be attained and by the obstacles to its attainment," he went on. "But Smith has no conception that this overcoming of obstacles is itself an exercise of freedom." Marx meant that it can sometimes be an exercise of freedom—whenever "the external goals, ceasing to appear merely as necessities of nature, become goals that the individual chooses for himself." In part, what is at stake here is the control of work, the distribution of power in the workplace and in the economy at large—an issue I will come back to in a later chapter. But Marx also wanted to hint at some grand transformation in the way mankind relates to nature, an escape from the realm of necessity, a transcendence of the old distinction between work and play. Then one won't have to talk, as I have been doing, of work carried on at a leisurely pace or incorporated into a life of leisure, for work will simply be leisure and leisure will be work: free, productive activity, the "species life" of mankind.

For Marx, it is the great failing of bourgeois civilization that most men and women experience this sort of activity, if they experience it at all, only in spare and scattered moments, as a hobby, not as their life's work. In communist society, by contrast, everyone's work will be his hobby, everyone's vocation his avocation. But this vision, glorious as it is, is not a proper subject for the theory of justice. If it is ever realized, justice will no longer be problematic. Our concern is with the distribution of free time in the age before the transformation, escape, and transcendence have taken place—that is, here and now, when the rhythm of work and rest is still crucial to human well-being, and when some people, at least, will have no species life at all if they have no break from their usual occupations. However work is organized, however leisurely it is—and these are crucial questions—men and women still need leisure in the more narrow and conventional sense of a "cessation from work.". . .

## Two Forms of Rest

Though the rhythm and periodicity of work has been radically different among, say, peasants, artisans, and industrial workers, and though the length of particular working days shows great variation, the working year does seem to have had a normative shape—at least, a shape reiterated under a wide variety of cultural conditions. Calculations for ancient Rome, medieval Europe, and rural China before the revolution, for example, suggest something like a 2:1 ratio of work to days of rest. And that is roughly where we are today (figuring a five-day week, a two-week vacation, and four to seven legal holidays).

The purposes of rest vary more radically. Marx's description is typical of nineteenth-century liberals and romantics: "time for education, for intellectual development, for the fulfilling of social functions and for social intercourse, for the free play of . . . bodily and mental activity." Politics, which played such an important part in the free time of the Greek artisan, is not even mentioned; nor are religious observances. Nor is there much sense here of what any child could have explained to Marx, the value of doing nothing, of "passing" the time—unless "free play" is meant to include random thoughts, stargazing, and fantasy. We might incorporate Aristotle's definition of leisure and say that purposelessness, the state of being without fixed goals, is one (though only one) of leisure's characteristic purposes. . . .

### A Short History of Vacations

In the year 1960, an average of a million and a half Americans, 2.4 percent of the workforce, were on vacation every day. It is an extraordinary figure, and undoubtedly it had at that point never been higher. Vacations have indeed a short history—for ordinary men and women, very short: as late as the 1920s, Sebastian de Grazia reports, only a small number of wage earners could boast of paid vacations. The arrangement is far more common today, a central feature of every union contract; and the practice of "going away"—if not for many weeks, at least for a week or two—has also begun to spread across class lines. In fact, vacations have become the norm, so that we are encouraged to think of weekends as short vacations and of the years after retirement as a very long one. And yet the idea is new. The use of the word *vacation* to mean a private holiday dates only from the 1870s; the verb *to vacation,* from the late 1890s.

It all started as a bourgeois imitation of the aristocrat's retreat from court and city to country estate. Since few bourgeois men and women owned country estates, they retreated instead to seaside or mountain resorts. At the beginning, ideas about relaxation and pleasure were masked by ideas about the health-restoring qualities of fresh air and mineral or salt water: thus eighteenth-century Bath and Brighton, where one went to eat and talk and promenade and also, sometimes, "to take the waters." But the escape from city and town was soon popular for its own sake, and the entrepreneurial response slowly multiplied the number of resorts and cheapened the available amusements. The invention of the railroad made a similar escape possible for nineteenth-century workers, but they had no time for anything more than the "excursion"—to the sea and back in a single day. The great expansion of popular leisure began only after the First World War: more time, more places to go, more money, cheap lodgings, and the first projects in communal provision, public beaches, state parks, and so on.

What is crucial about the vacation is its individualist (or familial) character, greatly enhanced, obviously, by the arrival of the automobile. Everyone plans his own vacation, goes where he wants to go, does what he wants to do. In fact, of course, vacation behavior is highly patterned (by social class especially), and the escape it represents is generally from one set of routines to another. But the experience is clearly one of freedom: a break from work, travel to some place new and different, the possibility of pleasure and excitement. It is indeed a problem that people vacation in crowds—and, increasingly, as the size of the crowds grows, it is a distributive problem, where space rather than time is the good in short supply. But we will misunderstand the value of vacations if we fail to stress that they are individually chosen and individually designed. No two vacations are quite alike.

They are, however, designed to the size of the individual (or familial) purse. Vacations are commodities: people have to buy them—with pay forgone and money spent; and their choices are limited by their buying power. I don't want to overemphasize this point, for it is also true that people fight for their vacations; they organize unions, bargain with their employers, go on strike for "time off," shorter work days, early retirement, and so on. No history of vacations would be complete without an account of these fights, but they are not the central feature of contemporary distributions. We might indeed conceive of time off in terms directly relative to those of work, so that individuals could choose, as Shaw suggests, hard and dirty work and long vacations or leisurely work and shorter vacations. But for most workers, right now, time is probably less important in determining the shape and value of their vacations than the money they are able to spend.

If wages and salaries were roughly equal, there would appear to be nothing wrong with making vacations purchasable. Money is an appropriate vehicle for individual design because it imposes the right sorts of choice: between work and its pay, on the one hand, and the expenses of this or that sort of leisure activity (or inactivity), on the other. We can assume that people with similar resources would make different choices, and the result would be a complex and highly particularized distribution. Some of them, for example, might take few or no vacations, preferring to earn more money and surround themselves with beautiful objects rather than escape to beautiful surroundings. Others might prefer many short vacations; still others, a long stint of work and a long rest. There is room here for collective as well as individual decision making (in unions and cooperative settlements, for example). But the decisive decisions must come at the individual level, for that is what vacations are. They bear the mark of their liberal and bourgeois origins. . . .

But all this assumes the centrality of the vacation, and it is important to stress now that the vacation is an artifact of a particular time and place. It isn't the only form of leisure; it was literally unknown throughout most of human history, and the major alternative form survives even in the United States today. This is the public holiday. When ancient Romans or medieval Christians or Chinese peasants took time off from work, it was not to go away by themselves or with their families but to participate in communal celebrations. A third of their year, sometimes more, was taken up with civil commemorations, religious festivals, saint's days, and so on. These were their holidays, in origin, holy days, and they stand to our vacations as public health to individual treatment or mass transit to the private car. They were provided for everyone, in the same form, at the same time, and they were enjoyed together. We still have holidays of this sort, though they are in radical decline; and in thinking about them it will be well to focus on one of the most important of the survivals.

### The Idea of the Sabbath

According to the Deuteronomic account, the Sabbath was instituted in commemoration of the escape from Egypt. Slaves work without cease or at the behest of their masters, and so the Israelites thought it the first mark of a free people that its members enjoy a fixed day of rest. Indeed, the divine command as reported in Deuteronomy has the slaves of the Israelites as its primary object: "that thy man-servant and thy maid-servant may rest as well as thou" (5:14). Egyptian oppression was not to be repeated even though slavery itself was not abolished. The Sabbath is a collective good. It is, as Martin Buber says, "the common property of all"—that means, of all who share in the common life. "Even the slave admitted into the household community, even the *ger*, the stranger [resident alien], admitted into the national community, must be permitted to share in the divine rest." Domestic animals are included, too—"thine ox, . . . thine ass, . . . thy cattle,"—since animals presumably can enjoy a rest (though they can't take a vacation).

Max Weber argued that the strangers or resident aliens were required to rest in order to deny them any competitive advantage. There is no reason for saying this—no evidence in the sources—beyond the conviction, not always associated with Weber, that economic motives must in principle be paramount. But it is true that, even in a pre-capitalist economy, it would be difficult to guarantee rest to everyone without imposing it on everyone. Public holidays require coercion. The absolute ban on work of any sort is unique, I think, to the Jewish Sabbath; but without some general sense of obligation and some enforcement mechanism, there could be no holidays at all. That is why, as obligation and enforcement have declined, holidays have ceased to be public occasions, have been attached to weekends, have become undifferentiated pieces of individual vacations. One can see here an argument for "blue laws," which can be justified much as taxation is justified: both have the form of a charge on productive or wage-earning time for the sake of communal provision.

Sabbath rest is more egalitarian than the vacation because it can't be purchased: it is one more thing that money can't buy. It is enjoined for everyone, enjoyed by everyone. This equality has interesting spillover effects. Insofar as the celebration came to require certain sorts of food and clothing, Jewish communities felt themselves bound to provide these for all their members. Thus, Nehemiah, speaking to the Jews who had returned with him from Babylonia to Jerusalem: "This day is holy to the Lord, your God. . . . Go, eat of the richest food and drink of the most delicious wines, and send portions to those who have nothing provided." (8:9–10). Not to send portions would be to oppress the poor, for it would exclude them from a common celebration; it is a kind of banishment that they have done nothing to deserve. And then, as the Sabbath rest was shared, so it came to be argued that the work of preparing for the Sabbath should also be shared. How could people rest if they hadn't first worked? "Even if one is a person of very high rank and does not as a rule attend to the marketing or to other household chores," wrote Maimonides, thinking first of all of the rabbis and sages, "he should nevertheless himself perform one of these tasks in preparation for the Sabbath. . . . Indeed, the more one does in way of such preparations, the more praiseworthy he is." So the universalism of the seventh day was extended at least to the sixth.

It might be said, however, that this is only another case where equality and the loss of liberty go together. Certainly the Sabbath is impossible without the general commandment to rest—or, rather, what survives without the commandment, on a voluntary basis, is something less than the full Sabbath. On the other hand, the historical experience of the Sabbath is not an experience of unfreedom. The overwhelming sense conveyed in Jewish literature, secular as well as religious, is that the day was eagerly looked forward to and joyfully welcomed—precisely as a day of release, a day of expansiveness and leisure. It was designed, as Leo Baeck has written, "to provide the soul with a broad and lofty space," and so it seems to have done. No doubt this sense of spaciousness will be lost on men and women who stand outside the community of believers but are still submitted, in one degree or another, to its rules. But it isn't their experience that is determining here. Holidays are for members, and members can be free—the evidence is clear—within the confines of the law. At least, they can be free when the law is a covenant, a social contract, even though the covenant is never individually designed.

Would people choose private vacations over public holidays? It isn't easy to imagine a situation in which the choice would present itself in such sharp and simple terms. In any community where holidays are possible, holidays will already exist. They will be part of the common life that makes the community, and they will shape and give meaning to the individual lives of the members. The history of the word *vacation* suggests how far we have come from such a common life. In ancient Rome, the days on which there were no religious festivals or public games were called *dies vacantes*, "empty days." The holidays, by contrast, were full—full of obligation but also of celebration, full of things to do, feasting and dancing, rituals and plays. This was when time ripened to produce the social goods of shared solemnity and revelry. Who would give up days like that? But we have lost that sense of fullness; and the days we crave are the empty ones, which we can fill by ourselves, as we please, alone or with our families. Sometimes we experience the fear of emptiness—the fear of retirement, for example, conceived now as an indefinite succession of empty days. But the fullness that many retired people long for, the only one they know, is the fullness of work, not of rest. Vacations, I suspect, require the contrast of work; it is a crucial part of the satisfaction they give. Are holidays the same? That was Prince Hal's view, in Shakespeare's *Henry IV, Part I:*

> If all the year were playing holidays,
> To sport would be as tedious as to work;
> But when they seldom come, they wish'd for come.

Hal's view is certainly the common one, and it seems to fit our own experience. But according to the ancient rabbis, the Sabbath is a foretaste of eternity. The messianic kingdom, which will come, as the old phrase has it, in the fullness of days, is a Sabbath (but not a vacation) without end.

# Joseph Epstein, "Observing the Sabbath"

The sun shines through the shutter slats. An eye opens and sights, on the digital clock upon the night table, the numbers 8:12. More than two hours have elapsed beyond the time when one is accustomed to wake. Avarice for time is no less a compulsion than avarice for money, perhaps a greater. How to make up those missing hours? Then, creeping up from the edge of subconsciousness, comes the sweet realization that this is not a regular day at all; and hence the regular rhythms of regular daily living can be relaxed. It is Sunday, blessed Sunday.

Under Christianity, of course, Sunday is literally blessed. The third century *Didascalia Apostotolum* held, "On Sunday be always joyful, for he who is afflicted on Sunday commits a sin." Gibbon reminds us that in 321 A.D. the Emperor Constantine published an edict which "enjoined the solemn observance of Sunday." The Constitution on the Sacred Liturgy (1963) of the Second Vatican Council says: "The Lord's day is the original feast day," and should be observed "as a day of joy and of freedom from work." Yet if Sunday be officially a Christian day, one does not—to work a twist on an old rye bread advertisement—have to be Gentile to love it.

Not that everyone everywhere has loved Sunday. At the beginning of his essay "The Superannuated Man," Charles Lamb speaks of his own gentle reservations about Sunday, his one day free from his job at the countinghouse. "In particular," he wrote, "there is a gloom for me attendant upon a city Sunday, a weight in the air. . . . Those eternal bells depress me. The closed shops repel me." In *Little Dorrit* Dickens has not a single good word for Sunday. "Nothing for the spent toiler to do but to compare the monotony of his six days, think what a weary life he led, and make the best of it—or the worst, according to the probabilities." "Heaven forgive me," says Mr. Arthur Clennam, the Dickens character who thinks these thoughts, "and those who trained me. How I have hated this day!" But then as now Sunday has never had a very good press in England, where, more recently, it has been thought of as *Sunday, Bloody Sunday*. . . .

Fortunately, here in the United States the worst that Sunday has ever brought us is boredom. Yet it has generally been boredom of a rather luxurious kind. In *Origins,* his etymological dictionary, Eric Partridge informs us that the ice-cream sundae doubtless derives from the word Sunday, perhaps because "whereas an ordinary ice-cream was good enough for a weekday, only this special kind was good enough for a Sunday." The specialness of Sunday was, in an America of another day, denoted by dress: by the idea of Sunday clothes. As a child growing up in Oklahoma City, Ralph Ellison has recalled:

> As a kid I remember working it out this way: there was a world in which you wore your everyday clothes on Sunday, and there was a world in which you wore your Sunday clothes every day—I wanted the world in which you wore your Sunday clothes every day. I wanted it because it represented something better, a more exciting and civilized and human way of living; a world which came to me through certain scenes of felicity which I encountered in fiction, in the movies, and which I glimpsed sometimes through the windows of great houses on Sunday afternoons when my mother took my brother and me for walks through the wealthy white sections of the city. I know it now for a boy's vague dream of possibility. . . .

Much of the specialness as well as the boredom of Sunday derived from its being the Lord's day. Churchgoing dominated Sunday, and among many sects—most commonly in the South—one attended church not only in the morning but yet again after the evening meal. Unless one felt a strong sense of religious calling or a heightened sense of tradition, the strain of boredom could be excruciating—especially among the very young, who, it could be argued, stood most in need of religious instruction and in temperament were least prepared to receive it. But religious boredom—or rather the boredom with religion—was not suffered by the young alone. Not so many years ago, writing about the then intellectually fashionable God Is Dead controversy, Malcolm Muggeridge recalled attending an Anglican church in England. No sooner did the vicar open his mouth to intone the text of that Sunday's sermon, Muggeridge remarked, than God would be gone. But now, he concluded, with fewer and fewer people attending church, there was really scarcely anything else to think about but God. . . .

Inevitably, our American Sunday has changed—and so drastically as scarcely to seem the same day it once was. How has it changed? Why has it changed? What are the discernible consequences of the change?

The most patent change in the American Sunday is in the fairly recent alteration of commerce, and chiefly that of retailing. Where once stores stayed closed on Sundays, today Sunday has come to be a major shopping day. Blue laws—so termed because commonly ascribed to puritanical bluenoses who wished to tell people what they could and could not do on Sunday—once made such shopping illegal in most states. Sometimes enforced, sometimes not, blue laws provided a strange congeries of impermissible Sunday activities. Under these laws, barbers, for example, could cut hair on Sunday in California, though they were forbidden to do so in Arizona, while in Massachusetts barbers were permitted to shave an aged invalid. Retail sales were fined $100 in Virginia, though the state's smoked and cured hams were excluded from the ban. The advent of the shopping center and of the discount store, both following much of middle-class life out to the suburbs, eventually caused the removal of many of the old blue laws from the books of many of the states. Once the turnstiles were opened, Americans by the millions brushed through them.

I note that Salisbury College in Maryland has instituted something called "Leisure Studies." Do they, I wonder, consider shopping a leisure-time activity? If not, perhaps they should, for not only is much shopping now done on Sunday—some years ago discount stores claimed that as much as 35 percent of their gross sales were made on Sunday—but shopping has become something on the order of a major American sport. Nor is it solely a spectator sport. Along with shopping in shops, the last few years have witnessed the emergence, in rather a widespread way, of the garage sale—or yard, house, or apartment sale—which more often than not takes place on Sunday. Everyman his own Wanamaker. . . .

Dr. Johnson believed in the strict observance of Sunday. "It should be different," he observed, "from another day. People may walk but not throw stones at birds. There may be relaxation, but there should be no levity." While I have not, to the best of my recollection, thrown stones at birds, I have most certainly violated the Johnsonian stricture against levity. Growing up when I did, in the 1940s, Sunday always began precisely on a note of levity. I refer to the chief interest of children in the Sunday newspapers: the comics, or, as they were sometimes called, the funny papers. In my childhood, my father read these to me; then I recall a local radio show that read the funny papers along with me; and later, with passion for them only slackening in early adolescence, I read them, Sunday and daily, myself. My own children have never consistently read the Sunday funnies—perhaps, having been surfeited by the cartoon offerings of television during the week, they had no hunger for them—but I remember loving them unabashedly.

For me, nowadays, Sunday morning begins with the *New York Times,* which is, as everyone knows, devoid of comics, but not by any means of comedy. As with so many other Americans, I have for some time been a member of the church called the Gray Lady of the Sunday *New York Times,* worshiping at the altar of cultural and current events. As with church, so with the Sunday *New York Times:* a sense of duty is involved, but how pleasant it is on those mornings when one remains in bed. Still, most Sunday mornings one gets through it, not so secretly pleased when there is nothing that requires reading in either the *Magazine* or the *Book Review.* Of late, I note that the *New York Times* has tried to spread Sunday throughout the week, with its special "Weekend" section on Fridays, and, more recently, its "Living Section" on Wednesdays and now "Sports" Mondays, "Science" Tuesdays, and "Home" Thursdays.

I gather that these special sections have been a commercial success, resulting in greater circulation on the days when they appear, yet I feel somewhat resentful toward them. Somehow one can accommodate all the added trivia on Sunday, but it does not go down so easily on weekdays—it is, in fact, rather like watching musical comedy at breakfast.

The essence of the current Sunday is that on it we are more tolerant, if not more indulgent, of ourselves. Not so much a letting go as a letting up is involved. For some it takes the form of lying abed, for others of getting out: on tennis courts, ski slopes, lakes, and links. The most disciplined man I know used to allow himself to take Sunday morning off for reading, with no motive but pleasure. Pace everywhere slackens. In cities in summer, older couples seek the beach; younger couples—because both parties work during the week—seek the laundromats. Such rhythm as the day has is barely perceptible. At their best, Sundays are hibernant, digressive, restorative. William James somewhere speaks of the dues that are owed to oneself, the small change of self-indulgence that is necessary to each of us if we are to achieve mental equilibrium, and Sunday seems the day on which these dues are best paid.

One of the chief ways of paying them has been through sport, which, in our time, has grown much more popular through democratization. Such sports as golf and tennis, once almost exclusively the Sunday pastimes of those who could afford to belong to a country club, are now played without bar by anyone who is interested. Something similar can be said of the more exotic—and more costly—sports of skiing and sailing. To walk through large American sporting goods stores—open, almost all of them, on Sunday—is to realize afresh what a wealthy country we are. Apart from the essentially boyish sports of baseball, football, basketball, and hockey, one finds in these stores rifles and rafts, tennis and jogging clothes, 10-speed bicycles, equipment for court sports of all sorts, darts and Frisbees and soccer balls and Ping-Pong tables, and scores of models of different kinds of sneakers. An up-to-date theory of the leisure class in the United States would very nearly have to be a sociological study of the nation, for we are almost all leisure class now.

This is not to speak of more strictly spectator sports, which remain by and large a masculine preoccupation and which can take up a good part of Sunday in almost any season. Going to ball games—football or baseball, major or minor league—has long been an established Sunday outing, as has listening to them over the radio been a traditional Sunday afternoon activity (lapsing, in my experience, into another traditional Sunday afternoon activity: the nap). But with television this has changed, and radically. Viewing sports can now easily fill the day. Not one but two or three pro football games are offered in the autumn and winter; in spring and summer, golf follows baseball or tennis as night follows day. Now divisional play-off baseball games are played on Sunday nights. The motive is clearly commercial—they are scheduled so as not to lose any serious portion of the audience to the pro football games also broadcast on Sunday afternoons—but the break with tradition is complete.

Deeper as well as more general changes have been at work altering the nature of the traditional American Sunday. Not least among these changes has been the gradual, but by now thorough, evolution of American work patterns. For one thing, over roughly the past two decades the American work week has largely gone from a six- to a five-day week; for another, more women, especially wives, have gone to work out in the world. From these two changes all sorts of others have followed.

With two days free, rather than one, the specialness of Sunday has been somewhat diluted. The weekend, in this new scheme of things, looms larger than the Sabbath. With two days off one can make plans, invest enterprise in leisure. Hitting the road in one's recreational vehicle, taking off for a skiing, tennis, or gambling weekend, retreating to one's country cottage—things once only possible to the privileged—are now more widely accessible to the multitudes. As Sunday was once an at-home day, the weekend now frequently provides the reverse possibility: a chance to get away from home.

With more women working at jobs, the weekend, and Sunday as part of it, belongs fully as much to them as to men. When only the men in the household worked, in many homes Sundays were devoted to the ease of men, the breadwinners. For obvious reasons this is no longer so. In how many homes in America is Sunday dinner still the serious event it once was? (In England, more than two centuries ago, Dean Swift complained: "That Luxury and Excess men usually practice upon this Day . . . dividing the time between God and their Bellies, when, after a gluttonous meal, their senses dozed and stupefied, they retire to God's House to sleep out the Afternoon.") Now, working themselves, women can no longer fairly be charged with the responsibility for an elaborate Sunday meal. Two breadwinners in the home has meant, increasingly, more sandwiches.

Along with the Sunday dinner, another Sunday institution that appears to have gone by the board—one that my own generation, now in its forties, may be the last to remember—is the Sunday drive. The idea of a drive as a pleasure in and of itself now seems rather bizarre. Unless one lives in certain attractive rural sections of the country, whatever can be the point of a Sunday drive, for whatever is there to see? Apart from convenience, no delights are to be found on the freeways, nor any surprises on the franchise-lined Ventura Boulevards of our nation. Since freeways did not then exist, as often as not one used to drive through the city. Although the purpose of the Sunday drive was more lighthearted—its purpose was, simply, a family outing—one of its side benefits was a lesson in sociology, for as one drove through neighborhoods both richer and poorer than one's own, one saw how the other half, or (in the case of middle-class families like my own) the other two halves, lived. The Sunday drive usually had no greater goal than a longish ride for an ice-cream soda or sundae. Sometimes, though, its destination would be the cemetery. But more often it would be a visit with cousins living in another part of the city. Customs that nowadays seem almost quaint accompanied these visits—bringing along a box of chocolates to the living or planting flowers on the graves of the dead. Visits to the cemetery perplexed and bored me, for death is, I think, perplexing and boring generally to the young. Visits to living relatives I found a pleasure; I had a number of cousins of my age almost all of whom I adored. Death, relocation, estrangement have, over the decades since those days, taken their toll, and I no longer see these cousins. Were I to set out on a Sunday drive today, I am not at all sure in which direction I would head.

Sunday may indeed be fun day, as a commercial for a schlock clothing store in the Middle West has it, but not so long ago it used to be, for better or worse, family day all over America. Nearly everything about it seemed to be organized around the family, and around an extended family at that: children, cousins, bachelor uncles, widowed aunts, grandparents. I say "for better or worse" because many people find it worse. So much family seems to them suffocating, sordid, oppressive in the extreme. When they hear the word Sunday, they reach for their blanket, so as to pull it over their heads; or for their telephones, so as to call their psychoanalysts. Yet it is those people without family who seem to yearn for it most. Is family one of life's pleasures—peace and quiet are two others—that is most earnestly desired when it is absent, almost unbearable when one is immersed in it?

I do not know if this is an emotion universally felt, but I have discovered that I am not alone in feeling what I have come to think of as "Sunday night *triste*," a feeling of the blues that comes upon me dependably each Sunday, roughly at dusk. What does this tinge of sadness signify? Expectations disappointed? A yearning for a time now gone and not ever to be recaptured? Regret for the winding down of another week, during the course of which one achieved (yet again!) less than one had hoped? Sorrowful anticipation of still another week ahead? Or is it—more simply and more persuasively—sadness at the passing of Sunday itself, one of life's minor pleasures that is now once again no less than a full six days off?

# Abraham Joshua Heschel, *The Sabbath*

## Architecture of Time

Technical civilization is man's conquest of space. It is a triumph frequently achieved by sacrificing an essential ingredient of existence, namely, time. In technical civilization, we expend time to gain space. To enhance our power in the world of space is our main objective. Yet to have more does not mean to be more. The power we attain in the world of space terminates abruptly at the borderline of time. But time is the heart of existence.

To gain control of the world of space is certainly one of our tasks. The danger begins when in gaining power in the realm of space we forfeit all aspirations in the realm of time. There is a realm of time where the goal is not to have but to be, not to own but to give, not to control but to share, not to subdue but to be in accord. Life goes wrong when the control of space, the acquisition of things of space, becomes our sole concern.

Nothing is more useful than power, nothing more frightful. We have often suffered from degradation by poverty, now we are threatened with degradation through power. There is happiness in the love of labor, there is misery in the love of gain. Many hearts and pitchers are broken at the fountain of profit. Selling himself into slavery to things, man becomes a utensil that is broken at the fountain.

Technical civilization stems primarily from the desire of man to subdue and manage the forces of nature. The manufacture of tools, the art of spinning and farming, the building of houses, the craft of sailing—all this goes on in man's spatial surroundings. The mind's preoccupation with things of space affects, to this day, all activities of man. Even religions are frequently dominated by the notion that the deity resides in space, within particular localities like mountains, forests, trees or stones, which are, therefore, singled out as holy places; the deity is bound to a particular land; holiness a quality associated with things of space, and the primary question is: Where is the god? There is much enthusiasm for the idea that God is present in the universe, but that idea is taken to mean His presence in space rather than in time, in nature rather than in history; as if He were a thing, not a spirit.

Even pantheistic philosophy is a religion of space: the Supreme Being is thought to be the infinite space. *Deus sive natura* has extension, or space as its attribute, not time; time to Spinoza is merely an accident of motion, a mode of thinking. And his desire to develop a philosophy *more geometrico*, in the manner of geometry, which is the science of space, is significant of his space-mindedness.

The primitive mind finds it hard to realize an idea without the aid of imagination, and it is the realm of space where imagination wields its sway. Of the gods it must have a visible image; where there is no image, there is no god. The reverence for the sacred image, for the sacred monument or place, is not only indigenous to most religions, it has even been retained by men of all ages, all nations, pious, superstitious or even antireligious; they all continue to pay homage to banners and flags, to national shrines, to monuments erected to kings or heroes. Everywhere the desecration of holy shrines is considered a sacrilege, and the shrine may become so important that the idea it stands for is consigned to oblivion. The memorial becomes an aid to amnesia; the means stultify the end. For things of space are at the mercy of man. Though too sacred to be polluted, they are not too sacred to be exploited. To retain the holy, to perpetuate the presence of god, his image is fashioned. Yet a god who can be fashioned, a god who can be confined, is but a shadow of man.

We are all infatuated with the splendor of space, with the grandeur of things of space. Thing is a category that lies heavy on our minds, tyrannizing all our thoughts. Our imagination tends to mold all concepts in its image. In our daily lives we attend primarily to that which the senses are spelling out for us: to what the eyes perceive, to what the fingers touch. Reality to us is thinghood, consisting of substances that occupy space; even God is conceived by most of us as a thing.

The result of our thinginess is our blindness to all reality that fails to identify itself as a thing, as a matter of fact. This is obvious in our understanding of time, which, being thingless and insubstantial, appears to us as if it had no reality.

Indeed, we know what to do with space but do not know what to do about time, except to make it subservient to space. Most of us seem to labor for the sake of things of space. As a result we suffer from a deeply rooted dread of time and stand aghast when compelled to look into its face. Time to us is sarcasm, a slick treacherous monster with a jaw like a furnace incinerating every moment of our lives. Shrinking, therefore, from facing time, we escape for shelter to things of space. The intentions we are unable to carry out we deposit in space; possessions become the symbols of our repressions, jubilees of frustrations. But things of space are not fireproof; they only add fuel to the flames. Is the joy of possession an antidote to the terror of time which grows to be a dread of inevitable death? Things, when magnified, are forgeries of happiness, they are a threat to our very lives; we are more harassed than supported by the Frankensteins of spatial things.

It is impossible for man to shirk the problem of time. The more we think the more we realize: we cannot conquer time through space. We can only master time in time.

The higher goal of spiritual living is not to amass a wealth of information, but to face sacred moments. In a religious experience, for example, it is not a thing that imposes itself on man but a spiritual presence. What is retained in the soul is the moment of insight rather than the place where the act came to pass. A moment of insight is a fortune, transporting us beyond the confines of measured time. Spiritual life begins to decay when we fail to sense the grandeur of what is eternal in time.

Our intention here is not to deprecate the world of space. To disparage space and the blessing of things of space, is to disparage the works of creation, the works which God beheld and saw "it was good." The world cannot be seen exclusively *sub specie temporis*. Time and space are interrelated. To overlook either of them is to be partially blind. What we plead against is man's unconditional surrender to space, his enslavement to things. We must not forget that it is not a thing that lends significance to a moment; it is the moment that lends significance to things.

The Bible is more concerned with time than with space. It sees the world in the dimension of time. It pays more attention to generations, to events, than to countries, to things; it is more concerned with history than with geography. To understand the teaching of the Bible, one must accept its premise that time has a meaning for life which is at least equal to that of space; that time has a significance and sovereignty of its own.

There is no equivalent for the word "thing" in biblical Hebrew. The word "*davar,*" which in later Hebrew came to denote thing, means in biblical Hebrew: speech; word; message; report; tidings; advice; request; promise; decision; sentence; theme, story; saying, utterance; business, occupation; acts; good deeds; events; way, manner, reason, cause; but never "thing." Is this a sign of linguistic poverty, or rather an indication of an unwarped view of the world, of not equating reality (derived from the Latin word *res,* thing) with thinghood?

One of the most important facts in the history of religion was the transformation of agricultural festivals into commemorations of historical events. The festivals of ancient peoples were intimately linked with nature's seasons. They celebrated what happened in the life of nature in the respective seasons. Thus the value of the festive day was determined by the things nature did or did not bring forth. In Judaism, Passover, originally a spring festival, became a celebration of the exodus from Egypt; the Feast of Weeks, an old harvest festival at the end of the wheat harvest (*hag hakazir,* Exodus 23:16; 34:22), became the celebration of the day on which the Torah was given at Sinai; the Feast of the Booths, an old festival of vintage (*hag haasif,* Ex. 23:16), commemorates the dwelling of the Israelites in booths during their sojourn in the wilderness (Leviticus 23:42f.). To Israel the unique events of historic time were spiritually more significant than the repetitive processes in the cycle of nature, even though physical sustenance depended on the latter. While the deities of other peoples were associated with places or things, the God of Israel was the God of events: the Redeemer from slavery, the Revealer of the Torah, manifesting Himself in events of history rather than in things or places. Thus, the faith in the unembodied, in the unimaginable was born.

Judaism is a *religion of time* aiming at *the sanctification of time.* Unlike the space-minded man to whom time is unvaried, iterative, homogeneous, to whom all hours are alike, qualitiless, empty shells, the Bible senses the diversified character of time. There are no two hours alike. Every hour is unique and the only one given at the moment, exclusive and endlessly precious.

Judaism teaches us to be attached to *holiness in time,* to be attached to sacred events, to learn how to consecrate sanctuaries that emerge from the magnificent stream of a year. The Sabbaths are our great cathedrals; and our Holy of Holies is a shrine that neither the Romans nor the Germans were able to burn; a shrine that even apostasy cannot easily obliterate: the Day of Atonement. According to the ancient rabbis, it is not the observance of the Day of Atonement, but the Day itself, the "essence of the Day," which, with man's repentance, atones for the sins of man."

Jewish ritual may be characterized as the art of significant forms in time, as *architecture of time.* Most of its observances—the Sabbath, the New Moon, the festivals, the Sabbatical and the Jubilee year—depend on a certain hour of the day or season of the year. It is, for example, the evening, morning, or afternoon that brings with it the call to prayer. The main themes of faith lie in the realm of time. We remember the day of the exodus from Egypt, the day when Israel stood at Sinai; and our Messianic hope is the expectation of a day, of the end of days.

In a well-composed work of art an idea of outstanding importance is not introduced haphazardly, but, like a king at an official ceremony, it is presented at a moment and in a way that will bring to light its authority and leadership. In the Bible, words are employed with exquisite care, particularly those which, like pillars of fire, lead the way in the far-flung system of the biblical world of meaning.

One of the most distinguished words in the Bible is the word *qadosh,* holy; a word which more than any other is representative of the mystery and majesty of the divine. Now what was the first holy object in the history of the world? Was it a mountain? Was it an altar?

It is, indeed, a unique occasion at which the distinguished word *qadosh* is used for the first time: in the Book of Genesis at the end of the story of creation. How extremely significant is the fact that it is applied to time: "And God blessed the seventh *day* and made it *holy*." There is no reference in the record of creation to any object in space that would be endowed with the quality of holiness.

This is a radical departure from accustomed religious thinking. The mythical mind would expect that, after heaven and earth have been established, God would create a holy place—a holy mountain or a holy spring—whereupon a sanctuary is to be established. Yet it seems as if to the Bible it is *holiness in time,* the Sabbath, which comes first.

When history began, there was only one holiness in the world, holiness in time. When at Sinai the word of God was about to be voiced, a call for holiness in *man* was proclaimed: "Thou shalt be unto me a holy people." It was only after the people had succumbed to the temptation of worshipping a thing, a golden calf, that the erection of a Tabernacle, of holiness in *space,* was commanded. The sanctity of time came first, the sanctity of man came second, and the sanctity of space last. Time was hallowed by God; space, the Tabernacle, was consecrated by Moses.

While the festivals celebrate events that happened in time, the date of the month assigned for each festival in the calendar is determined by the life in nature. Passover and the Feast of Booths, for example, coincide with the full moon, and the date of all festivals is a day in the month, and the month is a reflection of what goes on periodically in the realm of nature, since the Jewish month begins with the new moon, with the reappearance of the lunar crescent in the evening sky. In contrast, the Sabbath is entirely independent of the month and unrelated to the moon. Its date is not determined by any event in nature, such as the new moon, but by the act of creation. Thus the essence of the Sabbath is completely detached from the world of space.

The meaning of the Sabbath is to celebrate time rather than space. Six days a week we live under the tyranny of things of space; on the Sabbath we try to become attuned to *holiness in time*. It is a day on which we are called upon to share in what is eternal in time, to turn from the results of creation to the mystery of creation; from the world of creation to the creation of the world.

———————

## Beyond Civilization

Technical civilization is the product of labor, of man's exertion of power for the sake of gain, for the sake of producing goods. It begins when man, dissatisfied with what is available in nature, becomes engaged in a struggle with the forces of nature in order to enhance his safety and to increase his comfort. To use the language of the Bible, the task of civilization is to subdue the earth, to have dominion over the beast.

How proud we often are of our victories in the war with nature, proud of the multitude of instruments we have succeeded in inventing, of the abundance of commodities we have been able to produce. Yet our victories have come to resemble defeats. In spite of our triumphs, we have fallen victims to the work of our hands: it is as if the forces we had conquered have conquered us.

Is our civilization a way to disaster, as many of us are prone to believe? Is civilization essentially evil, to be rejected and condemned? The faith of the Jew is not a way out of this world, but a way of being within and above this world; not to reject but to surpass civilization. The Sabbath is the day on which we learn the art of *surpassing* civilization.

Adam was placed in the Garden of Eden "to dress it and to keep it" (Genesis 2:15). Labor is not only the destiny of man; it is endowed with divine dignity. However, after he ate of the tree of knowledge he was condemned to toil, not only to labor. "In toil shall thou eat . . . all the days of thy life" (Genesis 3:17). Labor is a blessing, toil is the misery of man.

The Sabbath as a day of abstaining from work is not a depreciation but an affirmation of labor, a divine exaltation of its dignity. Thou shalt abstain from labor on the seventh day is a sequel to the command: *Six days shalt thou labor, and do all thy work.*

"Six days shalt thou labor and do all thy work; but the seventh day is Sabbath unto the Lord thy God." Just as we are commanded to keep the Sabbath, we are commanded to labor. "Love work . . . " The duty to work for six days is just as much a part of God's covenant with man as the duty to abstain from work on the seventh day.

To set apart one day a week for freedom, a day on which we would not use the instruments which have been so easily turned into weapons of destruction, a day for being with ourselves, a day of detachment from the vulgar, of independence of external obligations, a day on which we stop worshipping the idols of technical civilization, a day on which we use no money, a day of armistice in the economic struggle with our fellow men and the forces of nature—is there any institution that holds out a greater hope for man's progress than the Sabbath?

The solution of mankind's most vexing problem will not be found in renouncing technical civilization, but in attaining some degree of independence of it.

In regard to external gifts, to outward possessions, there is only one proper attitude—to have them and to be able to do without them. On the Sabbath we live, as it were, *independent of technical civilization:* we abstain primarily from any activity that aims at remaking or reshaping the things of space. Man's royal privilege to conquer nature is suspended on the seventh day.

What are the kinds of labor not to be done on the Sabbath? They are, according to the ancient rabbis, all those acts which were necessary for the construction and furnishing of the Sanctuary in the desert. The Sabbath itself is a sanctuary which we build, *a sanctuary in time.*

It is one thing to race or be driven by the vicissitudes that menace life, and another thing to stand still and to embrace the presence of an eternal moment.

The seventh day is the armistice in man's cruel struggle for existence, a truce in all conflicts, personal and social, peace between man and man, man and nature, peace within man; a day on which handling money is considered a desecration, on which man avows his independence of that which is the world's chief idol. The seventh day is the exodus from tension, the liberation of man from his own muddiness, The installation of man as a sovereign in the world of time.

In the tempestuous ocean of time and toil there are islands of stillness where man may enter a harbor and reclaim his dignity. The island is the seventh day, the Sabbath, a day of detachment from things, instruments and practical affairs as well as of attachment to the spirit.

# Prayer at the Close of Day

O Lord, support us all the day long of this troubled life, until the shadows lengthen and the evening comes and the busy world is hushed, the fever of life is over, and our work is done. Then, Lord, in your mercy, grant us a safe lodging, and a holy rest, and peace at the last; through Jesus Christ our Lord. Amen.

# CREDITS

The editor and the publisher are grateful to the owners of copyright for their permission to reprint the following selections:

Angell, Roger. "Goodbye Tom," and "One Hard Way to Make a Living," from *Late Innings,* pp. 36 and 350–51. New York: Ballantine Books, 1982. © 1982 by Roger Angell. Reprinted with the permission of Simon & Schuster, Inc..

Aristotle. *Nicomachean Ethics,* translated by Martin Oswald, pp. 286–94. Indianapolis: Bobbs-Merrill, 1962. © 1962. Reprinted by permission of Prentice-Hall, Inc.

Augustine. *The City of God,* translated by Henry Bettenson, Book XIX, chapter 19, p. 880. Penguin Classics, 1972. © Henry Bettenson, 1972. By permission of Penguin UK.

Barth, Karl. *Church Dogmatics,* vol. 3, part 4, pp. 607–17. Edinburgh: T. & T. Clark, 1961. By permission of T. & T. Clark, Ltd.

Callahan, Sidney. *Parents Forever: You and Your Adult Children,* pp. 73–84, 88–90. New York: Crossroad, 1992. © 1992 by Sidney Callahan. Reprinted by permission of Crossroad Publishing Company.

Drucker, Peter F. "The Age of Social Transformation," *Atlantic Monthly* (November 1994), pp. 53–72. © 1994 Peter F. Drucker. By permission of Peter F. Drucker.

Ellul, Jacques. *The Ethics of Freedom,* translated by Geoffrey Bromiley, pp. 495–506. Grand Rapids, Mich.: William B. Eerdmans, 1976. © 1976 Wm. B. Eerdmans Publishing Company, Grand Rapids, Mich. Reprinted by permission of the publisher; all rights reserved.

Epstein, Joseph. Selections from "Observing the Sabbath," in *Familiar Territory: Observations on American Life,* pp. 194–204. New York: Oxford University Press, 1979. © 1979 by Joseph Epstein. Reprinted by permission of Georges Borchardt, Inc. for the author.

Heschel, Abraham Joshua. *The Sabbath: Its Meaning for Everyday Life,* pp. 3–10, 27–29. New York: Farrar, Straus & Giroux, 1951. By permission of Farrar, Straus & Giroux.

Hochschild, Arlie Russell. "There's No Place Like Work," *The New York Times Magazine* (April 20, 1997), pp. 50–55, 81, 84. © 1997 by Arlie Russell Hochschild. First appeared in *The New York Times.* Reprinted by permission of Georges Borchardt, Inc. for the author.

Kaus, Mickey. "Getting Sleepy," *The New Republic* (July 5, 1993), p. 6. © 1993 The New Republic, Inc. Reprinted by permission of *The New Republic.*

Kirk, Kenneth. *The Vision of God,* pp. 179–86. Abridged ed. Greenwood, S.C.: Attic Press, 1934. By permission of James Clarke & Co., Ltd.

Lindbergh, Anne Morrow. *Gift From the Sea,* pp. 99–103. New York: Vintage Books, 1955. © 1955, 1975, renewed 1983 by Anne Morrow Lindbergh. Reprinted by permission of Pantheon Books, a Division of Random House, Inc.

MacIntyre, Alasdair. *After Virtue: A Study in Moral Theory,* selections from pp. 84–102. Notre Dame, Ind.: University of Notre Dame Press, 1981, pp. 84–102. By permission of the Press.

Martin, Judith. *Common Courtesy,* selections from pp. 36–53. New York: Atheneum, 1985. © 1985 by Judith Martin. Reprinted with permission of Scribner, a Division of Simon & Schuster, Inc.

Marx, Karl. *The Grundrisse,* edited and translated by David McLellan, pp. 123–24. New York: HarperCollins, 1971. © 1971 by David McLellan. Reprinted by permission of HarperCollins Publishers, Inc.

Marx, Karl. "The German Ideology: Part I," from *The Marx-Engels Reader,* 2d ed., edited by Robert C. Tucker, p. 124. New York: W. W. Norton & Company, 1972. © 1978, 1972 by W. W. Norton & Company, Inc. Reprinted by permission of W. W. Norton & Company, Inc.

May, William F. *The Physician's Covenant: Images of the Healer in Medical Ethics,* pp. 182–86. Philadelphia: Westminster John Knox Press, 1983. © 1983 by William F. May. Used by permission of Westminster John Knox Press.

Moore, George Foot. Excerpt from *Judaism in the First Centuries of the Christian Era,* vol. 2, p. 177. New York: Schocken Books, 1971. © 1955 by Alfred H. Moore. Reprinted by permission of Harvard University Press.

Novak, Michael. *Business as a Calling: Work and the Examined Life,* pp. 34–36, 119–25, 177–82. New York: Free Press, 1996. © 1996 by Michael Novak. Reprinted with the permission of The Free Press, a Division of Simon & Schuster, Inc..

Orwell, George. *The Road to Wigan Pier,* chapter 2. New York: Harcourt Brace, 1958. © 1958 and renewed 1986 by the Estate of Sonia B. Orwell. Reprinted by permission of Harcourt, Inc.

Josef Pieper, "Leisure and Its Threefold Opposition," in *Josef Pieper, An Anthology,* pp. 137–40, 141–44. San Francisco: Ignatius Press, 1989. © 1989 by Ignatius Press. All rights reserved.

Robinson, John P., and Geoffrey Godbey. "Are Average Americans Really Overworked?" *The American Enterprise* 6 (September/October, 1995), p. 43. © 1995 *The American Enterprise.* Reprinted with permission from *The American Enterprise.*

Rybczynski, Witold. "Waiting for the Weekend," *The Atlantic Monthly* (August, 1991), pp. 35–37, 50–51. © 1991 by Witold Rybczynski. Reprinted by permission.

Sayers, Dorothy L. "Why Work?" in *Creed or Chaos?* pp. 47–64. London: Harcourt Brace, 1947. Reprinted by permission of David Higham Associates Limited.

Seneca. "On the Shortness of Life," in *Moral Essays,* vol. 2, translated by John W. Basore, pp. 333, 335, 337. London: William Heinemann, 1951; and Cambridge, Mass.: Harvard University Press, 1932. Reprinted by permission of Harvard University Press and the Loeb Classical Library.

Sennett, Richard. *The Corrosion of Character: The Personal Consequences of Work in the New Capitalism,* selections from pp. 15–27. © 1988 by Richard Sennett. Reprinted by permission of W. W. Norton & Company, Inc.

Taylor, Charles. *Sources of the Self: The Making of the Modern Identity,* pp. 211–26. Cambridge: Harvard University Press, 1989. © 1989 by the President and Fellows of Harvard College. Reprinted by permission of Harvard University Press.

Tilgher, Adriano. *Homo Faber: Work through the Ages,* chapter 23. Chicago: Henry Regnery Company, 1958. Reprinted by permission of Ayer Co. Pubs., Inc.

Tolstoy, Leo. *Anna Karenina,* translated by Louise and Alymer Maude, edited by George Gibian. Part III, chapters 4–6. Oxford: Oxford University Press, 1918, revised 1939. Reprinted by permission of Oxford University Press.

Tolstoy, Leo. *The Death of Ivan Ilyich,* translated by Lynn Solotaroff, chapter 2. New York: Bantam Books, 1981. Translation © 1981 by Bantam, a division of Bantam Doubleday Dell Pulishing Group, Inc. Used by permission of Bantam Books, a division of Random House, Inc.

Walzer, Michael. *Spheres of Justice: A Defense of Pluralism and Equality,* selections from pp. 185–88, 190–95. New York: Basic Books, 1983. © 1983 by Basic Books, Inc. Reprinted by permission of Basic Books, a member of Perseus Books, L.L.C.

Whitehead, Barbara Dafoe. "Lost in Work," *The American Enterprise* 6 (September/October 1995), pp. 39–40. © 1995 *The American Enterprise.* Reprinted with permission from *The American Enterprise.*

Will, George F. *Men at Work: The Craft of Baseball,* pp. 4–6, 329–30. New York: Macmillan, 1990. © 1990 by George F. Will. Reprinted with permission of MacMillan Library Reference USA.